90297

DATE DUE		
JAN 14 '85		
~~SEP 27~~		
~~APR 16 1991~~		
~~APR 18 1992~~		
NOV 4 1995		

Imaginary Social Worlds

John L. Caughey

Imaginary
Social
Worlds

A Cultural Approach

University of Nebraska Press

Lincoln and London

Portions of this book have previously been
published in different form: parts of Chapter 2
as "Artificial Social Relations in Modern
America," *American Quarterly* 30 (Spring 1978),
70–89, copyright 1978 by the Trustees of the
University of Pennsylvania, and as "Media Mentors,"
Psychology Today 12, no. 4 (September 1978),
44–49, copyright 1978 by Ziff-Davis Publishing Co.,
and parts of Chapter 4 as "Ethnography,
Introspection, and Reflexive Culture Studies,"
Prospects 7: 115–39 (1982), copyright 1982 by
Burt Franklin and Co., Inc.

The paper in this book meets the guidelines for
permanence and durability of the Committee on
Production Guidelines for Book Longevity of the
Council on Library Resources.

Library of Congress Cataloging in Publication Data

Caughey, John L., 1941-
Imaginary social worlds.
Includes index.
1. Interpersonal relations. 2. Fantasy.
3. Psychology, Pathological. 4. Mass media –
Psychological aspects. 5. Popular culture. I. Title.
HM132.C38   1984   302   83-6702
ISBN 0-8032-1421-9

Contents

Preface

This is a book about imaginary social relationships. It deals with American dreams, fantasies, anticipations, media involvements, and hallucinations, and especially with the social interactions that pervade these imaginary worlds. My interest in the subject began with fictional literature. However, the orientation of this study reflects the work I have carried out over the last fifteen years in anthropology and American Studies. I have drawn on the diverse social science literature on imaginary processes, but much of the material presented here is based on my own research.

For comparative perspectives, I have relied heavily on my own fieldwork in two non-Western societies. In 1968 I carried out field research on the social organization of Fáánakkar, a Pacific island in the Truk group of the Caroline Islands in Micronesia. In 1976–77 I did a similar study with a band of Sufi fakirs in the Margalla Hills of Pakistan. During that year I also interviewed urban intellectuals, many of whom were associated with a northern Pakistani university where I was teaching. My American material includes data on schizophrenic imaginary systems obtained during a field study of an urban psychiatric ward from 1972 to 1975. But the bulk of my information about American imaginary relationships is drawn from some 500 persons within my own social circles, that is, from personal acquaintances and also from interviews and survey work with faculty, staff, and students at the two eastern universities where I have taught. While published sources suggest that the patterns I have explored here are widespread, they probably vary considerably among the complex subcultures of contemporary America.

For help in this study—direct and indirect—I would like to thank my former teachers and colleagues at the University of Pennsylvania, particularly the anthropologists Ward H. Goodenough, A. I. Hallowell, Anthony F. C. Wallace, Ruben Reina, Igor Kopytoff, Olga Linares, and William Davenport; and the Americanists Murray G. Murphey, Michael Zuckerman, and Melvyn Hammarberg. I would also like to thank my colleagues at the University of Maryland, especially Gene Wise, Myron Lounsbury, R. Gordon Kelly, Lawrence E. Mintz, Carl Bode, Carol Pearson, and Neil Isaacs.

I am particularly grateful to my wife, Frannie. A linguistic anthropologist, she helped with the research in Micronesia and Pakistan, listened to my ideas, offered many helpful suggestions, and provided expert editorial assistance. Katie Helene and Pearl Leopard expertly typed and retyped the manuscript.

During various phases of research and writing, grants were provided by the National Institute of Mental Health, the University of Pennsylvania, the Council for the International Exchange of Scholars, the Ford Foundation, and the General Research Board of the University of Maryland. I am very grateful for this support.

However, I owe the most thanks to those many people in America, Fáánakkar, and Pakistan who shared with me accounts of their imaginary experience.

Prologue

Three Fantasy Relationships

On 14 June 1949, there was a shooting in a Chicago hotel. Eddie Waitkus, first baseman for the Philadelphia Phillies, was staying in the downtown hotel with his team for a series with the Chicago Cubs. Late in the evening Waitkus received a call in his room from Ruth Steinhagen, an eighteen-year-old girl who had just checked into the same hotel. She had never spoken to Waitkus, never met him, never communicated with him in any way. But she had to see him, she said, about "something important." When Waitkus knocked on her door, Ruth told him to come in. When he entered, there she was—with a .22 rifle.

"For two years you have been bothering me," she said. "And now you are going to die." And then she shot him in the stomach.

Waitkus was rushed to the hospital. He survived and lived to play professional baseball again. But who was Ruth Steinhagen and what was her motive? At first the press was mystified. Then it emerged that although she had never met Waitkus, she had a strong emotional attachment to him. She was "one of his greatest fans." She had been "in love" with him for two years. In a psychiatric report to felony court, the events leading up to the shooting were reconstructed as follows.[1]

Steinhagen had first noticed Eddie Waitkus in April 1947, two years before the shooting, when she and a girl friend had attended a baseball game at Wrigley Field. At the time Waitkus was playing for the Chicago Cubs and Steinhagen became very interested in him. Her interest developed into a strong emotional attachment or "crush," a highly intense, totally one-sided fantasy romance.

1

Steinhagen frequently went to baseball games in order to see Waitkus play and, with other girls, sometimes waited afterwards to watch for him when the players left the stadium. However, she hid herself and never actually approached him to talk or get his autograph. She collected all kinds of media information about him, including press clippings and photographs, and at night was accustomed to spreading these out in a kind of shrine. She slept with one of his pictures under her pillow. She became preoccupied with 36, his uniform number, and because of his background developed a strong interest in things associated with Lithuania and Boston (she wanted baked beans "constantly"). This artificial romance also affected many of her actual relationships. She talked about "Eddie" sentimentally and incessantly with her family and girl friends.

She also engaged in a variety of fantasy relations with him. She talked out loud to pictures of him, dreamed about him, held imaginary conversations with him, and had daydreams about meeting, dating, and marrying him. When he was traded to the Phillies she cried for a day and a night, saying she could not live if he went away.

The relationship went on for many months, but as Steinhagen put it, "After a year went by and I was still crazy about him I decided to do something about it." She decided to resolve the situation by murdering Waitkus: "I knew I would never get to know him in a normal way, so I kept thinking I will never get him and if I can't have him nobody else can. And then I decided I would kill him."[2] Despite shooting Waitkus, she did not stand trial for attempted murder. Instead she was ruled insane—"schizophrenic"—and committed to a state mental hospital.

This shooting was not unique. The years since have seen dozens of attacks on celebrities, ranging from the assassinations of the Kennedys, through the beating of rock star Frank Zappa, to the shooting of Larry Flynt, the publisher of *Hustler*. There have also been thousands of death threats against sports figures, politicians, popular musicians, and other public figures. The problem has become a pattern in American society. Sometimes a desire for personal fame seems to have motivated the assailants, and in other cases political considerations were involved. But in many cases

2

there is also evidence that a fantasy relationship influenced the attackers. This is apparent in two recent shootings.

John Lennon was killed 8 December 1980 by a man he did not know, Mark David Chapman. The only previous meeting between the two had occurred earlier the same day on the sidewalk outside Lennon's apartment. It was a typical fan-celebrity encounter. Chapman stepped from a group of fans and asked Lennon to autograph a copy of his new album, *Double Fantasy*. Lennon complied. "John Lennon signed my album," [Chapman] exulted to Goresh (another fan) . . . after the Lennons had left. 'Nobody in Hawaii is going to believe me'"[3] Six hours later, as Lennon returned from a recording session, Chapman shot him dead on the same sidewalk.

Lennon knew nothing about Chapman. They had never communicated, never talked, never met. But to Chapman, Lennon was very familiar. Evidence gathered from newspaper interviews with former friends and acquaintances clearly shows that Chapman had a strong relationship with Lennon—he had been a major figure in Chapman's life for fifteen years. His fantasy relationship has some parallels to Steinhagen's involvement with Waitkus. Here, however, the basis of the imaginary relationship was not romantic love, but admiration and hero worship. It began when Chapman was a teenager collecting Beatles albums and pictures. Lennon became his favorite. As a friend reports, "He tacked John Lennon's pictures on his wall and played the 'White Album' over and over."[4]

Later, the relationship developed into patterns of emulation and identification. Chapman developed a mystical fascination with Lennon's lyrics. At least once he claimed to know Lennon. Several times he signed his name as "John Lennon." He also imitated Lennon. He wore Lennon-style wire-rimmed glasses and took up the guitar. He "yearned to be a rock star like Lennon but lacked the talent." According to a close friend, "I have a feeling that in his mind, he wanted to become Lennon."[5] Others who knew him cited additional evidence: they noted "how he used to play Beatles songs constantly on his guitar, how he taped the name 'John Lennon' over his own on the ID badge he wore as a maintenance man at a Honolulu condominium, how he emulated Lennon by marrying a Japanese woman several years his senior."[6]

Citing the interpretations of psychiatrists and psychologists, the

3

media presented the details of Chapman's relationship with Lennon as symptoms of mental abnormality. Chapman's concern for Lennon was characterized as a "lethal delusion" and an "obsessive identification." Chapman was said to have obscured his own identity by making Lennon his alter ego.[7]

This identification with Lennon was not only seen as evidence of mental pathology; it was also presented as the motive behind the shooting. Because of the identification, several psychological experts suggested that the murder was really a substitute for suicide, a "suicide turned backwards." Given Chapman's frustrated musical career, resentment was also said to have been a motive. "Lennon with his expensive apartments and happy marriage represented a symbol of stability and success that the killer himself wanted."[8]

On Monday, 30 March 1981, there was another shooting, this time in Washington, D.C. In an attempted assassination, President Ronald Reagan was shot in the chest and Press Secretary James Brady, a Washington policeman, and a Secret Service agent were gunned down with him. The gunman was described as the "son of a wealthy Colorado oil executive" and a "drifter." At first no motive was apparent. By Wednesday, however, the press reported that the assailant, John Hinckley, had a strange connection to eighteen-year-old movie starlet Jodie Foster. "He did it for her," one source reported. "She's the key."[9]

While Hinckley never met Foster, he developed an interest in her through her movies and other appearances in the media. According to some sources, Hinckley saw *Taxi Driver*—a movie in which Foster plays a teenage prostitute who is saved by a gun-wielding anti-hero—at least fifteen times. He is also known to have assembled media information about her various movie roles and to have carried several pictures of Foster in his wallet.[10]

Six months before the shooting, in September 1980, Hinckley traveled to Connecticut and spent several days in New Haven, where Foster had just enrolled as a freshman at Yale. He hung around her dormitory with other fans and, like many others, sent her love letters. He evidently hoped to meet Foster, but she threw his letters in the garbage. Later Hinckley wrote to Paul Schrader, scriptwriter on *Taxi Driver*, and asked him to arrange an introduction. Again he was unsuccessful. In early March, Hinckley returned to New Haven. During his stay he told a bartender and two Yale students that Jodie Foster was his girl friend. Again Hinckley hung around Foster's dorm. This time he left several love notes, but again she did not respond and again he was unable to meet her. After several days in New Haven, Hinckley returned to Colorado. There, apparently, he developed his plan to assassinate Reagan.

Before the shooting, Hinckley's life had been marginal but unremarkable. He was an ordinary high school student and a college dropout. For a time he saw a psychiatrist in Colorado. He became an unemployed wanderer, alienated from his family, disconnected from any close relationships, and given to traveling about the country and living in cheap hotels.

On the basis of such sketchy and limited information, the media developed a psychological portrait of Hinckley. Through their own descriptions and the quotes of laymen, the press immediately characterized him as mentally ill. He had a "mental condition." He was a "desperate man," a "kook," a "screwball," and a "lone nut." Many experts quickly agreed. Psychiatrically he was speculatively diagnosed as a "pathological case" suffering from "sexual inadequacy," "self-loathing," "isolation," "schizophrenia," and "sexual and psychological confusion." His imaginary relationship with Foster was seen as prime evidence of his mental abnormality. His fantasy relationship was a "fanatic relationship" which went far beyond the normal fan's aesthetic appreciation of a star. It was an "obsession," a "monumental obsession," an "erotomanic obsession."[11] Later, of course, this interpretation was officially sanctioned. At the conclusion of his trial, Hinckley was found "not guilty by reason of insanity."[12]

In fact, the precise nature of Hinckley's mental condition remains controversial and unclear. What is evident is that he had a strong fantasy relationship with Foster, and that this was an important motive in the shooting. Shortly before he shot Reagan, Hinckley wrote a "last" letter to Foster. He made it clear that his attempt to "get Reagan" was designed to impress Foster and to persuade her to change her mind about him. The letter ended as

5

follows: "Jody, I'm asking you to please look into your heart and at least give me the chance with this historical deed to gain your respect and love. I love you forever. [signed] John Hinckley"[13]

All three of these shootings developed out of an intense emotional connection between the assailant and someone he or she did not actually know. This connection was not an actual social relationship—there had been no real interaction—but rather something that parallels a social relationship, a connection which we will here call an *imaginary* or *fantasy relationship*. In each of the cases, the common interpretation is that the assailant was mentally disturbed. Primary evidence for this interpretation is the description of the imaginary relationship which had preceded the shooting. On one level there is justification for this interpretation. On another it is erroneous.

Ironically, these brutal shootings are seen as "pathological" largely because they do not seem to have been motivated by "normal" criminal thinking. If Waitkus had been shot by a jealous girl friend, if Lennon had been killed in a robbery attempt, or if Reagan had been shot by political rivals, the shootings would have been no less tragic, but they would not have been characterized as "abnormal" or "crazy." In the absence of such "normal" motives, the shootings seem senseless and bizarre.

And yet there is a pattern here—one that is not confined to these three cases. As we shall see, imaginary relationships of the kind described above are characteristic of many of those persons who are diagnosed as mentally disturbed in American society. In this sense these fantasy relationships are not merely individual symptoms but part of a widespread psychiatric complex, or *cultural syndrome*, characteristic of many American psychotics.

But there is another, more significant way in which the characterization of these three cases as "abnormal" is problematic. A primary source of evidence for the diagnosis of "pathology" is the imaginary relationships which these three individuals had before they decided to shoot their victims. Would these fantasy relationships have been viewed as pathological if they had *not* led to a shooting? The conventional answer, implicit in the reports quoted above, would be yes. Each of these relationships is described in the language of pathology—as "obsessive," "abnormal," "delu-

6

sionary," "fanatical," and "schizophrenic." In fact, such an interpretation is untenable. It is probable that these three individuals were in some sense psychiatrically ill before they decided to shoot their victims—but this cannot be determined solely by reference to the prior imaginary relationship.

Some evidence of this can be found within the commentary accompanying the above reports. Hinckley was but one of many fans outside Jodie Foster's Yale dormitory. His love letters were merely a fraction of the many she received each week from unknown admirers. Chapman was but one of the many fans outside John Lennon's apartment, and those he talked with sensed nothing amiss. Much of the background on Chapman is supplied by his longtime friend Gary Limuti; not only did Limuti share Chapman's teenage admiration for Lennon and the Beatles, but he himself became a Beatles style rock musician.[14] While Ruth Steinhagen's crush on Waitkus was irritating and disturbing to some members of her real social world, especially her father, it was considered entirely acceptable by others, including her sister and girl friend. Not only did they know all about it—and see nothing amiss—but they were involved in similar celebrity love relationships themselves.[15]

This is not to claim that Ruth Steinhagen, Mark Chapman, and John Hinckley were "sane," but only to raise the question whether or not, in this society, fantasy relationships such as these can properly be characterized as abnormal. As we shall see, an examination of the structure and dynamics of such imaginary relationships shows that they are an important, powerful, and pervasive aspect of contemporary American life. Indeed, intense imaginary relationships through fantasy, media, dreams, and the stream of consciousness are characteristic of contemporary American society.

Chapter 1

Introduction: Culture
and Social Relationships

Imaginary experience has been commonly approached through psychological schemes of interpretation. Thus Ruth Steinhagen's fantasies about Eddie Waitkus were officially explained as a product of her personal mental pathology—the "schizophrenia" that rendered her incapable of recognizing "reality." Such interpretations, constructed from current psychological theories, focus on peculiarities of individual personality to the neglect of social and cultural patterns. Here, by contrast, I will develop a *cultural* approach to imaginary experience. I will be concerned with exploring how an individual's imaginary experiences—Steinhagen's fantasies as well as yours and mine—are connected to recognizable patterns in cultural systems.

Culture, that which makes us a stranger when we are away from home, is a *learned* system. By its complexity, it differentiates humans from other animals; through its variation from place to place, it differentiates one society of humans from another. Beyond this level of description, there are a variety of competing definitions and theories.[1] Traditionally, culture has often been equated with "customs," "ways of life," and "patterns of behavior." Here I will adopt a widely accepted alternative approach and assume that culture is best understood as a conceptual system of beliefs, rules, and values that lies behind different ways of behaving. As Ward Goodenough writes, "As I see it, a society's culture consists of whatever it is one has to know or believe in order to operate in a manner acceptable to its members and do so in any role that they accept for any one of themselves."[2] From this point of view, the

9

description of a particular way of life involves an investigation of the system of knowledge with which people operate. A crucial step, therefore, is to explore the *inner* world of one's subjects, to discover and describe the perspective from which they experience their world.[3]

One way to do this is through anthropological ethnography, that is, through participant observation and interviewing. In 1968 I spent a year doing ethnography on Fáánakkar, an island in the western Pacific. It was a very different world, a place of green mountains, white sand, a blue lagoon—and a strong traditional culture. I lived for eleven months in a native house on the edge of a lagoon. I observed and participated in the activities of daily life, fishing expeditions, breadfruit cooking, and religious rituals. I learned the language and spent hundreds of hours in intensive interviewing. I also studied esoteric systems of magical knowledge. In studying *rong*—sorcery, curing, love magic, divination, and the like—I interviewed ordinary people and experts, observed the use of magic in everyday life, and studied with specialists. I wanted to learn what it was like to live in a world where magic was real. I did this not because I was interested in recording local behavior in terms of an outside classification system but because I wanted to understand how their beliefs and assumptions structured behavior. In other words, I wanted to get at their *experience* of their world.[4]

Cultural knowledge is highly relative. People of different subgroups and societies live in different worlds because their systems of knowledge are fundamentally different. Cultures vary greatly in their values and fundamental premises about what is important. The specific concepts in terms of which people perceive, think, and evaluate also differ from group to group. Particular cultures may have concepts not found in other societies, and different cultures may draw different distinctions within areas they all recognize. Seemingly straightforward universal categories may also have different meanings.

When I first went to Fáánakkar, for example, I noticed that certain young women of the village were "obviously" more attractive than others. But I soon learned that, in terms of Fáánakkar knowledge, I had it all wrong, because Fáánakkar people perceived beauty in terms of standards significantly different from my own. A round face is considered attractive, as are thick eyebrows and a pointed nose—and the ideal figure, for men as well as women, is considerably heavier than that currently in vogue in American society. Once I had learned this aspect of culture I could make judgments the people of Fáánakkar would accept as valid. ("Yes, you've got it now, *that* is a pretty girl.") But given my own cultural programming I could never quite empathize with them, nor they with me. The men would sometimes take me aside and say, "Tell us again who you think is pretty among the village girls." And when I told them they would laugh. Such evidence shows that people of different societies live in different worlds; the cultural categories in terms of which they perceive, think, and evaluate are significantly different.

People in different societies also live in different worlds because their mental plans, or how-to-do-it recipes, differ. All plans are linked cognitively to values and conceptions of reality. On Fáánakkar, for example, it is simply taken for granted that people eat heavily in order to become more attractive; that Americans diet to achieve this end they find absurd. Different societies have specialized plans which are totally absent in other societies— plans for using love magic, milking camels, or preparing betel nut. Even instinctive, biologically based activities are subject to massive cultural patterning. What is considered desirable or even edible as "food" varies, as do the methods of preparation, the techniques and rituals of food consumption, and the social meaning of food sharing. We are seldom aware of such cultural programming, but it shapes virtually all of our daily behavior.

Cultures are relative over time as well as space—even though this may not be immediately evident. Systems of knowledge seem to have a structural stability viewed from both within and without. As Peter Berger puts it, the typical societal inhabitant is locked in his culturally structured reality as comfortably as a horse in its stable.[5] Everyone in a given society may "know" that the world is flat or that heaven and hell await the human soul at death. Such stability preserves the peace of mind of a society's inhabitants, maintains a predictable social order, and allows us, as cultural analysts, to describe culture as system, not chaos.

Yet viewed over time, change is evident. What is "true" now is not what was true before, and it will be false again later. Reality does change. Even in relatively isolated, small-scale societies the system "drifts," partly through the development of its own inner logic, partly through diffusion and invention, and partly in response to environmental changes that require new modes of adaption.[6]

From an analytic perspective, two different and almost contradictory processes are important to the survival of any social group. Because reality is relative, precarious, and subject to disintegration and disruption, the current system of knowledge must be protected and maintained. All societies have therefore developed elaborate systems of social control to keep people thinking and acting in conventional ways. On the other hand, to meet the need for readjustment and change, societies need individuals to create new ways of thinking and acting. Hence, in some cases, imaginative ways of thinking will be regarded not as witchcraft, insanity, or deviance, but as desirable innovation. How a particular instance of new thinking is categorized depends partly on its inherent value but even more on the societal reaction—that is, on whether the innovation is perceived by others as a threat to their values or a solution to their felt needs.

Human beings are social animals much given to regular interactions with others of their kind.

From the moment of conception which is itself the result of the intimate union of two human beings, until death, each of us lives in a world of people. Birth, the physical separation of mother and child, begins the lifelong experience of social interaction. As infants we get our food from other people. Adults clothe us and protect us. For the rest of our lives we eat, sleep, play, work, and live in close proximity to other people. Even at death the human body is often placed with other corpses where the living can look after it. The daily experience of men and women in every society is characterized by social interaction. . . . Always there will be other people.[7]

In part, social interaction is enforced. The economic, educational, political, and religious institutions by which human groups maintain themselves require cooperative social action. All societies develop mechanisms that encourage and, when necessary, force their members to cooperate. But individuals also become personally driven to engage others socially. They develop strong emotional orientations to others. They acquire a sense of self whose maintenance depends on social interactions. They learn compelling goals whose accomplishment demands particular relations with others and whose fulfillment requires social recognition. Finally, most humans come to feel that social interaction is gratifying in itself.

Like other areas of experience, social relationships are relative over space and time and intricately structured by systems of cultural knowledge. Patterns of actual social interaction are influenced by the general cultural ethos or value orientation. Social relations in a society with a harmonious, self-effacing, cooperative value system will differ significantly from those in a society with a competitive, aggressive, individualistic ethos. Cultural knowledge also influences social conduct through conceptions about people.[8] Two general kinds of identities seem to exist in all societies. First are social roles or *social identities*, such as "lawyer," "professor," or "uncle," which refer to occupational, age, sex, kinship, and other social categories. These involve rules of conduct that specify what someone in one social position—such as magical curer or lawyer—owes to and can demand from someone in a matching social position—such as patient or client. As a person moves from one social situation to another, he or she drops certain social identities and takes on others. Social identities exert a pervasive influence on social interaction in all societies. Given a context in which I am *this* and you are *that*, much of our conduct is already at least broadly defined.

A culture's catalogue of social roles is not, however, the only means it has for categorizing its members. *Personal identity* categories like "beautiful," "emotional," "stingy," "aggressive," and "arrogant" are also part of the cultural knowledge with which people classify, think about, and relate to others in society. The social behavior of two people operating in the social roles of lawyer and client may be significantly affected by the way each of them appraises the other's personal identity.

13

Cultural knowledge about kinds of persons affects the individual's classification of others, but it also structures another crucial aspect of social organization—the way in which the individual understands and thinks about himself. The cultural repertoire of identity labels provides the only means with which the individual can answer the implicit or explicit question, "What kind of a person am I?" Social role and personal identity labels as self concepts influence social conduct because they include assumptions about the consequences that are expected to befall a person who does or does not conform to a given cultural category. A powerful source of motivation in social interaction is the individual's concern with achieving a self image and public image as a person with culturally favorable roles and personality attributes.

Attention to the culturally constituted motives behind role and self-image formation is important to an understanding of *actual* social worlds. As we shall see, attention to these cultural factors is also crucial to an understanding of *imaginary* social worlds. But before considering the importance of culture in imaginary relationships, I want to examine two actual social scenes, one from Fáánakkar and one from Pakistan. I will return to these scenes periodically throughout this book as I develop contrasts between American and non-Western social systems. Before considering the imaginary dimension of these scenes, I want to introduce certain actual patterns of social interaction.

A magical curer on Fáánakkar does not begin the morning in that role. He begins the day in a thatch-roofed, sand-floored, one-room building occupied by about twenty-five other people. His wife and children are with him in a corner of this room, but they are merely part of the extended family group including his wife's "mothers" and "sisters" and their immediate families. The house is the residential center of his wife's matrilineage, and it is presided over by the oldest of his wife's mother's brothers. As *mweno*, lineage leader, this man exercises considerable authority over the curer and his wife. If the curer fails to fulfill his obligations, the lineage leader may retaliate—as by terminating his marriage. The curer's relationships with the other persons in this lineage center are also structured by social roles. For example, he has the right to sleep with his wife's younger sister, whom he also addresses as "wife."

In the middle of the day the curer walks across the village to his own lineage center to treat a sick relative suffering from fevers and delirium. He suspects that the patient is suffering from a disease called *sáát*, but on his way across the village he stops at another specialist's house to check his diagnosis. There a local medium enters a trance state and verifies his suspicions. Entering his own lineage house, he takes on the role of *mwáání*, "older brother," to his sisters' husbands and exercises authority over them, but here he also assumes the role of curer. Preparing his treatment, he heats small stones in the fire and drops them into bowls of herbal medicine. Then, to the accompaniment of spells, he steams the patient with this medicine. The patient's lineage has already presented him with valuables, and if the cure is successful he will receive a larger payment. He will also enhance his status in his ongoing battle with the other magical curers of the village.

High in the craggy Himalayan foothills of northwestern Pakistan, a Sufi holy man, or fakir, awakens on the stone floor of a shallow cave. He rolls out from under his blanket and looks down over the valley below. Dressed in baggy white clothing, he also wears black iron bracelets and a necklace of colored stones. Outside the cave huge black and green banners sway in the breeze, and grey wood smoke drifts up from the mud-walled village in the valley far below.

With him in the cave are five other men rolled in their blankets. None of them is related to him by blood, but all are linked to him by social ties considered stronger than kinship. Each of them is a *muriid*, a spiritual disciple, who has left the worldly life of the villages and cities in order to pursue a difficult path of spiritual development. The holy man serves in the role of their spiritual guide (*murshid*). He supervises their progress along the stations and states of the path and he assigns them spiritual exercises, including forms of self-mortification intended to remove negative personal attributes. At various stages the disciple may be asked to meditate for several hours a day in a dark hole in the ground, or to fast and keep a vow of silence, or to wear 100 pounds of iron chains. As the disciple progresses along the path, he not only changes his personal identity but gradually acquires magical powers with which he can cure illness and help other people to attain their wishes. Along with their spiritual exercises, the disciples must also assist the holy man with the work of helping the many pilgrims who visit this shrine each day.

By midmorning the first of the pilgrims are climbing slowly up the steep rocky path. They arrive in groups of relatives and friends, usually from the same caste, village, or city district. Some come to visit or to offer general prayers, but many come with specific problems. A man is suffering from bodily pains, depression, and strange visions; a woman can bear no male children; a man's business is failing; a ten-year-old girl is subject to fits of raving and violent anger.

When the group with the girl has reached the top of the trail, they leave their sandals at the steps and move out the stone walkway to the cave where the holy man is sitting. The pilgrims greet him deferentially, chat for a few minutes, and then sit the girl down before him. The holy man talks to the child gently and touches her arm. Then he sits quietly for a few moments and enters a mild trance state. When he returns he whispers a short prayer and ties a strip of sacred cloth on the child's arm. He tells her family to take her out to the "court." They proceed further along the walkway to a small, narrow, balcony-like structure on the face of the cliff wall. There they light candles at the altar, rub the child with black stones, gather ash from the fireplace, write a prayer on a strip of paper, and hang it on the altar. Then they return past the cave to the lower part of the shrine. There they eat the sacred food prepared by the apprentice fakirs and prayed over by the holy man. Later they will give the child a pinch of the sacred ash to eat. If the cure is successful the pilgrims will return again to thank the fakir, and they will bring him money, food, and a goat to sacrifice.[9]

The descriptions of these two social scenes illustrate a standard focus of traditional ethnography. It is taken for granted that a description of "social organization" is crucial to ethnography because "social relationships constitute the single most important feature of life in every society."[10] It is also taken for granted that "social relationships" means *actual social relations between real people*. Whatever the theoretical orientation of the ethnographer, matters like those discussed above are what get described in accounts of social organization. Social scientists are concerned with patterns of actual social conduct.

While valid as far as it goes, this view of social relationships is incomplete. As A. I. Hallowell has pointed out, such a supposedly objective approach to social organization actually represents an ethnocentric projection of certain narrow assumptions in Western social science. It may seriously misrepresent the inner worlds of other cultures. A description of social relationships restricted to actual interactions between real people may not begin to encompass the subjective social experience of people in other societies. "In other words, the 'social' relations of the self when considered in its total behavioral environment may be far more inclusive than ordinarily conceived. The self in its relations with other selves may transcend the boundaries of social life as objectively defined. This is a fact of some psychological importance since it is relevant to the needs, motivations, and goals of individuals under certain circumstances."[11]

Emphasizing the importance of understanding another society from the inside—that is, in terms of the cognition of its members—Hallowell showed that non-Western social systems commonly include categories of beings other than those "real" humans with whom an individual engages in actual face-to-face relations. Among the Ojibwa Indians it is taken for granted that additional "persons"—thunder gods, fabulous giant monsters, and deceased ancestors—not only exist but interact with human beings. Many of the encounters humans have with these beings involve dreams and other "hallucinatory" states of mind, but they are an important part of the individual's subjective social experience. "The more deeply we penetrate the world view of the Ojibwa the more apparent it is that 'social relations' between human beings (anicinavek) and other-than-human 'persons' are of cardinal significance."[12]

The importance of this perspective can be appreciated through a reconsideration of the two social scenes described above. The

Sufi shrine is located where it is, on this particular cliff, because it was here that a famous local saint, a long dead fakir, used to come and meditate. The court is built on the ledge where he stayed, the present fire is in his fireplace. The shrine is holy because the saint's spirit (*ruh*) is still present here. When pilgrims climb the trail to this shrine, they do so to visit the saint's spirit. It is to him that they bow when they reach the court, it is to him that they make their requests, and it is to him that they address their prayers. While praying, they sometimes feel his mysterious power, but his presence is also evidenced by more tangible effects such as the visible form of his fresh handprint in wet clay during the annual death ceremonies. His presence is also evident in the cures which are effected by him on the pilgrims who come to visit.

The fakirs of the shrine have even more direct interactions with the saint's spirit, and much of what they do is based on his directions. Sometimes he guides them through cryptic signs or "indications," sometimes he communicates with them in dreams, and sometimes he appears to them in trance states. When the fakir went into a trance during the visit of the sick girl, he heard the saint's voice tell him that the girl was possessed by evil jinn spirits; his choice of remedies was based on the saint's diagnosis. The world of these Sufis is thus pervaded by social interactions with the saint's spirit.

The Sufis are a magical-religious group, but human-spirit relationships may be of similar importance in ordinary societies as well. This will be evident from a reexamination of Fáánakkar social organization.

First, spirits are crucial to Fáánakkar magic. All magical knowledge was directly taught to humans by spirits in the past. They continue to provide the active power behind magic, and most spells invoke the name of a particular spirit. However, spirits are important not only to magical curers. The existence and importance of spirits is an aspect of reality that is taken for granted by all members of Fáánakkar society. Everyone knows the names, personalities, and special attributes of dozens of spirits; there is a widespread lore about their past accomplishments, and people talk about them regularly.

Ordinary people not only know about these beings—they also

have social relationships with them. Good ancestral spirits maintain an active interest in their descendants and often engage in indirect interactions with living people—by, for example, punishing an offender with illness. Spirits also interact directly with people. Sometimes they communicate through mediums, men or women who have a special gift for spirit interactions. One medium, the "canoe of the ghosts," enters a trance state and is temporarily possessed by spirits who speak through her, giving orders, warning of sorcery attacks, or identifying the cause of an illness. Spirits also appear visually before ordinary people, and sometimes they converse with them in the local language. Occasionally they establish a special relationship involving regular interactions. For example, evil sea spirits—nine of whom live in the lagoon around Fáánakkar—have the power to appear to people in the form of handsome men or beautiful women. Sometimes, as in the following account, they establish love relationships with their victims.

While he was out fishing by himself one night, a man fell asleep on his paddling canoe. He was awakened by a beautiful girl who asked him for a cigarette. When he said he had none, she told him to wait for her. She went over the side of the canoe and returned half an hour later with a pack of cigarettes. He was very attracted to the girl. When she asked that they "marry" he quickly agreed and they made love on the canoe. Afterwards the girl ordered him to tell no one. She also asked him to return to the same spot the next night, promising that he would catch many fish. The next night he returned and slept with the girl again. Each night he went out to meet the sea demon. Afterwards he began to go crazy.[13]

While such love relationships are not common, most people have had some dealings with spirits, and these interactions often have important effects on actual social conduct. A lineage leader who was wondering what to do about a dispute between two of his living kinsmen told me about one spirit encounter a few hours after it had happened. "I was lying on my sleeping mat," he said, "when the ghost of M. appeared. It was like a dream but it was not a dream. She said that I should not participate in the dispute between N. and W. She said that if I ignored her orders she would take one of my 'eyes' [that is, sicken or kill one of his lineage mates]."

For the Pakistani Sufis and the people of Fáánakkar, as for the people of many other societies, the social world includes a set of spirit beings, some of whom play roles in the social system. Interactions with spirits represent an important part of the individual's subjective experience. Often these relations are emotionally intense. As Yi-Fu Tuan suggests, belief in supernatural beings "enables a person to see and live in phantasmagorical worlds of witches, ghosts and monsters; these figures embody a weight of dread unknown to other animals. . . . Imagination adds immeasurably to the kinds and intensity of fear in the human world."[14] Yet relations with spirit beings may also be experienced as intensely satisfying, meaningful, and gratifying.

Spirit relationships are subjectively significant; they also exert a strong influence on actual social behavior. They are a common topic of conversation, they influence decision making, and they affect the manner in which people interact with each other. Given their psychological and social effects, spirit relationships are often important to the functioning of a social system. Discussing spirits on the tiny Micronesian island of Ifaluk, Melford Spiro shows that spirit interactions deflect hostility and aggression from actual relationships in a society where cooperation is crucial. He argues that an "irrational belief" in spirits actually performs an essential social function. Without spirit relationships, he says, the actual social system would disintegrate.[15]

The "reality status" of spirit relationships poses an interesting question. In terms of Fáánakkar and Sufi knowledge, spirit relations are more than subjective experiences. They are special but real experiences with beings who exist not only in the mind but out there in the world. Spirits are assumed to be independent actors with their own histories, personalities, and motives. However, from a secular, Western, social science perspective, belief in spirits is "irrational." While there are problems with this perspective, I will adopt it here. I will assume, that is, that spirit relationships are imaginary social relationships.

To say this, however, is not to say that these relationships are insignificant. As we have seen, spirit relationships can be important both to individual experience and to the functioning of society—which is to say that understanding imaginary social

20

relationships is often crucial to an understanding of society. As Hallowell properly insists, a study of non-Western social organization that excludes spirit relationships must be regarded as incomplete.

Hallowell's critique of traditional studies of social organization is based entirely on his concern that relationships with spirits should be included in an inside description of non-Western social structure. But his perspective applies to the study of modern American society as well. Spirit beings are sometimes important in contemporary Western society, and for many members of American religious groups, spirit relations are just as significant as they are to Pakistani fakirs or the people of Fáánakkar. However, rather than examining American spirit relationships, I will argue here that there are hundreds of significant beings different from but somewhat analogous to spirits who haunt the lives of contemporary secular Americans. Given a slight twist, Hallowell's insight into social systems opens up an important perspective on a significant but neglected dimension of American social experience.

The "real" social world of an American consists of the people with whom he actually interacts. Commonly numbering 200 to 300 persons, this group consists of various relatives, friends, co-workers, and acquaintances. Such relationships—the focus of studies of American social organization—are obviously important. But the average American also knows about a swarming throng of other beings who may be very significant to him, but with whom he does *not* engage in actual face-to-face relations. There are three main classes of these beings.

First, there are the media figures—all those beings with which the individual is "familiar" through television, movies, books, newspapers, magazines, and other forms of the media. The beings in this media world—the movie stars and politicians, the talk show hosts and soap opera characters, the sports figures and comic strip characters—are typically more numerous than the persons in anyone's actual social world. It may be objected that since the individual only knows *about* these media beings, he does not (by definition) interact with them, and they cannot be part of his social experience. In fact, media figures do play important roles in the individual's subjective social experience.

While an American does not have real face-to-face interactions with media figures, he does have artificial interactions with them. Every time he turns on a television or opens a book or magazine, he shifts mentally into a world of vicarious social experience. As we shall see, the intensity of such media relations can be very high. The individual's pseudo interactions with media figures are not restricted solely to media involvements. People regularly encounter media figures in imaginary contexts. Ruth Steinhagen "met" Eddie Waitkus as "lover" in fantasies, dreams, and solitary conversations. Such imaginary processes remove the individual psychologically from his or her objective situation, but they take the individual into a system of *social* relationships.

The purely imaginary figures produced by the individual's own consciousness constitute a second class of artificial beings. These private constructs include the enormous number of imaginary beings that float through the individual's sleep world in dreams and nightmares. Often these dream figures seem vividly real. They act, talk, cry, and smile. And again these creatures do not just appear; they also approach the dream self and engage the individual in imaginary social interactions. Such relations, charged with powerful emotions, are subjectively significant within the dream, and often they are important to actual experience as well. Numerous other private imaginary beings, from the imaginary friends of childhood to the fantasy figures of adult daydreaming, also figure significantly in waking imaginary experience.

Finally, there are the several hundred persons one actually knows as they appear in imaginary experience. Imaginary replicas of friends, kin, and lovers play important roles in all forms of inner experience—as when the individual visualizes future encounters with friends or meets family members in memories and dreams. Like media beings and private creations, imaginary replicas of known others engage the individual in *imaginary social interactions*.

Even such a preliminary sketch of imaginary social relationships points up the presence of a neglected but important aspect of American society. We have here a situation that parallels the problem which Hallowell identified. Traditional studies of social organization, focused on "actual" social interactions, have neglected a complex, pervasive, and significant dimension of American social life. Yet an approach to American society that ignores imaginary social relationships is incomplete. An adequate understanding of American social experience demands analysis of imaginary social interactions.

But granting the importance of imaginary relationships, how can they be studied? Unlike actual social behavior, imaginary processes are not susceptible to direct "objective" observation. The only way to obtain data on such processes is through asking one's subjects to engage in introspection. But introspection, it is often assumed, is unreliable, erroneous, and distorted—not, therefore, a legitimate "scientific" method. This attitude reached its extreme in psychology during the reign of behaviorism, when psychological processes not subject to direct laboratory measurement were banished from the field. In some circles, behavioristic thinking continues to affect, and sometimes to distort, research on inner experience. As Kamiya writes, "One of the chief difficulties [in the study of private experience] is that it is very difficult when an individual says, 'I had a dream last night,' to know whether in fact he is telling the truth. This emerges as a problem because we have no independent way of indexing the occurrence of a dream, or the occurrence of a hope, etc." [16]

Noting that we can now use laboratory methods to electronically monitor the occurrence of brain activities, Kamiya suggests, "We can put electrodes on the scalp and observe patterns of electrical activity that reflect brain activity." [17] Thus we can *prove* whether or not our subjects are telling the truth when they report a dream, an image, or a hope. This triumph of objective measurement, however, does not take us very far. Through the use of electrodes we may be able to tell whether or not the subject in fact had a dream, but we can tell nothing about what we really want to know—what the dream was *about*. If our interest is in the contents of dreams or images, we must still rely entirely on the subject's introspective reports. For the strict behaviorist this means that imaginary experience should not be studied. For the rest of us the question is one of trying to devise reliable forms of research based on self reports. Since Kamiya's article was published, there has been a shift

23

towards greater reliance on introspective self-reports. A considerable portion of this research has, in fact, been directed toward the psychological study of imaginary processes, a notable example being the careful work of Jerome Singer and his colleagues on daydreaming.[18] Some of the methods and findings of these studies are of considerable interest for the development of a cultural approach to imaginary social experience.

In social science as well, introspection has traditionally been regarded as taboo. Anthropologist Jacques Maquet expressed the conservative view when he asserted that "anthropological techniques exclude introspection."[19] This sounds noble; it is also patently false. As Anthony F. C. Wallace has shown, introspection is and always has been central to traditional ethnography. In the field, ethnographers routinely ask their informants questions which require them to engage in personal reflection. For example, a great deal of the data on social organization actually come not from direct observation but from interviews in which informants introspectively reflect on social knowledge and on their experience of past interactions. Data so generated can often be shown to have a great deal of validity. As Wallace observes, the anthropologist actually obtains much of his data through asking his informant to introspect.[20] Since this is an accepted method for studying actual experience, there is no reason not to apply it to the study of imaginary experience.

Wallace goes on to argue not only that introspection is a legitimate method, but that it is also relevant when the anthropologist is studying his own society. The researcher can employ introspection to ethnographically study his own personal experience by using himself as the informant. "For the anthropologist to record, by writing or dictating, his own thoughts about his own culturally relevant behavior involves only a minor difference in method from standard procedure."[21]

In his essay "Driving to Work," Wallace explores the knowledge he uses each morning to drive from his home to his office. "Thus the description of the process of driving to work will depend upon the introspective consultation of memory by an anthropologist-informant, sitting at his writing table, recalling patterns of experience in specific activity which he has personally experienced approximately five hundred times."[22] While the use of such methods has been increasingly employed in recent anthropology, there has been some criticism. Hayano points out that Wallace's "self-ethnography" involves no attempt to show how the researcher's individual knowledge compares to that of other members of American society. He implies that self-ethnography is problematical because it is confined to a sample of one, and that data from a single informant cannot produce reliable results.[23]

Here the solution is simple enough. Just as one can sit down after an experience—real or imaginary—and record one's memory of it, so one can ask an informant to do the same. Informants can be enlisted as coethnographers and asked to report on their own memory of their own experience immediately after the experience has occurred. Such an approach allows for the possibility of systematically checking and comparing independent reports of the same experience.[24]

Since this is a book about imaginary experience, it is based largely on introspective self-reports. While I have drawn to some extent on published autobiographical accounts, I have relied more heavily on data obtained from my own informants. I have used ethnographic interviews to obtain self-reports from informants in Pakistan and Fáánakkar and I have used similar methods in my research in the United States. Most of my American informants were associated with one of the two eastern universities where I have taught. Some were faculty or staff; many were students in my graduate and undergraduate classes on imaginary social worlds. While less familiar in anthropology and American Studies, the use of students as subjects is, of course, a well-established tradition in psychology and social psychology.[25] In studying American imaginary processes I have also used myself as an informant; that is, I have monitored and recorded my own imaginary experiences. Where some new aspect of imaginary experience seemed to emerge from my own introspections—as from the introspections of any other single informant—I have systematically checked this information against independent reports from many other informants. While I have relied heavily on in-depth work with particular informants, I have dealt with many different subjects. My total sample of American informants now runs to over 500 people.

With this kind of sample, an ethnographic approach has certain advantages over clinical methods, laboratory research, and questionnaire surveys. In the clinical approach, one's subjects are "disturbed" and hence nonrepresentative. In laboratory research and questionnaire surveys, one's subjects are strangers and distortion is likely to be a problem. In the ethnographic approach, one comes to know informants over a period of weeks or months. As a working relationship is established, the informant is probably less likely deliberately to withhold data or distort its contents, let alone lie about whether or not he or she had a dream last night. Moreover, as the ethnographer comes to know the informant, he can more adequately evaluate his reports; he gains a better sense of a given informant's reliability, self-awareness, and insight. This is not to say that introspective self-reports obtained through ethnographic methods are totally accurate records of the experiences they represent. Even a trustworthy and open informant may sometimes withhold certain embarrassing details from the description of a dream. Nevertheless, using the methods outlined above, one can obtain a quite reliable body of data.[26]

Usually, deliberate distortion is less of a problem than lack of recall. The evidence is overwhelming that most Americans pass large amounts of time engrossed in imaginary experiences, but many people are only dimly aware of the shape and contents of these experiences. People dream extensively every night, but since Americans pay little attention to these experiences, dream details tend to fade rapidly upon awakening. As with questionnaire research, straightforward interview questions ("Tell me about your recent dreams") often produce sparse results. However, this problem can be overcome by the use of alternate ethnographic strategies. In research on all forms of imagination, I have asked informants to recall their own imaginary experience outside the interview situation immediately after the experience has occurred. Thus, in studying dreams, I asked informants to keep a notebook beside their beds and to record the contents of dreams immediately upon awakening. I have employed a similar approach in studying daydreams and other forms of imagination. Using such techniques, most informants can produce highly detailed reports of their imaginary experiences.

Granting that we can obtain detailed texts of imaginary experience, how can we analyze and interpret them from a *cultural* perspective? In seeking to answer this question, we can turn to the work of those few writers who have taken a social science approach to experiences similar to those that concern us. The work of the phenomenological sociologists Alfred Schutz, Peter Berger, and Thomas Luckmann is particularly pertinent. They note that, in all societies, "Everyday life is taken for granted as reality." [27] This "reality" is, in fact, culturally constructed and culturally relative— it varies from society to society. But to the individual member of society, this culturally constructed drama seems to be solid, universal reality. He experiences the routines of daily life, particularly social interactions with family, coworkers, and friends, as taken-for-granted reality. However, as Schutz observes, the individual also experiences certain "interruptions" or "shocks" in his ordinary everyday life. These include "the shock of falling asleep as the leap into the world of dreams; the inner transformation we endure if the curtain in the theater rises as the transition into the world of a stageplay; the radical change in our attitude if, before a painting, we permit our visual field to be limited by what is within the frame as the passage into the pictorial world. . . ." [28] These interruptions take the individual into states of mind that are beyond the ordinary and to a greater or lesser degree contrary to ordinary reality. Schutz and Berger mention many other examples of such nonordinary states, including violence, sexual experience, boxing and similar sports, mathematics, puppet shows, madness, vacations, and police interrogations. In each case the activity carries the individual outside ordinary reality. Sexual activity, for example, is viewed as "a breach in the structures of everyday reality" because in "tearing the masks of their social roles from the faces of men and women" it reveals "a howling animality beneath the civilized decorum." [29]

In discussing such interruptions, Schutz and Berger observe that these nonordinary experiences have their own distinctive "structure" and "cognitive style." They argue, therefore, that they should be considered other "realities" outside the paramount reality of everyday life. When the individual engages in these activities, he is transported to another reality, or to what Schutz and Berger often refer to as "other worlds." Such a perspective is of particular importance to the study of the phenomena that concern us here.

For my purposes, it is useful to distinguish imaginary experience from other kinds of alternate realities. While boxing, making love, and taking vacations are somewhat different from everyday routines, they are still culturally patterned forms of actual social behavior. Even in the throes of sexual experience, men and women are engaged in culturally structured actual interaction. In this study, I will put aside these actual interactions and focus on *imaginary* interruptions of daily life, considering imaginary experiences mentioned by Berger and Schutz, such as dreams, and other forms of imagination as well. In doing so, I will seek to develop an aspect of Berger and Schutz's approach by treating such experiences as visits to "other worlds."

If we focus on imaginary experiences, the "other world" perspective becomes particularly useful and illuminating. When an individual falls asleep, he is indeed transported outside the reality of everyday life into another world with its own distinctive structures and patterns. And the same is true of other imaginary experiences. Adopting such a perspective allows us to approach these experiences with methods from social science. If we treat dreams and other imaginary experiences as other worlds, we can bypass psychological interpretations and apply instead the culturally oriented ethnographic methods that have been developed for the exploration and analysis of actual other worlds. That is, we can approach the dream world with methods similar to those we apply in trying to describe the inner world of a Pacific island society or a subculture within our own society. We can describe the basic settings and objects of these worlds, analyze their patterns of action and knowledge, and consider how their characteristics are similar to and different from those of ordinary American daily life.

Imaginary worlds have one important characteristic which makes them broadly similar to actual worlds. When an individual enters an imaginary realm, he typically finds himself in a place

where he is not alone—usually he meets other beings and engages in social interactions with them. In imaginary worlds, as
in actual worlds, always there will be other people: like actual
worlds, imaginary worlds are *social* worlds. This means that we
can apply methods of *social* analysis to them. In this study, I will
apply ethnographic methods used in the cultural analysis of actual
social relationships to the analysis of imaginary social experience.
I will consider the kinds of beings who appear, the kinds of roles
and identities they play, the values and goals they pursue, and the
social satisfactions and frustrations they endure. In short, I will seek
to analyze the patterns governing social interactions in imaginary
worlds.

I will also be concerned with the way in which imaginary social
relationships connect to society and culture. Here again I will
adopt standard ethnographic procedure. In studying an institution
or subculture in America, we are not concerned solely with the
inner world of this social system, but also with how it connects to
the general society and culture. It has often been assumed that
imaginary social experience is a trivial process with little or no
significance for the actual social world. This is one reason why
such experiences have been widely neglected. However, such an
attitude is in itself a cultural myth. Not only do imaginary experiences consume much of the individual's life; they also have multiple, complex, and significant connections to actual social conduct.
Like spirit relationships on Fáánakkar, American imaginary relationships play important roles in the American social system. As
we have seen in the prologue, imaginary relationships can lead to
real shootings. In the chapters which follow, I will show that
imaginary relationships have many other direct as well as subtle
influences on actual social behavior.

As Schutz and Berger point out, the paramount reality of everyday life is not as solid as it seems. Because it is fragile and precarious and subject to disruption and collapse, the social order of
everyday life needs to be enforced, protected, and maintained.
Other realities—including visits to imaginary worlds—constitute
potential threats to the stability of the social order and to the
peace of mind of individual societal inhabitants. Thus indulgence
in fantasy may be taken as a dangerous sign that the individual is

no longer appropriately loyal to official, socially sanctioned reality. In our society, psychiatry functions to keep potential "emigrants" from migrating too far into imaginary social worlds and seeks to bring back or isolate those who are reluctant to return.[30]

Imaginary processes do constitute a real threat to the social order. People can and do become "lost" in imaginary social worlds, and imaginary social relationships sometimes have highly negative effects on actual social interaction. However, to view the connections between imaginary relationships and society exclusively in this light is to fall prey to our culture's traditionally negative view of these experiences. Imaginary relationships also have many positive functions, both for the individual and for society. In this book I will examine how imaginary social relationships both threaten and support cultural reality.

Chapter 2

Social Relations with Media Figures

In order to act acceptably, or pass as a member of society, an individual is required to know about particular people.[1] On the Pacific island of Fáánakkar, a person unable to tell the names, salient characteristics, and personal histories of members of his or her own matrilineage would immediately be unmasked as an outsider. A member of Fáánakkar is also expected to know the names, characteristics, and personal histories of Fáánakkar spirits.[2] In any given society it may not be enough to have information about those one "knows"; one may also be required to possess information about beings one has never actually met. In American society it is not spirits that one is required to know about—it is media figures.

There are several classic tests of whether or not a person is truly "American." In Europe during World War II, strangers dressed in American uniforms and speaking fluent English might be Americans lost from their own units or German spies. Standard interrogation questions designed to test American affiliations included inquiries about persons the individual could not be expected actually to know—for example, "Who plays first base for the Philadelphia Phillies?" Answering such questions successfully was literally of life or death significance. A similar situation occurs during psychiatric interviews in American mental hospitals. Here failure to answer questions about American media figures—"Name the last four presidents"—is taken as a serious symptom of mental abnormality.[3]

The true American knows about more than a handful of baseball players and politicians; he knows about hundreds of different examples from many different fields. It is simply taken for granted that an American will know about a huge swarming throng of unmet figures through his consumption of the various media— through television, movies, radio, books, magazines, and newspapers. Within this group will be many sports figures, politicians, historical personages, actors, musicians, authors, columnists, announcers, disc jockeys, talk show hosts, and other celebrities, as well as all the fictional characters in the novels, plays, movies, television shows, and comic strips that are familiar to him.[4] The enormous number of beings in this artificial social world—commonly numbering well over 1,000—includes several times as many "persons" as those in his real social world. As one informant noted, "When I sat down and started to list media figures that were significant to me, my mind was overwhelmed by the volumes of names and faces. . . . We are bombarded by thousands of media figures."

And it is not enough merely to know who these beings are. An American is expected to possess extensive information about them. Even an average fan knows more than a baseball player's name. He also knows his team, uniform number, position, batting average, salary, and something about his appearance, personality, medical history, and off-the-field conduct. In the fall of 1980 millions of Americans knew about George Brett's hemorrhoids and Terry Bradshaw's marital difficulties. Would Terry's problems with JoJo Starbuck affect his quarterbacking? The *Washington Post*'s sports columnists presented not only Terry's views of the situation, but also his coaches' views, his teammates' views, and even JoJo's views.

Extensive information of this sort is absolutely essential for adequate participation in many standard American activities. It is necessary for adequate media comprehension, since media productions of all kinds are sprinkled with allusions to the characteristics of media figures who are identified by name alone. Sometimes only first names ("Jackie," "Reggie," "Bo," "Elvis," "Goldie," "Liz") or even initials ("JR," "RMN," "MM") are offered. Such knowledge is also socially necessary, since many American conversations revolve around the activities of media figures.

For example, *all* members of a minor league baseball team, the Alexandria Dukes, faithfully watch the soap opera "General Hospital." Partly they do so for aesthetic reasons ("It's one of the most exciting soap operas around"), but partly they watch out of social necessity. As a pitcher says, "Can't miss GH. You have to keep up. We talk about it everywhere, on the field, in the batting cage. . . ." What they talk about is the social entanglements of the fictional characters such as "vulnerable" Laura, "clever" Luke, "stoic" Jessie, and "conniving" Heather. Pseudo mutual acquaintances of this kind often provide American strangers in airplanes, taxicabs, or bars with the primary basis for socializing. Of "General Hospital" the baseball player adds, "Besides, when we go out to the bars and talk to girls, they all know about 'General Hospital.' It's something we can talk about. . . ."[5] In other social situations, analogous information is de rigueur.[6] Information about media figures is a core aspect of American cultural knowledge.

But Americans not only know about media figures. Despite the complete lack of real face-to-face contact, they also feel strongly about them. They are indifferent to a few, but they like or dislike others, and toward some they feel truly powerful emotions. In discussing their feelings, informants sometimes use terminology associated with the evaluation of performers ("talented," "entertaining"); more commonly they evaluate media beings personally. For example, those they dislike are characterized as "shallow," "phony," "manipulative," "dishonest," "mean," "pompous," "crude," and "snobbish." People characterize unmet media figures as if they were intimately involved with them, and in a sense they are—they engage in pseudo-social interactions with them. Just as the people of Fáánakkar engage in social relations with spirits, Americans involve themselves with their particular "gods." A major form of artificial social involvement is through media consumption.

As Peter Berger and Thomas Luckmann observe, the theater illustrates our participation in "multiple realities" outside ordinary social life. In attending the theater a person is psychologically drawn out of his objective social world into the realm of the play. At one moment he is talking with his companion in the next seat. At the next moment both are absorbed in the fictional doings of an eighteenth-century drama.

The transition between realities is marked by the rising and falling of the curtain. As the curtain rises, the spectator is "transported to another world," with its own meanings and an order that may or may not have much to do with the order of everyday life. As the curtain falls, the spectator "returns to reality," that is, to the paramount reality of everyday life by comparison with which the reality presented on the stage now appears tenuous and ephemeral. . . .[7]

Such vivid "transporting" experiences characterize *all* forms of media consumption. Every time an American enters a movie theater, turns on a media machine, or opens a book, newspaper, or magazine, he or she slips mentally out of the real social world and enters an artificial world of vicarious social experience.

Americans pass much of their lives in the "other worlds" of the media. By age sixteen, a contemporary child has spent more time watching TV than attending school. The average adult watches more than three hours of TV per day. Mass media consumption in general occupies 50 percent of all leisure time.[8] Take an American adult's evening of leisure. Picking up the evening newspaper, unmet reporters take the reader into a parade of national and international situations, from a mass murder in New York, through a Middle Eastern coup, to a strike in Japan. For relief the individual turns to the comic page. As he reads down the page from strip to strip, he shifts from the realm of fifteenth-century English knights ("Prince Valiant"), through French Foreign Legionnaires ("Crock"), to futuristic outer space ("Star Wars"), and back home to the realm of middle-class American suburbanites ("Hi and Lois"). And this is just the first ten minutes. He picks up a popular novel and enters the "romantic" world of the antebellum South. After an hour, he turns to TV, and spinning the dial, he flips from reality to reality, from "The Waltons" to "Dallas" before settling on "Buck Rogers." Even here commercials interrupt this reality and transport him back and forth from outer space to twentieth-century supermarkets, bathrooms, and bars.

The cultural variability of these multiple realities is less than might be expected. Comic strips, popular novels, television programs, and commercials present outer space monsters, Nazi Germans, fifteenth-century knights, and nineteenth-century Southern plantation owners who not only speak late twentieth-century

American English, but who operate with values, motives, and roles firmly locked to the assumptions of the contemporary American middle class. But the lack of cultural variability does not contradict the important fact that the average American's media experience takes him daily through a large number of complex "scenes" beyond those of his actual experience.

It is essential to recognize that these other worlds are *social* worlds. In each form of media consumption, the individual is not transported to deserted landscapes or empty rooms, but into crowded social scenes peopled by hundreds of different human or humanlike media creatures. He is tangled temporarily in elaborate systems of *social interaction*. How does an individual connect to such artificial social worlds?

First, an individual connects to a media world because it *seems* vividly real. Our familiarity with the media tends to obscure this point, but it is evident in the reactions of people exposed for the first time to movies or television. On Fáánakkar many of my informants were just beginning to see movies. While visiting the nearby district administrative island, they would sometimes go to a rusty old Quonset hut where American musical, cowboy, and war movies were occasionally shown. Typically, the islanders assumed that the moviemakers had somehow recorded ongoing events in the lives of real soldiers and cowboys; they took these vivid images as real records of actual behavior. An even more striking example is provided by the reactions of early American movie audiences. "They accepted the flat flickering images as reality. When locomotives thundered down the track, when waves rolled towards the camera, people in the front rows ran screaming for the exits."[9]

Contemporary American children, attracted early by the seemingly real quality of television, have to learn to make reality distinctions between different kinds of programs. A five-year-old who was already familiar with the distinction between "live" sportscasts and staged fictional productions misinterpreted his first view of professional TV wrestling: Bill Blackthorn was set upon by the huge villain who, despite the referee's frantic efforts, resorted to the most vicious tactics. Grabbing Bill by the shoulders, he repeatedly smashed his head—battering ram style—into the ring corner post. Picking up Bill, he spun him around over his head and hurled him down on the floor of the ring. Bill lay motionless on the floor of the ring. "Bill Blackthorn is down . . . ," the announcer intoned. The five-year-old interrupted and said with horror, "Bill Blackthorn is dead!" Whether the person thinks that what seems to be happening is fictional or "live," that which absorbs him in the production is its seeming "reality." To an important extent the flickering images are apprehended as *people*.

An individual connects to media experience through learned systems of knowledge for processing perceptions about human social conduct. To understand the contents of any media production, the individual must use culturally encoded cues to recognize social situations, personality types, and social roles. One must be capable of determining each character's intended place in the situation—broadly speaking, that so-and-so is the "villain" or the "hero" or, more narrowly, that so-and-so is having certain feelings about what is happening but is disguising these to fool some other character.[10] All this involves wielding an enormous amount of complex information about symbolic social relations. The cultural structuring of this process is clearly revealed when people misconceptualize foreign media productions. South Sea islanders, for example, may construe information in American cowboy movies intended to show friendship between the hero and his sidekick as indicating that the two are members of the same matrilineal kin group.

The individual also connects to a media production by assuming a social role that links him structurally to the social drama he consumes. In the least intricate form, the individual watches (or listens to, or reads about) the social interactions of media figures in the passive role of "observer." He watches the action in much the same way he watches his neighbors arguing through a lighted window. Although behaviorally passive, the individual must be emotionally interested in what he beholds, or he will shift his attention to other matters. Media productions, of course, are deliberately structured to engage the "human interest" of the audience; they focus relentlessly on what are culturally considered the "highlights," such as violent moments, of the social situations and relationships they portray. This is so effectively accomplished that a child watching a boisterous cartoon or even an adult reading a suspense novel typically becomes so fascinated that it may be difficult to catch his attention. The intensity of this absorbed state leads some researchers to compare media consumption to the trance-like altered states of consciousness induced by drug consumption.[11] Manipulated by a steady stream of dramatic dialogue and tense or amusing interaction, the individual becomes so absorbed that the proper label for this role is not "observer" but "voyeur."

Often the individual is drawn more directly into the media drama. He or she shifts from the role of observer to that of participant and "enters" the other world. Sometimes the individual remains himself but is drawn into a pseudo relationship with the media being. Thus the individual may find himself "interacting" with media beings when literature takes a conversational tone ("Dear Reader . . .") or when a TV figure such as an announcer, politician, or comedian speaks directly out of the television and addresses the audience personally. Here media consumption directly parallels actual social interaction. D. Horton and Richard Wohl have analyzed this artificial or "seeming face-to-face relationship between spectator and performer" and demonstrated that it is "closely analogous to and in many ways resembles social interaction in ordinary primary groups." In order to engage the audience, the "greatest pains are taken by the persona to create an illusion of intimacy," as by facing the camera and imitating the conversational style, tone, and mannerisms of personal relationships. Watching such a performer's image, the spectator does not remain "passive." His or her "psychological response is closely analogous to that in an actual social relationship." In apprehending the total communication and in decoding gestural, situational, and linguistic cues, the spectator is compelled to select some role complementary to that assumed by the performer. This may involve psychologically playing "the admiring dependent to his father-surrogate" or "the earnest citizen to his fearless opponent of political evils" or even "the loved one to the persona's lover."[12]

A vivid example was the popular 1951 radio program "The Lonesome Gal." This program consisted entirely of a female voice engaged in a conversational monologue. "Darling, you look so tired and a little put out about something this evening . . . you are worried, I feel it. . . . Come, lie down on the couch, relax, I want to stroke your hair gently. . . ." She spoke to the individuals in her audience "as if she was addressing a lover in the utter privacy of some hidden rendezvous."[13]

Of course, the spectator may reject the performer's gambit and react with antagonism; in doing so he is still engaged in pseudo interaction with the media image. As Alan Blum has shown, lower-class blacks commonly engage in hostile joking relationships with white TV performers. Sometimes this role playing is overt, as when "the spectator would chide the performer, cajole him, answer his questions directly, warn him of impending dangers, compliment him, and so on."[14] The strategies employed by an audience usually represent "some variant of the role or roles normally played in the spectator's primary social groups."[15]

Such role playing sometimes transcends psychological reactions and linguistic responses and extends to physical action—as when the viewer kisses the TV, makes a rude gesture at the TV image, or even hurls objects at the screen. Seizing on the commercial possibilities of this pseudo interaction, an American firm markets styrofoam "TV Bricks" which can be safely hurled at offending media beings.

A third form of artificial role playing involves the complex processes of "identification."[16] Here people temporarily abandon their own identities and social roles and, by imaginatively projecting their consciousness onto the media image, take on alternate personal and social identities. Sometimes media identification involves living celebrities. Frederick Exley offers an example from American sports.

I spent . . . Sundays with a few bottles of beer at the Parrot, eyes fixed on the television screen, cheering for my team. *Cheering* is a paltry description. The Giants were my delight, my folly, my anodyne, my intellectual stimulation. With Huff I "stunted" up and down the room among the bar stools, preparing to "shoot the gap"; with Shofner I faked two defenders "out of their cleats," took high, swimming passes over my right shoulder and trotted, dipsy-doodle-like, into the end zone; with Robustelli I swept into backfields and with cruel disdain flung flatfooted, helpless quarterbacks to the turf.[17]

In a similar way, people may also vicariously live out the experiences of totally fictional characters. Through identification they may feel the hero's or heroine's emotions, endure the character's personal tragedies, and achieve his or her social triumphs. The constructors of media worlds lavish considerable effort on techniques that not only invite but virtually force this kind of identification. A telling example is their success in inducing identification not only with imaginary humans but also with imaginary dogs, rabbits, and pigs.

Most media productions employ a variety of techniques to induce pseudo involvement. A cowboy drama may employ camera work that switches the audience back and forth between the roles of voyeur and identified participant—as in the following hypothetical movie script.

(1) Shot from across the room of the hero picking up a pair of binoculars. We can see him standing at the window looking out.

(2) Shot through the binoculars of distant Indian warriors riding toward us across the plain. Here we are the hero; we see what he sees.

(3) Shot of the heroine in a low-cut dress walking over and looking tenderly at the hero. We see them both from the middle distance facing each other. They think they are alone but we are watching.

(4) Close-up shot of the heroine's face and upper trunk, full face, as she stares lovingly up at the hero. Here we become the hero again and get fully the look she is sending at him.

In practice the techniques are often more subtle, but the effect is the same. The individual is pulled out of the objective social world and transported into the midst of an imaginary social world in which he or she participates in the most intense and intimate fashion. In a single week an average American plays roles in hundreds of social situations beyond those of actual social experience.

Social involvement with media figures is not confined to periods of actual media consumption. Even when the TV is turned off, the book closed, or the newspaper thrown away, people continue to engage in artificial social relationships with the figures they have "met" in the media. Our fuzzy thinking about media beings is reflected in the lack of a precise vocabulary with which to specify the kinds of relationships that actually exist between media figures and media consumers. Virtually everyone with any interest in a media being is classified simply as a "fan." The derivation of this term is significant. The word "fan" comes from the term "fanatic," which is derived from the Latin *fanaticus*, "someone inspired to frenzy by devotion to a deity," a person "possessed."[18] However, as ordinarily used, both in common parlance and in social analysis, the term "fan" is inadequate. It does not begin to do justice to the variety of attachments to media figures that exist in American society—and it does not do justice to the real structure of these attachments. Psychiatrist Lawrence Freedman suggests that "most fans are normal individuals who become involved in a continuing esthetic appreciation of a star."[19] In fact, the basis of most fan attachments is something much more than this.

Interviewed about their interest in a given figure, many fans attempt to explain their attachment by specifying an actual social relationship whose emotional quality is similar to that which they feel to the star—one celebrity will be seen as a "father figure," another as a "sister type" or a "friend." This leads us in the right direction. The basis of most fan relationships is not an esthetic appreciation but a social relationship. Fans have attachments to unmet media figures that are analogous to and in many ways directly parallel to actual social relationships with real "fathers," "sisters," "friends," and "lovers." I will consider two other major varieties below, but I will begin with the most dramatic example, "artificial romance." Here the fan casts the media figure in the role of imaginary lover.

Ruth Steinhagen had a romantic attachment to baseball player Eddie Waitkus. She was not engaged in an "esthetic appreciation" of Waitkus; she was in love with him. The psychiatric report argues that her relationship was abnormal from the start, but this is not the case. All the patterns of behavior that Steinhagen engaged in prior to the time she decided to murder her imaginary lover are standard among those many—probably millions—of normal Americans who have love relationships with unmet media figures. The data for the analysis that follows come partly from published sources, but most of the detailed information comes from my own research with seventy-two Americans who are or have been engaged in such artificial love relationships. Fifty-one of these relationships involved females (ranging in age from eight to sixty-two), all of whom had intense romantic attachments to male celebrities they had not actually met. The objects of their affections included Paul McCartney, John Lennon, John Travolta, Donny Osmond, Elton John, Roger Daltrey, Gary Cooper, Frank Sinatra, O. J. Simpson, Bill Bradley, Marlon Brando, Rudolf Nureyev, Richard Chamberlain, Dick Cavett, James Dean, Charlton Heston, Rhett Butler, Bobby Sherman, Jonathan Hart, Clint Eastwood, Robby Benson, Richard Dreyfuss, Cat Stevens, Burt Reynolds, and Robert Redford.

Like Steinhagen, most of my informants explicitly described their relationships in romantic terms. They were "infatuated with," "fixated on," "obsessed with," "crazy about," or (most commonly) "in love with" the favored media figure. Erotic attraction is a basic part of the appeal. "At this time I did not have a boyfriend, so Elton John filled that role. . . . I was in love with him. Even though he was far from what people would view as sexually appealing, I was highly attracted to him." For one seventeen-year-old, it was the eyes. "I fell in love with him [John Travolta] when he appeared in *The Boy in the Plastic Bubble*. I liked his beautiful blue eyes. . . . Although I have somewhat outgrown my teenage fetish, I can't help but think of him from time to time. When I see those blue eyes, I still melt." Another informant, age twenty-one, is even more explicit.

It almost takes my breath away to look at him or even think about him, and seeing him magnified on the movie screen makes him look even more like a Greek God. . . . He's elegantly dark, with short, thickly waving hair pushed hurriedly away from his face. . . . His nose is precisely formed, his lips thin but soft and sensitive. Coarse, dark, curling hair covers his chest, arms and legs, and this masculine look is heightened by the contrasting softness of his back and his fingers. . . .

The intensity of these love relationships is often as strong as that of a "real" love affair. As an Elvis Presley admirer put it, "No one will ever understand how I feel. I love him! He has given me happiness and excitement in my life that will never die."[20]

But aside from these intense feelings, what do such relationships involve? First, they involve regular, intense, romantically structured media consumption. "I saw the film [*Saturday Night Fever*] not only once, twice, but six times." In viewing a dramatic production, the individual sometimes projects herself into the female lead and plays out romantic interactions with her media lover. "I put myself in the wife's role; my personality took over her part." In other cases, the individual personally responds in the role of romantic partner.

I lust for him in a daydreamy way when I watch him in the show.

He sang a song he wrote with such feeling and conviction that I was enchanted. The fact that he wrote it indicated to me that those were powerful emotions he personally felt. I wanted to climb right through the screen.

From the moment he first walked on stage, I was completely enchanted. His movements and speech were spellbinding, and I found that I couldn't take my eyes off him.

One twenty-year-old with a crush on Roger Daltrey of The Who describes her first concert as follows:

As I sat in my seat waiting for the concert to begin, my heart was pounding with the excitement. Then the lights went out and The Who appeared on stage. From that point on, I was totally absorbed in the concert. I didn't speak to my friend, who was sitting next to me, nor did I move my eyes away from the stage. I felt as though The Who were playing their songs just for me. I was surrounded by their music. When I left the concert, I felt exhilarated, as though I had actually met The Who in person.

This reaction is described again and again. The individual feels that the TV singer is singing directly to her. Mass media productions—including those in magazines and posters—are taken as *personal* communications.

I would go grocery shopping with my mother just so I could leaf through the various teen magazines that contained heartthrob stories about Donny, who at twelve years old was made out to be a loving, sensitive and caring young man. I, too, covered my walls with posters of Donny, which were inscribed with personal statements such as, "To you, from Donny" or "I love you, Donny." I secretly thought that the messages on his posters and on his records were directed towards me, and often I would become openly emotional over them. For instance, in one of his records he cried out, "Help me, help me please," and I played it repeatedly while crying for poor Donny.

Such relationships are not confined to media consumption. Typically they develop into elaborate patterned forms of behavior that constitute symbolic substitutes for actual interaction. Several parallel the behavior of separated real lovers. We have noted that Ruth Steinhagen collected and treasured all sorts of mementoes and media information about Eddie Waitkus, including photographs and press clippings, and that at night she spread these out in a kind of shrine. Such collecting behavior is standard.

At this time, I decided that I was going to live and die for my man Elton John. I started collecting every album he made and memorized every word of every song. Whenever I found an article in a newspaper or magazine, I cut it out and placed it in a scrapbook. Of course, this was the scrapbook that I would present to him once he met me and fell in love with me. My world became Elton John. I had four huge posters of him in my bedroom.

Steinhagen was preoccupied with Eddie's uniform number and, because of his background, she developed a special interest in Lithuania and Boston. My informants report the same kind of interest in seemingly insignificant details. A Beatles fan put it this way:

I relished every little detail I could find out about Paul. If I read that he ate scrambled eggs and bacon for breakfast, I developed a sudden love for scrambled eggs—one food I had always hated. Details of his life became extremely important to me. I wanted to know when he woke up, when he went to bed, what color socks he wore, and if he liked french fried or mashed potatoes.

More important aspects of the beloved's life assume critical significance. The figure's career successes and setbacks are taken seriously and emotionally, as are personal events such as a sickness in the celebrity's family. Of particular concern are events that affect the individual's role orientation to the beloved. Several informants were distraught by media reports that Elton John was bisexual.

Since I was emotionally involved with Elton John, his announcement of his bisexuality was devastating to me. I no longer could view him as a suitable boy friend, lover, or marriage partner.

While reading the newspaper I came upon an article stating that he was gay. No way, I thought. Not my Elton. He just hasn't met me yet. If he knew me, he would become "normal." But then the articles and stories started pouring in from every source about him. Could it be true? The love of my life, gay? I took down all but one poster of him in my room. . . . He had let me down. . . . How could he do this to me!

A similar, if slightly less distressing, problem occurs when the media figure marries someone else. "I still remember the hurt and loss I felt in my senior year of high school when I was told by a friend that Donny Osmond was going to get married . . . . No, he's a Mormon. He'll *never* get divorced. It really dashed my hopes."

People are not only interested in the beloved's life events; they typically take up parallel activities. A 1974 letter to "Dear Abby" offers an illustrative, if extreme, example.

DEAR ABBY: How can I meet Prince Charles? I have always admired him, and it has been my dream to meet him one day, but I'm not having any luck. I've written him several letters, and each time his secretary has answered saying: "The Prince of Wales regrets that he is unable to meet you."

I am a normal, intelligent 20-year old college girl. I'm told I am pretty and have a pleasant personality. I've read everything I could find about the royal family in general and Prince Charles in particular. I'll bet I know more about the royal family than most people living in England and the rest of the United Kingdom.

I hope you won't think I'm crazy, but I have been taking horseback riding lessons, and I plan to take flying lessons when I can afford it because I know those are Prince Charles' favorite sports. Also, if we ever meet I will have something to talk to him about.

Abby, you're supposed to have all the answers. Can you help my dream come true?[21]

Such activity is often keyed to hopes of an actual meeting. Indirect communications are also often attempted. Many celebrities receive thousands of fan letters from their adoring lovers, but these letter writers probably constitute only a fraction of the star's actual romantic following. While several of my informants thought about writing to their imaginary lovers ("I wanted to write to him to ask him to wait for me until I got older"), few actually did so.

However, *pseudo communications* were standard. Ruth Steinhagen talked out loud to pictures of Eddie Waitkus. Such behavior is typical.

This poster [of Bobby Sherman] soon reigned alone on my closet door. I played the album constantly, singing along while staring into Bobby's eyes. Sometimes I would talk to the poster as if it was Bobby Sherman alive in my room.

He [Donny Osmond] had this song about pulling a string and kissing you. Everytime I'd hear this song, I'd pull a purple thread and kiss his poster.

Such external symbolic interactions are paralleled by something even more significant. Steinhagen had fantasies about meeting, dating, and marrying Eddie Waitkus. Far from being extraordinary, such fantasy interactions are *characteristic* of this kind of social relationship.

Certain fantasies occur again and again. One involves "the meeting," an imagined social situation in which the beloved first interacts with his fan.

I began to fantasize about meeting Roger Daltrey. I'd imagine myself sitting in a bar or at a pool and seeing Roger Daltrey walk over and sit next to me. We would start small talking and I would casually mention that he was one of the members of The Who. He'd smile shyly and say, "Yes."

Of course, the celebrity does not just notice the fan. He is smitten. One girl imagined how her beloved would spot her in a restaurant and, struck by love at first sight, would "send me a single rose with a note."

Another young woman, a law student, regularly conjures up a series of alternative meetings with O. J. Simpson.

Prince Charming crashes into the back of my brand new silver sports Mercedes with his sleek, red Jag. He races to the front of my car with every intent to curse me out, but once he notices the twinkle in my eyes, he asks me out for dinner instead.

This time O. J. Simpson is still active in the NFL. As he runs a fly pattern and makes the game-winning touchdown, he crashes into me and my cameras in the end zone. As he helps me up, he notices the twinkle in my eyes and I notice his twinkle. We fall in love and live happily ever after.

We sometimes meet because he needs help. On these occasions, I am the best lawyer in town. . . . a willing soul ready to do battle.

A fourth scenario involves an even more dramatic rescue. Ironically, this fantasy was related to me less than two weeks before John Lennon's death:

As a bystander in a crowd listening to O. J. Simpson give his farewell football speech, I notice a suspicious-looking man. He is about to shoot Simpson. Just in the nick of time I leap between Simpson and the bullet, saving his life but critically wounding my own. As I fall to the ground the six-foot-two-inch former running back catches me in his arms and gently places his coat under my head as he rests me on the ground. As a tear runs down his lean, smooth face, he says nothing and kisses me just as I close my eyes. Now I turn into the suffering heroine. Others realize the bravery and courage it took for me to risk my life. People from all over the world visit me in the hospital, and of course, immediately after a full recovery, O. J. Simpson and I get married and live happily ever after.

While many fantasies focus on the meeting and courtship aspects of the relationship, others picture the marriage that follows.

At that time I imagined I could communicate with Paul. I had long conversations with him. I imagined meeting him and having him fall in love with me. Of course, he begged me to marry him and we lived happily ever after. . . . He had to go away for concerts but he was always true-blue and loyal to me, of course. . . . He always came home from trips and told me how much he missed me.

Sometimes people seek to translate such fantasies into real meetings. Several of my informants not only hoped but expected to meet their lovers. Occasionally people actually succeed. "Groupies" represent a culturally recognized category of successful celebrity seekers who have managed to turn a fantasy attraction into a "real" relationship. Several of my informants made token efforts to meet their lovers by attending a "personal appearance." One of my Elton John fans gives a characteristic example.

Somehow time flew, and the night of the concert was here. I looked beautiful as I left the house, smiling from ear to ear, knowing that somehow this would be the night. Maybe he would see me in the audience and fall magically in love and invite me on stage to do a song with him. Or maybe he would spot me and send one of his guards for me. It didn't matter how, it just had to happen!

Relatively few people seriously attempt a meeting. Tacitly, at least, they often seem to realize not only that an actual meeting is virtually impossible, but that the fantasy is better than an actual encounter.

Although I dream of Prince Charming falling in love with me, I know in my heart that he never will, that I will never meet him and much less hold him. All this doesn't matter. What does matter is the creations of my imagination.

Most, while recognizing the unlikelihood of an actual meeting, retain a ray of hope. Recalling her adolescent crush, one young woman said, "I'd still like to meet him; I'd be perfect for him."

Romantic fan relationships are common among adolescent girls. An informant who grew up with the Beatles noted that in her day it was considered odd *not* to have a crush on one of the Beatles. Tacit cultural rules make it more acceptable for young females overtly to express such relationships than for people of other age or sex categories to do so. Nevertheless, such relationships are not confined to adolescent girls. A letter to a TV "answer man" makes this point forcefully: "I'm an adult so don't treat this question lightly, please. I am absolutely in love with Richard Thomas. . . . I don't mean a crush; I mean love. I think about him every waking moment of every day and I must write and tell him. Please, his private address so I can tell him how serious I am." [22] This letter is not unique. Many of my informants were well out of their adolescence, and one of my John Travolta fans was in her fifties. The following enjoyed by aging celebrities such as Frank Sinatra and Liberace demonstrates that such fantasy love relationships can extend far beyond adolescence. An elderly suburban matron with grown children still has a "special thing" for Frank Sinatra. When depressed, she pours herself a drink and listens to his romantic songs. Her attraction began some forty years ago. Like many of her age mates, she has had, in effect, a lifelong affair with Sinatra.

Men also have such relationships. John Hinckley is not an adolescent girl, nor was his relationship to Foster unusual. Although they tend to be more secretive about them, few of my male informants completely denied ever having had such relationships. Some of them described such attractions in detail. Among the female stars they have "loved" are Bonnie Raitt, Jane Fonda, Donna Summer, Princess Caroline of Monaco, Brooke Shields, Diane Keaton, Ann-Margret, Cheryl Tiegs, Joan Baez, and Yvette Mimieux. One man reported a series of such relationships extending through much of his adolescence. As this example suggests, most of the patterns described for female love relationships are paralleled among males.

I would read all I could about the actresses I had crushes on in *TV Guide*, *Life*, *Look* and, whenever I visited my grandmother, in *TV Screen* and *Movie Mirror*. Yet all these crushes pale in comparison to my love for Yvette Mimieux. I had a crush on YM for a long time—at least four or five years. It all started with an episode of Dr. Kildare called "Tyger, Tyger," in which YM played a devil-may-care Southern California surfer girl. From that time on, I watched every show that YM was in that I possibly could. I would imagine meeting her in one way or another. I imagined her coming to a basketball game in which I played really well, or would imagine heroically saving her life, sometimes sacrificing my own in the process— but never before she had a chance to kiss me and thank me.

Again, such relationships regularly extend beyond adolescence. Another Yvette Mimieux fan was only "turned off" in his mid-thirties, when he was disappointed by her "cruelty" in the movie *Three in the Attic*.

Homosexuals, too, engage in artificial love relationships, such as the TV newswriter who had a long-term crush on a black ballad singer. He found the singer "physically attractive and appealing," followed his career with interest, and kept several scrapbooks on him. He bought all the singer's records and collected information from friends who knew him personally. He was "overjoyed" to learn that the singer was gay, and then began "to fantasize in earnest."[23]

Ethnographic investigation shows that elaborate love relationships with unmet media figures are not characteristic just of American schizophrenics. On the contrary, such relationships represent a significant, and pervasive, culture pattern in modern American society. But *why* are Americans given to these relationships?

Both the forms and the contents of the contemporary American media are conducive to the development of such relationships. Especially through the vehicle of the electronic media, the individual is regularly transported into the midst of dramatic social situations involving intimate face-to-face contact with the most glamorous people of his time. The seeming reality of this experience naturally engenders emotional reactions—especially since these figures are deliberately and manipulatively presented in the roles of sexual objects and lovers. Given their intimate, seductive appearance, it would be peculiar if the audience did *not* respond in kind.

But in addition, these relationships often fill gaps in the individual's actual social world. As Elihu Katz and Paul Lazarsfeld observe, escapist media often serves as a direct substitute for socializing activity.[24] If the social situation is dissatisfying, an individual may compensate with artificial companions. When a person accustomed to company at dinner must dine alone, he or she typically substitutes artificial beings by way of a book, newspaper, or TV program. This suggests that an individual would be most likely to engage in a media love relationship when he or she is without a real or satisfying actual lover. While sometimes valid, such an interpretation does not fully suffice. It does not explain the suburban grandmother who had a lifelong "affair" with Frank Sinatra despite forty years of marriage. It does not explain why, in adolescence and in later years, artificial love relationships often persist after an actual lover is found. Take one of the fans introduced earlier. This young woman, like several other informants, explicitly offered the "substitute lover" interpretation herself:

Donny Osmond served to replace a missing element in my life. At this time I had little relationships with other boys. My sister and many of my friends did have these relationships. Donny and I had such a relationship, and I had yearned for one. . . . My feeling eventually began to fade as I did begin to have crushes on real boys in sixth and seventh grade.

However, as she herself remarked, the relationship with Osmond "faded" but did not end. It persisted through her senior year in high school and even now, at age twenty-two, she still buys Donny Osmond magazines and retains her fan club card. While she is now engaged in serious relationships with real lovers, she still has various artificial love relationships. "Now I have the same kind of relationship with Buck Williams [basketball star]. He's sooooo great, wow!"

In its simplistic form, the "substitute lover" theory assumes that the imaginary lover will disappear when the real lover appears. Tacitly it assumes that real love relationships are better than imaginary love relationships. The first assumption is often untrue, and the second may also be unwarranted. In some ways fantasy relations are often *better* than real love relationships. Media figures are more attractive than ordinary mortals, and they are carefully packaged—through makeup, costuming, camera angles, and film editing—to appear even better. Even when portrayed in a tired or disheveled condition, they seem cute, humorous, and "sexy." The media figure's prowess is typically almost supernatural. The hero is so strong and brave that the villains are always overcome ("His shoulders and arms are massive—secure comforters that are capable of doing away with any problem . . ."). The media figure's personality is also carefully sanitized, glamorized, and perfected. The continually brave, kind, interested, patient, and passionately devoted lovers of many media worlds are not to be found in reality. Celebrities are also more "successful" than ordinary people. This connects to a powerful American value. Extreme material wealth taps yet another basic American interest. Finally, since the figure is worshipped by millions of others, the star has a legitimacy and appeal lacking in a person who is not "somebody."

But it is fantasy that helps to make these relations superior to actual social interactions. To love a glamorous rock star through the media is to make a kind of intimate contact with a powerfully appealing figure—but you remain, in this dimension, only one of millions of other fans. However, through fantasy, the rock star moves from the public realm and picks you out of the crowd to be his special friend, lover, and wife. Landing such a widely adored figure confirms your self worth; it makes *you* somebody. It is analogous to landing the most popular boy or girl in high school, only better. One Donny Osmond fan put it this way:

I fantasized and dreamed about him constantly, thinking that if Donny ever bumped into me somewhere or met me, he would immediately fall in love with me and whisk me away. I wasn't really jealous of the other girls who liked him because I knew that if he met me he would forget about them.

One of her rivals had similar plans.

I felt we were meant for each other, and if only we could meet, all my dreams would come true. Since Donny was a famous superstar, this gave me a feeling of superstar worth also.

Sometimes this gratifying elevation of the self is based solely on becoming the beloved figure's chosen lover or spouse. In other cases the individual's fantasy includes stardom for himself or herself as well. Like several other informants, an Elton John fan pictured herself literally sharing the stage with her idol:

I saw Elton as the necessary contact I needed to break into the music business. I would frequently fantasize that Elton would hear me play the piano, fall in love with me, then take me on tour with him as an opening act. These fantasies were always very elaborate and intense and provided me with a way to fulfill all my dreams and desires.

Through fantasy, a media love relationship is exquisitely tuned not to the needs of the celebrity, but to the needs of the self. Imaginary lovers unfailingly do what you want with grace, enthusiasm, and total admiration. The whole course of the relationship is under your control. The relationship runs—and reruns—its perfectly gratifying course from dramatic and glamorous first meetings, through courtship and consummation, to happily-ever-after marital bliss. And through it all a fantasy lover smiles fondly, never complaining, never burping, never getting a headache, never wrecking the car or making you do the dishes. You owe her no obligations. He is there when you want him and gone when you do not. Real love relationships include all sorts of unfortunate realities: fantasy love relationships do not. It is not surprising that Americans sometimes prefer fantasy lovers to ordinary mortals.

A second media figure relationship, which also directly parallels an actual social relationship, is based on antagonism. Most informants can readily list media figures they despise. Controversial public figures like Howard Cosell, Jane Fonda, William Buckley, George Steinbrenner, Richard Nixon and villainous fictional characters like Alan Spaulding ("Guiding Light"), or JR ("Dallas") are commonly mentioned examples. Considering that the individual has never met these people, and that many of them are fictional beings, the level of hostility is often astonishing. Sometimes these negative feelings lead the individual to elaborate an artificial social relationship that is the inverse of the stereotypic fan relationship. Here the basis of the relationship is not esthetic appreciation, admiration, or love, but hatred, anger, and disgust.

As with love relationships, media consumption is often intense. Several informants have developed antagonisms to local talk show hosts, and sometimes they watch such shows for the pleasure of hating the celebrity. Soap opera fans are often as interested in characters they dislike as those they admire. "He is one of the most self-centered, arrogant, selfish, uncaring persons I have ever come across," said one informant. "His main purpose is to have power at the cost of others. . . . I watch him with feelings of hatred. . . . I am overjoyed to see other characters beat him at his own game." One set of three young men used to come together out of their mutual dislike of a TV evangelist. Their mutual relationships, both with each other and with this media figure, suggested the opposite of a fan club. They used to watch this evangelist's television show regularly because they thought he was an amusing "farce." When he appeared on the screen they would laugh and ridicule him.

Such relationships often have an important fantasy dimension. Serious participants conjure up fantasy meetings with their enemies and carry out imaginary arguments with them. Sometimes these pseudo interactions become violent. An otherwise peaceful informant described fantasies about torturing and killing "evil" politicians. These pseudo interactions, both in media consumption and fantasy, allow the expression of a hatred that is more extreme and presumably more satisfying than that which can safely be expressed in real social relations. The media figure's humanity can be denied in a way that a real person's physical presence makes difficult. One runs no risks of legal punishment or retaliation since the hated figure cannot fight back.

These relationships sometimes goad people to attempts at actual consummation. It may seem amusing that an actor who plays a villainous soap opera husband is regularly stopped on the street and berated for treating his "wife" so badly. Unfortunately, serious attacks sometimes result from such imaginary relationships.

A far more common and significant group of relationships are those in which the media figure becomes the object of intense admiration. Such relationships approximate the general stereotypic conceptualization of the fan, but much more is involved than esthetic appreciation. Characteristically, the admired figure comes to represent some combination of idol, hero, alter ego, mentor, and role model.

The media figures around whom informants have built intense admiration relationships are surprisingly diverse. Consider the following examples: John Wayne, Judy Garland, Loren Eiseley, Steve Carlton, Betty Ford, Neil Young, Ralph Ellison, Charles Manson, Frank Zappa, Jane Fonda, Arnold Palmer, Hawkeye Pierce, Jack Kerouac, Barbra Streisand, Woody Allen, Anne Frank, Bruce Springsteen, James Dean, Olivia Newton-John, James Bond, Diana Rigg, Tony Baretta, Isak Dinesen, Clint Eastwood, and Mary Tyler Moore. People express strong emotional orientations to such figures, speaking not only of "admiration" and "sympathy," but also of "worship" and (platonic) "love." Again people frequently characterize the attraction by comparing it to a real social relationship. They speak of their hero as a "friend," "older sister," "father figure," "guide" or "mentor."[25] As with the love relationships, the general source of the appeal is clear. Media figures are better than ordinary people. They have godlike qualities that are impossible for mortals to sustain. Furthermore, the emotional attachment is not complicated by the ambivalence that characterizes actual relationships; admiration is unchecked by the recognition of faults and limitations.

One man pointed out that the "father figure" he admired—a fictional John Wayne-type TV cowboy—outshone his real father in every respect. His father has several admirable qualities and he "loves him very much." But as a child he "needed someone to identify with," and his father did not measure up. A young woman described the perfection of her "TV mother," Mary Tyler Moore, and showed how Moore shifted from parent figure to role model.

It all began when I used to watch "The Dick Van Dyke Show" about eleven years ago, so I was ten years old at that time. The first thing I can remember from that time is how much I admired Mary; after all, she was slender, feminine, funny, talented, intelligent, cute, attractive, a kind mother, a loving wife, a caring friend, a good cook, a clean housekeeper, and more. . . . Mary became the person that I wanted my mother to be. . . . I would watch my mother cooking, for example, and I would imagine that my mother was just like Mary.

Things really took a turn when I got into junior high school about eight years ago. "The Mary Tyler Moore Show" had been on TV for about three years by that time, but I didn't pay much attention until I realized that I wanted to learn how to become a woman for myself . . . and I had the perfect person to model myself after: Mary. On her show she was a career woman and still as perfect as before; she dressed well, she was slender, she knew how to cook, she was independent, she had a nice car, she had a beautiful apartment, she never seemed lonely, she had a good job, she was intelligent, she had friends, etc. There was *still* nothing wrong with her.

From out of thousands of glamorous alternatives, why does the fan seize on one particular figure rather than another? The appeal is often complex, but the admired figure is typically felt to have qualities that the person senses in himself but desires to develop further. The admired figure represents an ideal self-image. Of course, it is sometimes difficult to establish whether the similarity existed prior to the "meeting" or whether it developed after the media relationship flowered. Sometimes, as in the following account, both factors are involved. As a high school student at an overseas international school, this informant did not have access to the most current American television fare.

I became familiar with the character Tony Baretta of the TV police series when newly arrived friends from the United States started to call me "Baretta." I learned that I looked a good deal like him—short, stocky, and black hair. The fact that I was from New York and had a tough guy reputation also helped.

Eventually the series came to Belgium and I saw who this character was. I was not displeased at our apparent similarity. He portrayed a hard but sensitive character, a heavily muscled tough guy who at the same time could be counted on to help people through thick and thin. I also enjoyed his speech, attitudes towards smoking, and life in general.

Once I started looking at the series, my behavior, largely because of peer expectation, started to resemble that of Baretta's more closely. . . . The next day after the series had been on friends and fellow students would say things like, "Man, I caught you on TV last night." Soon most people called me "Baretta" or "Tony" and I was sort of expected to play this character. . . . Often I would dress like him. Tight, dark blue T-shirts were a favorite during the warmer months. Naturally I was soon anxiously awaiting the weekly airing of the series and soon had assimilated many of his mannerisms. Although I never sounded like him, I do say many of his phrases: "You can take that to the bank," "Don't roll the dice if you can't pay the price," etc. . . . The TV character probably helped cement my character into the mold that is now me.

As this case also suggests, the media figure's appeal may be linked to the individual's actual social relationships. Here others made and supported the initial identification ("You are Tony Baretta"). One young woman's fifteen-year fixation on a soap opera character began with her social situation as a first grader. Arriving home from school she wanted to be with her mother, so she would sit down with her and watch "Guiding Light." A young golfer's attraction to Arnold Palmer developed in part because Palmer came from a neighboring town and because his father, also an avid golfer, deeply admired Palmer. Many people have been turned on to a given novelist or musician by a friend who admired the figure and gave the person his first book or record as a present. In some cases the initial interest may be insincere. One young man, charmed by a female Bob Dylan fan, feigned appreciation of this musician in order to ingratiate himself with the woman. In the process he gradually developed a genuine interest in Dylan that continues up to the present—long after the woman has gone.

Once the initial identification has been made, patterned forms of behavior typically develop. As with artificial love relationships, the individual typically collects totemlike jewelry, T-shirts, locks of hair, photographs, posters, first editions, records, tapes, news-clippings, and concert programs. Media consumption is also likely to be intense. The individual reads the author's work repeatedly ("I read the novel five times"), or travels long distances to attend a concert. During media consumption, personal involvement tends to be sympathetic and emotional. "From the minute she stepped on stage I was in a trance. I was mesmerized by everything she did and I could actually see myself doing the same singing. . . . It actually gave me the chills." As this passage implies, identification is usually significant. Sometimes it is partial ("When I watch the show I think to myself how much I would like to be like her"); sometimes it is complete ("When I see her I don't see a TV character, I see myself").

Admiration relationships with media figures also have an important fantasy dimension.[26] As with love relations, fantasies link the individual *socially* with the admired figure. Three types of fantasies are especially common. In the first the individual meets the idol, in the second the person becomes someone like the idol, and in the third he or she becomes the idol.

Fantasy encounters are not mere meetings. One does not just shake the celebrity's hand and move on. A close and intimate social relationship is established. Several informants played out elaborate scenarios with writers whose work they admired. One man imagined journeying to the reclusive writer's home, becoming fast friends, and going out on drinking bouts full of brotherly adventure. A young woman liked to imagine herself visiting Loren Eiseley. "I visualized the two of us drinking coffee while sitting at a comfortable old kitchen table in his house. We would talk about philosophy, time, exploring damp caves, and reactions to nights in the country."

A standard variant of this fantasy involves establishing a professional role relationship with the admired figure.

Steve Carlton is a six-foot five-inch 220-lb. pitcher for the Philadelphia Phillies. Since I myself am a frustrated athlete, I admire Carlton. He was given a great body and he has made the best possible use of it. Carlton possesses all the physical attributes I wish I had. . . . Carlton is also an expert in martial arts and is intellectual, having studied psychology and

Eastern philosophy. I admire the man because he is the type to accomplish tasks and achieve goals.

This fan has several fantasies about establishing a social relationship with his idol.

One has me in the big leagues pitching for the Phils and Carlton becomes my friend, takes me under his wing, and I become his protégé. I have also imagined that one day I will become Carlton's manager and that we have a great relationship. He admires me for my managing and coaching ability.

Another variant involves becoming, imaginatively, a close relative of the admired figure. One middle-aged woman, now herself a professional writer, described her attachment to Isak Dinesen. As a child she read and reread Dinesen and sought out all the biographical information she could find. She not only spent much time "reliving" scenes from the writer's adventurous life—"art school in Paris, her marriage to a Swedish count, the beginning of her African adventure . . ."—but she also constructed fantasies about growing up in Africa as Isak Dinesen's daughter. The dynamics of such fantasy interactions involve several different components but, again, a crucial dimension is the elevation of the self. Acceptance by the admired figure is the vehicle for indirect self-acceptance. (I admire them—I am like them—they accept me—I am a good person.)

In the second type of fantasy, the individual becomes someone like the admired figure and lives out experiences similar to those of the idol. An admirer of Jack Kerouac frequently imagined himself hitchhiking across the United States and Europe. Often a curious new self emerges, an imaginative combination of the fan and the admired figure. The following description comes from an admirer of *Gone with the Wind*.

In my fantasies I see myself dressed in one of those beautiful hoop skirt dresses complete with parasol, hat, and fan—making me your typical Southern belle. I would speak in a sweet Southern accent. I would belong to a very wealthy Southern family with a large plantation stretching out for miles. My family would entertain frequently and I would grow up becoming very well raised in the social graces. As a woman, I would be very at ease with others, hospitable, and charming in my relationships with men. In my fantasies I look like myself, and I still have some of my own peculiar habits and personality traits, but I do take on most of Scarlett's charming attributes—her vivaciousness and way of dealing with people, the way she carries herself, etc.

One step further, in the third type of fantasy, the fan abandons his or her self and *becomes* the media figure. This is a common desire ("I would change places with him in a moment," "If I could be anyone else it would be her"). In fantasy the desire is realized. A young man studying to be a doctor reported a special relationship with James Bond, agent 007. In reality he sees himself as very different from Bond. The young man is "afraid of decisive action," Bond is cool and calculating; he "thrives on security," Bond gambles; he "feels compelled to ask for advice and permission," Bond is independent; he is "sexually naive," Bond is a Don Juan. However, through his artificial relationship a transformation of self occurs. In his media consumption and fantasy he sloughs off his own "inadequate" personality and turns into James Bond. Here, in fantasy, the individual's consciousness is "possessed" by the media self; it colors perception, patterns decision making, and structures social behavior.

Such an influence is not confined to fantasy. In the actual world as well, the admired figure sometimes guides actual behavior. First, the fan may adopt the idol's appearance.[27] One teenage fan went to the barbershop with a picture of his hero and asked the barber to "cut my hair just like Fabian's." Writer Caryl Rivers describes a series of imitative identifications: "I had a Marilyn Monroe outfit—off-the-shoulder peasant blouse, black tight skirt and hoop earrings . . . When Grace Kelly came along, I swept my hair back and wore long white gloves to dances and practiced looking glacial. I got my hair cut in an Italian boy style like Audrey Hepburn. For a while I was fixated on lavender because I read that Kim Novak wore only lavender."[28] She goes on to describe how facial expressions were also borrowed and incorporated.

I wanted the kind that I saw in movie magazines or [on] billboards, the kind that featured THE LOOK. THE LOOK was standard for movie star pictures, although the art reached its zenith with Marilyn Monroe. Head raised above a daring décolletage, eyes vacant, lips moist and parted slightly—that was generally agreed to be looking sexy. I practiced THE LOOK sometimes, making sure the bathroom door was locked before I did.[29]

Such relatively superficial influences are often part of a deeper identification in which the media figure's values and plans are incorporated into the fan's social behavior. This is mentally accomplished in ways that directly parallel fantasy interactions. Operating in his or her own identity as someone who wants to act like the ideal figure, the individual may employ the media figure as a mentor or guide. Probably this is often unconscious. But sometimes the individual deliberately turns to the guide for help.

Especially when I am upset, I think about her [Anne Frank's] outlook. I look to her as a reference. Then I try to act like she did.

Woody Allen plays the role of my pseudo conscience. He discriminates what is silly and irrelevant from what is worthwhile. . . . In awkward situations, I tend to rely on what I've seen him do or say.

A Mary Tyler Moore admirer shows how such a process can move beyond advice to deeper forms of self-transformation.

I used her personality in my . . . anticipations about myself, especially when I had a problem. I would find myself thinking "What would Mary do?" . . . I would imagine myself in the situation that I wanted to be in . . . and also that I was exactly like Mary, that I had her sense of humor, her easygoing manner, etc. . . . This was a daily occurrence for me until about five years ago. . . . It was a way to solve my problems or to guide my behavior according to a model of perfection; a natural result was that I was pleased about how I conducted myself, especially with other people. I ended up regretting my behavior a lot less when I behaved as I thought Mary would behave. As a teenager I was very concerned about meeting role expectations, but with Mary inside my mind, it was much easier to meet those expectations.

As in certain fantasies, the fan here *becomes* the idol. Occasionally the fan consciously seeks to induce this self-transformation. "Sometimes I find myself saying, 'You are Carlton. Believe you are and so will everyone else.'" Here the fan overtly acts according to the hero's values, goals, and plans.

Because of such identification, media figures exert pervasive effects on many different areas of actual social life. Sports provide a good example. Many—probably most—American athletes are affected by media exemplars. Even the most successful professional athletes regularly report such role modeling. O. J. Simpson, for example, deliberately patterned himself after Jim Brown. This kind of imitation is so common that sports interviewers regularly ask their subjects about this aspect of their sports development. Many of my own informants reported on this process. The young golfer whose hero is Arnold Palmer reads all the Arnold Palmer how-to-do-it books, studies his games on television, practices his style of shots, and pretends to be Arnold Palmer while actually playing golf.

A successful college basketball player described her close relationship to a favorite professional player.

Many times I sit and stare at a basketball court and imagine Bill down there warming up with a series of left- and right-handed hook shots . . . and still there are other times when after seeing him play on TV I imagine myself repeating all his moves. . . . On the court I pattern many of my offensive moves from Bill Walton.

As is typical with such artificial relationships, the imitation of sports behavior is part of a more profound influence. A young tennis star shows vividly how his pattern of play is but one manifestation of a larger imitation of values and lifestyle.

I'm extremely aggressive on the court, I guess. I really like Jimmy Connors's game. I model myself after him. I read somewhere that he said he wants to play every point like it's match point at Wimbledon. . . . I like the individualism of tennis. It's not a team sport; it's an ego trip. You get all the glory yourself. That's what I thrive on, ego. . . . I want to become No. 1 in the world and become a millionaire. . . . I want to become like Vitas Gerulaitis, with the cars, the shopping in Paris, and the girls.[30]

As American idols, media figures do not influence merely one narrow aspect of life. They influence values, goals, and attitudes, and through this they exert a pervasive influence on social conduct.

Given such evidence, it may seem odd that the existence of imitative media effects is still debated. The focal area of research here has been antisocial conduct in general and violence in particular. While most researchers now conclude that violent media promotes imitative actual aggression, a few deny this.[31] They argue that violent TV fare "evaporates" or that it has a "cathartic," pacifying effect on the audience. One problem involves the behavioristic methods by which much of the research has been carried out. Many researchers seek only to assess the immediate observable effects of media consumption, as by experiments in which test children are shown a film of violence and then observed and rated as to level of aggressive action afterwards. Some such studies reveal imitative effects, others do not. However, this approach ignores a crucial intervening variable, the individual's consciousness and mind set.[32] How a viewer reacts to a given media figure's example may critically depend on the kind of artificial-imaginary social relationship he or she has established with the figure. A closely related variable is the effect the communications have not on immediate overt behavior but on the individual's consciousness and knowledge. Just because the individual does not immediately engage in imitative violence does not mean that he or she has not been affected. When the media figure is a personal hero, the individual's tendency toward violence may have been confirmed or increased. The individual may also have learned new ways of attacking, fighting, shooting, stabbing, or torturing other people.

People vividly remember the aggressive techniques of their heroes and they see an astonishing number of examples of aggression. One estimate suggests that between the ages of five and fourteen the average American child has witnessed the violent destruction of 13,000 human beings on television alone.[33] Furthermore, Americans often rehearse what they have witnessed in the media. American children regularly imitate the violent antics of their media heroes in play, sometimes immediately after media consumption, sometimes days, weeks, or even months after the original exposure. Playing *Star Wars*, playing "Guns," playing "Cowboys"—these media-derived games are among their most common pastimes. Children and adults also "practice" violent routines by adopting the hero's persona and playing out scenes of violence in their fantasies. The violence of American inner experiences can often be directly linked to particular media productions. Media violence does not evaporate. It affects attitudes, enters the stock of knowledge, and is acted upon in fantasy. It is thus readily available—in practiced form—for use in actual conduct as well. One American criminal who has spent fifteen years in jail spoke as follows:

TV has taught me how to steal cars, how to break into establishments, how to go about robbing people, even how to roll a drunk. Once, after watching a *Hawaii Five-O*, I robbed a gas station. The show showed me how to do it. Nowadays [he is serving a term for attempted rape] I watch TV in my house [cell] from 4 P.M. until midnight. I just sit back and take notes. I see 'em doing it this way or that way, you know, and I tell myself that I'll do it the same way when I get out. You could probably pick any ten guys in here and ask 'em and they'd tell you the same thing. Everybody's picking up on what's on TV.[34]

The following case shows how an antisocial media figure may guide an unmet fan. At the time, the informant, then thirty, was teaching at a California college. His mentor was Charles Manson.

At the time Manson was busted for the Tate-LaBianca murders, I was very much interested in his group and especially the power control he exerted over the women. At the time Manson was being tried in the Hall of Justice in Los Angeles, several of his followers were holding a vigil on the streets outside the courthouse. They had shaven their heads and carved swastikas on their foreheads. I had seen them on TV and wanted to talk with them. So I drove to L.A. and did just that.

I was very curious as to how such an insignificant person could garner such devotion from the women in his clan. Through brief talks with the willing group on the sidewalk, I soon got an inkling. The girls loved Charles because he was a forceful, dominant man whom they thought was godlike and was the savior for their kind: middle-class, confused, drugged, unstable, etc. youths. . . . Charles used biblical quotes, song lyrics, and drugs to partially control his flock; the real element of power, according to the girls, was the hypnotic spell his eyes could achieve in any face-to-face experience. . . . At the time I had been teaching a course in folklore and mythology and been caught up in the occult, mind games, mysticism, sexual myths, therapeutic processes, etc. Also at this time I was doing drugs heavily. . . . I was also experiencing a breakdown in my marriage. The point is that I was on the edge and very impressionistic. When I talked to the Manson girls who were convinced of the power of Charles's eyes, I acknowledged that sense of power in myself.

I began to experiment with "eye psychology" in my social relationships. I used it on colleagues, strangers, and especially on young . . . women in my classes. For the most part it worked. In my sensitive state, I saw positive control of others result through my hypnotic gaze. To wit: one young woman I concentrated on fell under my spell. She confessed her love for me and was convinced that my eyes, etc., brought her under my control. She would do anything for me. At this point I pulled a Charles Manson. I gave her drugs, told her what was good and what was bad, completely controlled her social behavior. She was obligated to me and I was in no way obligated to her. I was on a power trip; she was on a slave trip. I, the manipulator, was in control. . . . After I got off heavy drugs, and after my marriage broke up, I was guilt-ridden. In my drugged-out state I probably had had the same perverted dreams as Charles.

But it is not just relations with the antisocial types, the real or imaginary media villains, that promote antisocial conduct; it is relations with heroes as well. And not just the James Bonds and Barettas, but the all-American good guys, the Gary Coopers and the John Waynes. Their teachings on violence are clear. Violence may be regrettable, but it is often justified and required (only a coward would back down). Violence is the proper solution for difficult and threatening social situations. Vengeful violence is satisfying, and successful violence will be admired and rewarded (after the killing you get the girl). The mass media did not create these values. They have their roots deep in the American value system. But our mass media promotes these teachings in a more pervasive, glamorized, insistent, and unrealistic way than does any other social world the individual is likely to visit. Like Ruth Steinhagen, Mark Chapman, and John Hinckley, we are the children of this world.

Role modeling is one way in which media figures affect actual behavior. Throughout this chapter we have touched on many other ways as well. Because they invade the individual's fantasies, media figures also affect economic and political behavior and structure all kinds of decision making. I noted earlier that media figures as pseudo mutual acquaintances often provide the basis for socializing. The ultimate example here is fan clubs, organizations of real people who come together and interact out of their mutual attraction to a celebrity none of them may have actually met face to face.[35]

There are many other occasions when actual social interactions are affected because the people involved are simultaneously interacting imaginatively with media beings. Two people may "visit" while watching a TV program. In some cases, they switch their attention back and forth between the two worlds; at other times, they attend to both.[36] The typical American date often follows such a pattern. A young man and woman, attending a movie together, may be separately involved in the same public fantasy (the movie) while still retaining some minimal "real" contact, perhaps by holding hands. This kind of date, common in early stages of courtship, permits the couple to be together but removes the strain of confronting each other directly. After leaving the movie, people can simultaneously recall and comment on their personal reactions to the artificial social events they have just independently experienced together. A more dramatic example occurs when a man and a woman engaged in sexual intercourse are also each "away," experiencing separate sexual fantasies with media beings.

Definite rules govern the ways in which an individual who is physically present in a social situation may simultaneously involve himself with media figures. These tacit rules often specify the attention an individual owes to real relationships as distinct from that which he may legitimately devote to artificial interactions. A person is usually expected to abandon or lower his participation in the artificial world whenever a pressing claim is advanced by present real others ("It's time for supper," or "Someone is knocking on the door"). Tardiness in "coming back" usually calls for apologies. The presence of these rules is often revealed by their transgression, and people may become seriously annoyed when they receive less attention than media others. In many households, it is offensive for an individual to read at the dinner table. The seasonal laments of "football widows" constitute another case in point. Professional advice-givers like "Dear Abby" sometimes describe other examples. One woman worried about the time and attention her husband lavished on "girlie magazines." Another complained that her husband was angry when she revealed her fantasies. Here media figures are perceived as rivals.

Such social patterns, like other aspects of media relationships, typically strike people as amusing. Those who have been through intense media relationships often recall them with embarrassment, and those outside them often respond with derision. This reaction—so predictable as to have the status of a culture pattern—is worthy of analysis in its own right. Imitative role modeling in general tends to evoke amusement. There seems to be something funny about a person imitating someone else. But as Phillip Slater has pointed out, imitation is basic to our enculturation.[37] We are not born with social plans and identities. We have to develop these through cultural learning in social situations. We become our "selves" to a large extent through positive and negative role modeling on figures in our social environments. It is just that we like to pretend otherwise. Perhaps the humor of imitation involves a dimly felt sense of its unstated power, the incongruity between our pretended independence and our actual derivative dependence. Our amusement also comes from the sense of incongruity involved in choosing as hero or lover not a real person but an unmet image who appears only on the page of a book or the screen of a television—perhaps a totally fictional character as well, the figment of someone *else's* fantasy.

From one perspective this does seem strange—with so many real people to choose from, why pick a phantom? But from another perspective it makes perfectly good sense, because media figures are "better" than ordinary people. Another factor is the nature of the particular figure chosen. Older Americans often sneer at the idols of the young. They seem so one-dimensional, so discreditable, so unrealistic. An early Beatles fan had to "combat" her father over her infatuation with Paul McCartney since her father viewed him as "a long-haired bum." Here again, however, the problem is in the perspective. Like others of her time, this adolescent was not looking for a conventional establishment model but for an idol who expressed her own rebelliousness and her longing for romantic extremes beyond the boundaries of adult compromise.

Finally, the sense of ridicule merges with media criticism. Attachments to media figures seem undesirable because the media are seen as promoting antisocial, false, unrealistic, and shallow value orientations.[38] Few Americans would deny this, but it is also far from the whole story. As recent survey research suggests, even the popular mass media can be shown to have many "prosocial" effects.[39] My own ethnographic investigation also indicates that imaginary relationships with media figures can have many beneficial effects.

Artificial contact with an admired figure—whether through books, television, records, or imagination—is often felt to be subjectively beneficial. Like a meeting with a good friend, the artificial communication may lift the person out of a bad mood. Often the contact is sought for just this reason. The following informant speaks for the fans of many other musicians. "When I hear their music, I always feel good, even if I was feeling lousy. . . . I know every word and nuance of their songs. Their spirit lifts me up and makes me feel pleased with life. Their music helps my world to continue properly." Often, as with this informant, it is not only that the music is cheering but that the message is felt to be "inspirational," because it helps people develop and affirm strongly felt values. A twenty-seven-year-old nurse offered the following account:

When the antiwar protests of 1968 made headlines by attracting hundreds of thousands of demonstrators to Washington, Peter, Paul, and Mary performed at the monument grounds. . . . I remember hearing those folk heroes speak and sing, and I remember distinctly the feeling of camaraderie which they instilled in the crowd. Unlike other performers, they were able to inspire me toward ideals of the brotherhood of man. Through my contacts with the performances and appearances of this folk trio, I met other like-minded people.

Peter, Paul, and Mary were the embodiment of the sixties in their concerns for social justice and peace, and in their idealism, optimism, and enthusiasm. I identified with their values as did many of my peers. I admired their ideals and shared their concerns. After the Vietnam War ended, Peter, Paul, and Mary espoused new causes, including conservation. I continued to embrace the values they represented.

Gratitude for help of this kind is expressed toward many popular musicians, including John Lennon and the Beatles. If the figure dies, the person feels the loss of both friend and mentor.

Other kinds of media figures are similarly important. Like other autobiographies, *The Diary of Anne Frank* has been of enormous personal significance to several of my informants. "I admired her courage and strength and I tried to incorporate that aspect of her personality into my own." Fictional characters may have the same effect:

True, this novel is a work of art, is fiction, but in some ways it is more than that to me. It is a piece of art that contains knowledge on how to live. This novel is a how-to-do-it book containing countless mental recipes for a healthy existence, all of which comes from Ellison's head and is passed on through the persona of the "invisible man."

Often the individual credits a media figure with having helped him or her to reach traditional kinds of American values and ideals. Sometimes the model is a political figure—a notable example would be John F. Kennedy—but often it is a celebrity far outside the conventional political field.

Arnold Palmer played the role of model to me. He taught me several things which I still hold today. One thing Arnold taught me was competitiveness. He taught me to enjoy and to thrive on being a good, clean competitor. Arnie's determination not to give up and to keep on trying showed me the way to succeed in anything is never to give in. Secondly, Arnold Palmer illustrated to me how to be a good sportsman. He never once shouted out to an opponent, judge, or spectator. He demonstrated to me how to "keep my cool" under pressure and to be a gentleman on and off the golf course. Thirdly, Arnie showed to me that he never forgot about his "roots." In other words, Arnold Palmer was proud of where he came from.

Even conversions to traditional religious orientations have been directly attributed to relationships with media figures, as with a previously depressed woman for whom "God became real" through the autobiographical works of a religious writer whom she first encountered on a televised version of the Billy Graham Crusade.

As these examples indicate, a media relationship may influence the individual in the development of a variety of very different value orientations. Whether or not one personally agrees with a given orientation, we are talking here about positive media effects. Even the most silly and superficial of fictional mass communication figures can sometimes lead to something significant. One informant described his relationship with a character on the 1959–63 family situation comedy, "The Many Loves of Dobie Gillis." The show concerned the antics of a middle-class grocer's family and assorted friends and customers. For my informant, the significant figure was the "beatnik" character Maynard G. Krebs.

Maynard was clad in a sweatshirt with holes, chinos, and sneakers. His hair was longer than Dobie's crew cut and he sported a goatee. He had dropped out of school and the creators of the series made a point of having Maynard hiccup everytime he mentioned the word "work." Most of the time Maynard just hung around doing nothing. Maynard G. Krebs was the media's version of the "beatnik." Maynard had and has continued to have a profound effect on my personal development.

In order to understand Maynard's lasting influence, it is necessary to understand a little about me as an eight- or nine-year-old child. I was the classic 50-lb. weakling . . . someone who was bad at sports. I was so bad that not only was I always the last one chosen in team sports, but the team captains would argue over who would get stuck with me. At eight or nine sports were important, the rites of passage for one's boyhood. Since I was a failure at this test, I was ostracized, made to feel different from the other boys.

Maynard, although a friend of Dobie's, was clearly different from the other characters on the TV show. Hence the reason for the identification with the "beatnik." The identification lasted. . . . between 1964 and 1965 my hair got longer and from the beginning I identified with the counterculture. People would say things about the length of my hair and make fun of the way I looked. Again I was the different one, an outsider, a deviant.

In 1967 I read Ginsberg's *Howl* for the first time. Now, six or seven years after Maynard's caricature, I had "real" contact, through literature, with the Beats. Ginsberg, Kerouac, Snyder and the others were major forces in the counterculture and the fascination, influence, and sometimes imitation grew. . . . Later, in my twenties, I would occasionally grow a goatee, something I had wanted to do from the day I saw Maynard's.

From the late 1960s through today I spend much of my spare time reading the Beats—works about them and their literature. Through their writings I was introduced to the San Francisco poets, Black Mountain poets, as well as those who had influenced their writings from the past— Blake, Whitman, Thoreau, Miller and others. Many of my friends became musicians, poets, photographers, political activists, and other social misfits. . . . Twenty years later my emphasis in graduate school is bohemian-ism, the artist-intellectual and nonconformist, and his or her role in American cultural history. A lasting effect indeed.

The positive influence of media figures can extend throughout adult life. Sometimes these adult relationships involve less imita-tion and more in the way of a critical appreciation of the figure's life and philosophy. However, as in other media relationships, the individual often seeks regular forms of "contact" with the admired figure through personal fantasy, through the electronic media, and through repeated readings of an author's work. Sometimes the individual resorts to other devices as well. Robert Coles, often hailed as "a major social critic," and even a "saint," has been deeply affected by the life work of a variety of unmet beings. He feels that his own work has been helped by these figures and to heighten this influence he has hung their photographs in the study where he writes.

Here he has chosen to be scrutinized by pictures of people who, by their life and work, openly challenge him. Among them, Simone Weil, a tor-tured, frail French writer who literally starved herself to death when the Resistance wouldn't send her on a dangerous mission; George Orwell ("People think of '1984' and forget his exposes of capitalism, of the coal mines"); the Catholic Worker's Dorothy Day; Walker Percy ("Ten pages of 'The Moviegoer' are worth all the words I've written"); and George S. Bernanos, whose "The Diary of a Country Priest" is Coles's favorite book ("He fought the temptation to ignore life's uncertainties and ambiguities"). . . .[40]

Attachments to media figures do not have a simple, one-sided effect on American life. They have complex positive and negative consequences. But taken together it is clear that such pseudo-social relationships constitute a pervasive and powerfully signifi-cant influence. Any approach to American society that ignores these social relationships is seriously incomplete.

But how can we assess our contemporary American situation comparatively? How does our own set of media relationships compare with those of people in other times and places? A few brief observations are worth considering. For instance, latter nineteenth-century America provides an interesting point of contrast. Here we find a society in which the print media played a role similar in certain ways to that provided by the electronic media in twentieth-century culture. Serialized periodicals, children's magazines, and popular novels were enthusiastically read by a wide audience. In some cases these publications seem to have engendered artificial relationships of considerable intensity.

Novels, of course, were important long before the nineteenth century, and it would be useful to know more about their introduction in Europe. Even Miguel de Cervantes's *Don Quixote*, sometimes called the first novel, depicts the negative effects of reading fictions about the doings of heroic knights centuries before. Inspired by his immersion in these works, the character Don Quixote sloughs off his own identity and, imposing fantasy on reality, takes on the role of a knight-errant and sets off in armor to live out similar adventures.

> Now, everything that his adventurer of ours thought, saw, or imagined seemed to him to be directly out of one of the storybooks he had read, and so, when he caught sight of the inn, it at once became a castle with its four turrets and its pinnacles of gleaming silver. . . . Don Quixote drew up to the door of the hostelry and surveyed the two merry maidens, who to him were a pair of beauteous damsels or gracious ladies taking their ease at the castle gate.[41]

Cervantes explores a wide variety of crossovers between imagination and reality, including Don Quixote's encounters with imaginary beings. When he attends a puppet show enacting the fictional rescue of Melisandra from the Moors, Don Quixote is so caught up in this show that he pulls out his sword and attacks the puppets. Cervantes's book—first published in 1605—provides a classic study of media-based imaginary social relations.[42] Even works from the earliest phases of Western civilization—the Greek dramas and the Homeric epics—vividly show that the people of these societies were concerned with the doings of fictionalized humans beyond the circle of their actual social acquaintance. The works also portray social situations in which spirits interact with mortals. The gods of the Greeks, like the spirits of Fáánakkar, were not aloof from the human social world.

Given the limitations of the historical record—we can know

little about the fantasy life of people of prior eras—another important comparative perspective comes from ethnographic investigations of contemporary non-Western societies. While there are some good studies of mass communications in non-Western cultures, these works, like those in the West, typically ignore the artificial social relationships that people may develop with media figures. For the most part, the information does not even tell us whether or not such relationships exist.

When I did fieldwork in Micronesia in 1968, my anthropological interests were focused on traditional aspects of Fáánakkar culture, and I too paid little attention to this problem. Radios were becoming common, people were beginning to see movies, media figures sometimes served as a topic for conversation, and there were indications of more significant effects. However, I never learned whether people developed elaborate fantasy relationships with the beings they encountered through the media.

When I went to Pakistan in 1976, I was interested in exploring the effects of mass communications in that society. I knew from the published literature that there was a widespread popular radio broadcasting system, a flourishing print media system, a new but expanding television network, and a popular, well-established local movie industry—one estimate suggested that 70 percent of the urban population regularly attended movies.[43] What I did not know was whether or not Pakistanis had developed artificial relationships with media figures similar to those I had begun to study in America.

As it turned out, they had. Informants from very diverse backgrounds were enthusiastically interested in a wide variety of Pakistani media figures—poets like Igbal, singers like NurJahan, sports figures like Inoki, and movie stars like Shabnam. From the beginning, it was clear that people often elaborated admiration and hero relationships with these figures similar to those found in the United States. One woman described her admiration for a long dead political figure as follows: "He was a compassionate man. He was a man who was a leader in war, but who deeply believed in peace. He was an idealistic man . . . so there are certain personal qualities like heroism or wisdom or rocklike trustworthiness that make that character or person important for me.

71

. . . I feel much more calm and comfortable in my world of fantasy than in my real world."

Further research revealed that other types of relationships were also present, even in isolated rural areas. I learned of examples like a fourteen-year-old boy who had developed an imaginary love relationship with a Pakistani singer-actress. He used to rush from his work in the fields to hear her songs on the radio and afterwards, I was told, "he would admire her as if he had accomplished something himself." He used to praise her to others and would sneak away to see her movies when they came to the nearby village movie theater.

Artificial relationships were even more pervasive and significant in the urban centers. One university student described an intense imaginary romance she had developed with the leading character of a popular novel.

I was so impressed by the portrayal of its principal male character that for the following two years he was, for me, an incarnation of the ideal person to be in love with. I admired him for being a self-made man, and the fact that he was a deviant in his society and strong and confident enough to cope with the shortcomings of life undauntingly made me, sort of, identify myself with him. If the author meant to romanticize his arrogance, wit, cynicism and unscrupulous behavior, she certainly had the desired effect on me. However, I found him more human and closer to life than the heroes of other novels I had read, because, apart from his mocking attitude, there was a gentle and sentimental side to him; also the situation in which he is depicted is an historical fact, and this made him more credible and hence more realistic and appealing. I looked upon him as an actual person that I knew; to me, he represented the ultimate in manhood. . . .

I simply idealized the book. It was one of my most cherished possessions, and in spite of my slim pocket allowance I thought it was worth having a copy of each edition. . . . I had my name scrawled all over the book and was, of course, too possessive about it to consider lending it to anyone.

I had read the book at least a dozen times and reading extracts from it every now and then was my favorite pastime. I knew most of the dialogues by heart, especially those spoken by my favorite character.

This imaginary attachment was exclusively dear to me. I had an attitude of idealized fidelity and was almost jealous of another girl displaying a similar affection, though I loved to rave about him myself.

Since this character was played by a particular actor, he naturally became my favorite actor. I began to think of him as the character. I saw all his movies, read about him, and collected photographs and newspaper clippings concerning him.

I began to appreciate everything I associated with the character's personality—for example, men with a moustache, cigars, horses, etc. Imitating his attitude and mannerisms made me feel pretty elated, and I used his words (whenever applicable) in everyday situations as frequently and familiarly as though they were my own.

The values upheld in the novel were, for some time, quite seriously adopted and practiced by me in real life situations. In my daydreams as well, I projected conversations that would take place between me and this imaginary character, and needless to say, they went along the same lines as those described in the book. I imagined I was courted by men exactly like him. In fact, scenes described in the book took place between us. I firmly believed that life would be intolerable unless I married someone like him.

For two years I perpetually went around masquerading as this character incarnate. I tried to integrate most of his personality traits with my own. I behaved and reacted towards other people the way I thought he would in a similar situation. In fact, whenever possible I used his very words. I found only those men attractive who in some way reminded me of him. My attitude towards men was, for a couple of years, deeply inspired by the book. I thought it was proper behavior to be offhand, scornful, and perhaps a little rude to them, since that was the way the heroine was towards my hero; and I obviously expected a similar response in the bargain.

As this account nicely shows, Pakistanis elaborate their artificial social relations in much the same fashion as do people in the United States. The intense media consumption, the collecting, the fantasizing, and the imitative role modeling are similar to American media relationships. But what is particularly striking about this case is the identity of the character with whom the love relationship was established. This young woman, in traditional Pakistani dress and golden jewelry, had developed her relationship with a figure from an American novel. Her favorite novel—very popular in Pakistan—was Margaret Mitchell's *Gone with the*

Wind. Her female mentor was Scarlett O'Hara. The hero she loved was Rhett Butler.

Artificial relationships exist in Pakistan, they are similar to those in America, and they often involve exactly the same media figures—the gods of the American mass media. Many Pakistanis know a great deal about certain American media figures. Their favorite singers include local figures like Suhail Rana but also Don McLean and Joan Baez; their favorite movie stars include Ghulam Mohi-u-din, but also Clark Gable, Elizabeth Taylor, and Ali Mac-Graw; their admired sports figures include Hanif Mohamad but also Chris Evert and Muhammad Ali; their preferred writers include not only Niaz Mir, but also Robert Frost, Leon Uris, and Jacqueline Susann.

Contact with these American figures comes from imported media productions. While local films abound, many American films are also shown. Local Pakistani programs provide much of the television fare, but American programs are also aired. Some of these include "Six Million Dollar Man," "Mod Squad," and "Little House on the Prairie." Even ascetic Sufi fakirs are well aware of some Western media figures. When they visit the cities, they hear about English and American TV and movie characters. Even at home in their isolated mountain shrine, they are not without media contacts. In the evening they often listen to a portable radio; through this radio, media figures swarm into their consciousness.[44]

Since foreign media material is filtered through Pakistani cultural interpretations, it is to some extent assimilated into Pakistani cultural format. One young woman who had several crushes on American TV stars spoke as follows: "I'm sure you won't be able to write all my feelings down if I start describing them. All sorts of ideas come into my head. I want to be close to him, be near him, to find out more about him. If he's a foreigner like this one [Michael Landon], I wish he were a Muslim, a Pakistani Muslim. . . . After all, a woman must live where her husband lives. . . ." In fantasies people may transform foreign media figures into Pakistani identities and interact with them in terms of local situations and roles. Such relationships can also serve as a vehicle for Westernization. Through repeated media consumption and through fantasies based on such materials, the individual may be partially enculturated into Western assumptions, values, and modes of fantasy. As one informant rather guardedly noted, "Exposure and convincing evidence of alien thinking makes one review existing attitudes and, perhaps, become more accommodating."

Many Pakistanis, at all levels of society, are worried about the impact of mass communication on their own traditional Islamic value system. This includes concern not only about Western media imports, but also about popular Pakistani media productions. In conservative circles, all such material is viewed with suspicion. In order to restrict the supposedly pernicious effects of media productions, a high level of government control is exercised. In the mid-1970s various foreign books and films were banned, both local and imported media were heavily censored, and government propaganda newsreels were shown with every film. But this does not satisfy many of the critics of mass communications. An important component in the riots of 1977 was a concern with the reestablishment of stricter Islamic religious codes. Prime targets for the urban riots were the local movie theaters, many of which were burned to the ground. With the military takeover of General Zia, even stronger censorship has been imposed.[45] It remains to be seen how this will affect artificial social relations with media figures.

At the beginning of this chapter, I showed that an essential aspect of American cultural knowledge is information about media figures. But like the people of Fáánakkar with their spirits, Americans do not merely possess information about their particular gods. Americans not only know about media beings, they not only feel strongly about them, they also engage in pseudosocial relations with them.[46] Such relationships engage Americans in profoundly involving artificial social interactions—through "identified" media consumption, through external symbolic interactions, and through elaborate fantasies. These relationships also have important and pervasive effects on actual social interactions through processes such as imitative role modeling. It is not only American schizophrenics who have "obsessive identifications" or "erotomanic obsessions" with media figures. Few Americans have been totally untouched by a media relationship, and at one time or another most of us have been strongly affected by them. The American social system is pervaded by these imaginary yet powerful social relationships.

Chapter 3

Social Relations in Dreams

"Sleep," wrote Lord Byron, "hath its own world."[1] Like media consumption, sleep transports us to another reality. Falling asleep we drift away from the objective world of everyday waking life and enter the "kingdom of dreams." Here, entangled in phantasmagorical imaginary scenes, we are absorbed and lost, hour after hour, throughout the night. In the morning we awaken and "return to reality."

In twentieth-century America, dreams have been studied more than any other form of imagination. Numerous interpretive psychological theories have been elaborated, and an extensive dream literature has emerged. Since the early 1950s, there has also been much study of the biological aspects of dreaming. Through the use of objective measurement devices—especially electroencephalogram readings—we have acquired some interesting information on the frequency and duration of dreaming. We know that everyone dreams for long periods of time every night, and not just during periods of rapid eye movement. However, such objective approaches have their limitations. Commenting on the rise of "scientific" dream studies, Robert Van De Castle writes, "Dreams could now be indirectly observed unfolding as the pens charted their course across the slowly moving EEG paper. However, we seem to have remained fixated at the level of fascination with the ups and downs of the ink tracings and have neglected to study how these squiggles relate to the ebb and flow of phenomenological dream experience."[2]

The phenomenological experience of dreams has been neglected; so too have certain social and cultural aspects of dreaming. In this chapter I will develop an ethnographic exploration of the nature of American dreams as social experiences of the self, and I will examine the connections between dream interactions and actual social relationships. I will introduce this cultural approach to dreaming by considering some of the ways dreams have been interpreted by peoples of different societies.

In all cultures there are words for "dreams" and conceptions about their general nature. These conceptions have varied tremendously from society to society, and sometimes from group to group or even individual to individual, within a single society. One skeptical theory prevailed in certain circles of nineteenth-century European society. According to this view, dreams are meaningless. They are simply scattered shreds of consciousness produced by the rumblings of the digestive tract or some other "distemper of the inward parts." This conceptualization is still popular among a few biologically oriented modern American sleep researchers who treat dreams as meaningless "noise."[3] For the most part, however, humans have been strongly inclined to attribute some significance to their sleeping experience.

Across human history, dreams have been most commonly understood as a link between humans and the world of the supernatural.[4] In this view, dreams are not products of personal psychological processes—they are communications from supernatural beings. Sometimes a spirit appears in the dream, sometimes the dream itself is a message from the supernatural. In either case, dreams are explicitly *social*; they consist of interactions between people and spirits.

Among the Sufis of northern Pakistan, dreams are regularly interpreted as communications from the spirits of deceased holy men or "saints." One disciple reported the following experience.

Near the end of my business in the city, I was thinking about going home. But fifteen days before I was planning to go back, I had a strange dream in which I saw a graveyard, a forest, and a mountain shrine. I could not understand the meaning of the dream although I thought about it almost continually for the next fifteen days. On the day of my departure, I went to the bus stand to get a ticket. There was a huge crowd on the first bus so

I went to another bus and it was quite empty. As I put my foot up on the step, my mind was suddenly seized by a strong inclination to visit Saint B. So instead of going home I got a seat on the bus to Rawalpindi, where I spent the night. The next day I went to the tomb in the saint's village. I spent about a month there and I began to feel very pleased and content. One day I came up here to visit and as I climbed up the trail and saw this shrine it brought my dream back before my eyes. For this was the shrine I had been shown in my dream!

Here both the dream and the effects of the dream were understood as spirit "indications," messages from the saint that this man should abandon his worldly life and come and live at the shrines. That the man followed these directions was considered proper, even though it changed his waking life drastically.

Often the saint's "spirit" appears as a figure in the dream. Sometimes he speaks to the dream self, offering information, instructions, or warnings; sometimes the saint engages in more elaborate interactions with the dream self. "In the dream I saw the saint's face. I was in white and he asked me to ride with him on a white horse. Someone else held the bridle. I was taken by my master to many different [sacred] places in the dream, and I received the blessing of the saint. I felt myself flying through the air with my master, sitting behind him on the white horse." Occasionally pilgrims sleep at a shrine in an effort to receive a dream "indication."[5]

As Robert Van De Castle observes, such spirit contact theories played an important part in early Western civilization. "The earliest Greek view of dreams was that a visit was paid to a sleeping person by a dream figure in the form of a god or a ghost. Since Greek rooms had no entry except a door, it was thought that these figures entered through the keyhole, delivered their message while standing at the head of the bed, and then exited by the same keyhole."[6] In later Greek culture people were much concerned with "incubation"—the process of seeking supernatural dreams by sleeping in temples.[7] Borrowing heavily from the Greeks, the Romans also placed great emphasis on incubation and on the symbolic—but not Oedipal—interpretation of dreams. "Julius Caesar said he had a dream in which he was sleeping with his mother. The dream was interpreted as representing the mother city of

Rome and, thus bolstered, Caesar crossed the Rubicon and captured Rome without a drop of blood being shed."[8] The Bible also contains reference to many dreams that were understood as social communications from God, and in the Talmud it is written that "an uninterpreted dream is like an unread letter." In the Middle Ages it was believed that demons frequently entered peoples' dreams. As Van De Castle observes, "Martin Luther became so fearful that he would not be able to distinguish divine from demonic messages that he prayed to God not to speak to him in his dreams."[9]

With the rise of industrial society and "scientific" modes of thought, dreams began to receive secular, mechanistic interpretations. Dreams were now seen not as communications with the other world but as mechanical products of the individual's physiological and psychological processes. Such interpretive schemes, including those of Sigmund Freud and Carl Jung, include a tacit "communicational" dimension. As with certain religious interpretations, dreams were seen as cryptic messages. The personality was viewed as a system of separate parts and the dream was a "message" that traveled from one part of the self to another. For Freud, most dream elements, including dream figures, were seen as symbolic representations of unconscious infantile sexual elements.[10] In Freud's system, "Steps, ladders or staircases, or as the case may be, walking up or down them, are representations of the sexual act. . . . A woman's hat can very often be interpreted with certainty as a genital organ, and, moreover, as a man's. . . . Children in dreams often stand for the genitals. . . ."[11] Other dream figures, including "ghosts," were interpreted differently.

Robbers, burglars and ghosts . . . all originate from one and the same class of infantile reminiscence. They are the nocturnal visitors who rouse children and take them up to prevent their wetting the beds, or who lift the bedclothes to make sure where they put their hands in their sleep. . . . In every case the robbers stood for the sleeper's father, whereas the ghosts corresponded to female figures in white nightgowns.[12]

In Jung's system, the dream was to be understood as a message from the unconscious, a warning that some aspect of the self was being neglected.

80

The general function of dreams is to try to restore our psychological balance by producing dream material that re-establishes, in a subtle way, the total psychic equilibrium. This is what I call the complementary (or compensatory) role of dreams in our psychic make-up. It explains why people who have unrealistic ideas or too high an opinion of themselves, or who make grandiose plans out of proportion to their real capacities, have dreams of flying or falling. The dream compensates for the deficiencies of their personalities, and at the same time it warns them of the dangers in their present course.[13]

Again the specific interpretation of a given dream depended, in part, on the proper interpretation of specific dream figures. Jung believed that some of these beings had universal significance, that they appear and have the same meaning in dreams from all societies. There was, for example, the archetypal shadow figure who represents the animal side of the self and always appears as a figure of the same sex as the dreamer.

The "unconscious" psychological dream interpretation schemes developed by modern psychoanalysts are neither fully "scientific" nor fully "modern" theories. Each version is disputed by other psychologists who advocate partially or radically different interpretations, and such theories are virtually impossible to assess by the kind of quantifiable tests popular with laboratory dream researchers. Furthermore, these psychoanalytical interpretations cannot be considered exclusively a product of twentieth-century "scientific" thought. Similar cultural theories have been developed by people of other times and other places.

Anthony F. C. Wallace has demonstrated that the seventeenth-century Iroquois Indians employed a dream interpretation system that included a "psychoanalytic" dimension. The Iroquois recognized "visitation dreams" that involved social relations with spirit beings who "spoke personally to the dreamer," giving him a message of importance for himself and often for the community also.[14] However, the Iroquois also recognized "symptom dreams." These came not from supernatural beings but from the depths of the dreamer's inner self. Such dreams "expressed a wish of the dreamer's soul." This conception of dreams, Wallace shows, was "basically psychoanalytic" because it was based on the assumption that a dream "gave symbolic expression to unconscious wishes."[15]

In contemporary America, there is considerable diversity in the interpretations both psychologists and ordinary Americans place on their dreams. These interpretations are culturally significant, but it is important to remember that both folk interpretations and psychoanalytic theories are outside schemes for decoding dreams. They often tell us more about the interpreter's theory than the subject's dream. They are analogous to critical studies of media productions—they constitute a kind of waking gloss on the primary experience, and they are structured by the system of cultural standards with which the critic perceives and evaluates. Also, in the case of dream interpretation, the application of the "critical machinery" often involves scanty attention to the text itself—that is, to the internal structure and drama of the dream composition.

If we are to pursue the approach developed in this study, we must seek to understand the dream as "another world." If we adopt this perspective, we should shift our attention to the dream itself and seek to understand what the dream is like from the *inside* as a form of human experience. Instead of imposing meaning from the outside by trying to figure out what external referent some dream element might "stand for," we should seek to discover the meaning that exists phenomenologically in the dreamer's experience of his or her own dream. We then become concerned with questions like the following: What are the characteristics of the dream as another "reality" into which the dreamer is transported? What is the nature—within that reality— of the various dream elements including the dream self? What, if any, patterning or meaning is present? How are dream events similar to and different from those of waking American life? We should seek to approach the dream world ethnographically, as if we were trying to investigate the distinctive characteristics of an alien society or the fictional world of a science fiction novel.

Curiously enough, such an approach has rarely been taken in social science treatments of dreams. Anthropologists have paid more attention to dreams than to any other imaginary process, but they have been little concerned with ethnographic explorations of the inner worlds of dreams.[16] Commonly they have applied psychological or psychoanalytic theories to dreams in assessing the "national character" of some subgroup or society or in analyzing the life histories of particular individuals. In the latter case, dreams have sometimes been seen as private, "nonsocial" phenomena.[17] However, when dreams are viewed as "other worlds," they are seen to be highly social. Consequently, an ethnographic approach is fully appropriate.

As soon as one looks ethnographically at the inner world of dreams, one is struck by the high degree of cultural patterning. To a large extent, dreams are structured by the dreamer's culture. It may be true, as Jung argued, that some dream elements represent universal symbols found in the dreams of peoples in all societies. It may also be true that other dream elements represent highly individualistic residues of the peculiarities of one's early childhood experience. Nevertheless, it can be much more clearly and definitely documented that many dream elements are drawn from cognitive schemata in the culture to which the dreamer has been enculturated. They are structured by the categories, rules, roles, assumptions, beliefs, and values in terms of which the individual's waking world is constituted. The dreams of an individual from any given society will have many similarities to the dreams of other persons from that society, and these patterns will contrast markedly with those in dreams of people socialized in other cultural traditions.

This is evident in the settings within which the action of the dream world takes place. As with waking experience, dream experience occurs in particular places. These settings are meaningful because they are culturally constituted. It is often assumed that the dream world is characterized by mysterious, surreal, otherworldly landscapes vastly different from those of ordinary waking life. Sometimes this seems to be true. One dreamer, for example, reported, "I was in a room that was made of marble walls, floors, and pillars with mirrored ceilings. There was a bath that was also made of marble—it took up most of the floor." Other informants occasionally reported dreams which took place in "a cathedrallike castle," "a dark jungle," "a strange futuristic empty white hall," "the corridors of what appeared to be an ancient Mexican monastery," "an undersea world," "the pillar-enclosed hilltop of a witches' coven," and "a mysterious Sahara-like desert." Such striking scenes appear remarkably imaginative since they seem to be outside the dreamer's actual waking experience. However, these otherworldly settings are rare.

The vast majority of dreams—94 percent in my sample—take place in settings that directly parallel the dreamer's waking cultural experience.[18] "I am in a house. . . . I am looking out of a screen door in the back of the house. The weather is warm. It is a springlike day with the sun shining brightly, leaves on the trees, and the grass is green. There is camping equipment lying spread out on the back lawn." This dreamer is not in some strange never-never land, he is in an American *house* with a *screen door* and a *back yard* in what turns out to be *Baltimore, Maryland*. This is characteristic of most American dreams. They take place in culturally constituted scenes drawn directly from the individual's experience of American society. Often the dream occurs not only in a familiar category or setting; it occurs in a specific place. It is not just a house, it is "Grandma's house"; it is not a nameless beach, it is "Ocean City, Maryland"; it is not an anonymous dorm room, it is "Kathy's room"; it is not merely a highway, it is "Interstate 270"; it is not just a department store, it is "Bloomingdale's"; it is not just any drugstore, it is "the Dart Drug in Bethesda." Often the setting more or less exactly resembles its waking counterpart. "The two of them [the two dream figures] are standing in Susan's mother's kitchen, and I picture it exactly the way it really is. The colors and the placement of objects are exactly the same." Going to Bloomingdale's or to one's mother-in-law's kitchen may seem a rather prosaic kind of dream journey, but this appears to be standard in American dream experience.

While American dreams are typically situated in scenes drawn from the local cultural landscape, they do not precisely mirror this landscape. Despite the quote just above, there is usually some difference between the dream scene and its actual counterpart. The atmosphere and lighting are often different even when the scene is almost exactly parallel to the real-world vision. While Western artistic renderings of dream scenes, such as those of Salvador Dali, are often exaggerated, they accurately point to some of the subtle distortions of dream settings. If it were possible to project on a screen, side by side, the image of a room as seen in waking consciousness and as "seen" in a dream, the latter would have a distinctive quality. Often the dream scene is darker, more fragmentary, more "mysterious." Somehow the scene seems different. "When I was in the shoe store, it felt like a restaurant. I can't describe *how* it felt like a restaurant, it just did."

This sense of difference can sometimes be keyed to the fact that the dream scene includes items of material culture appropriate to some other setting—a college classroom has a kitchen table and a refrigerator, or an office has several church pews. The larger landscape may also be imaginatively restructured. In a dream version of her college campus, one informant noted the absence of some major buildings and the rearrangement of others.

In dreams, activities appropriate to one setting often occur in another. A wedding takes place not in a church but in the dreamer's office. A picnic takes place not in a park but on a city street. Dream settings are also much less stable than those of the real world; they often transform themselves from one type to another. At one moment one is in one's house; at the next moment the house has turned into a stadium. Both these characteristics are illustrated in the following text.

I had a dream that began at a wedding ceremony, and it was my wedding. I was marrying the same person, Robert, that I married in my real life. Both sides of our families were gathered together, but it was not a church, it was at the big mansion in Memorial Park, the cemetery I work at. . . . In my dream, the room had a few church pews in it. . . . We were all sitting on the pews waiting for the others to arrive. . . . The mansion turned into Robert's grandmother's house. . . . I don't know what happened to Robert, but all of a sudden I was walking down this hallway. There were boxes on one side of the hall that contained Christmas decorations. This hall exists in real life. It is in the house of the Smiths, who are friends of my family."

Dream characteristics, such as the transformation of settings and the mixing of incongruous elements, often seem "fantastic," "distorted," and "bizarre" *only* from the perspective of waking consciousness. Looking back at the memory of a dream from the standpoint of waking consciousness, the informant notices "distortions." However, within the dream, such characteristics may not be perceived as distortions at all; rather, they may be accepted as routine. If, in waking life, one's house turned into a stadium, one would be astounded. In dream life such changes are often accepted without surprise. Here again, there is a significant parallel with the ethnographic study of other societies. From the outside, the system seems bizarre. Once one has grasped the inner view, a logic is evident.

From an outside perspective, the dream as a whole is an imaginary production composed by the dreamer himself. However, if we adopt the inside view, we see that the dreamer is generally unaware of this. Typically the dreamer finds himself as an actor, an "I," moving through the scenes of the dream world:

"I am walking down a city street," "I am at Hecht's doing my last-minute shopping," or "I am driving a steel-grey convertible down Interstate 270." Such characteristic dream description phrases illustrate how the dream is experienced from the perspective of an actor who is unaware that it is he himself who constructs the settings and directs the plot. The dual nature of this process is nicely shown by the common phrase, "I dreamed I was. . . ." Here the first "I" represents the godlike unconscious: the composer-director who creates the dream world. The second "I" represents the subjective self who experiences the production as an actor moving through settings that seem objectively real. Somewhat like a movie viewer who identifies with an actor and hence becomes fully absorbed in the doings of the drama, the dreamer is *in* his or her own dream.[19]

This subjective dream self has numerous interesting qualities, several of which are of particular pertinence to the approach developed here. For the most part, the individual is fully identified with the dream self. Usually one does not feel that the dream events are happening to one's grandmother or to a stranger; one feels that they are happening to oneself. It is "I" who sees, feels, thinks, and acts. Sometimes the dream self has characteristics, abilities, and motives different from those experienced in waking consciousness. In the dream the person may have a different appearance, age, or even sex. Occasionally, the dreamer is unable to perform actions that are routine in the real world, as when the dreamer cannot run or walk effectively. Sometimes the dream self possesses powers beyond those he or she actually possesses, as when a child dreams of driving a car. Sometimes the dreamer possesses powers outside the range of human ability. In my sample, dreamers have sometimes been able to fly, to breathe under water, to sustain major injuries without diminution of physical functioning, and to see clearly through closed eyelids.

For the most part, however, the dreamer appears as a person of the same age and sex and much the same basic attributes as the waking self. As one informant put it, "I am myself in my dreams." Even if the dreamer possesses some unusual abilities or disabilities, these are mixed in with ordinary characteristics of the waking self. Generally, the dreamer operates with ordinary knowledge drawn from waking social experience. He or she perceives, thinks, and acts largely in terms of the categories of the culture's knowledge system. This is what "allows" the dreamer to look around and see or think "kitchen," "chair," "truck," "stadium," "Bloomingdale's." Usually, the dream self also operates with standard culturally constituted plans. This is what enables the dream self to talk English, drive cars, make sandwiches, ski down mountains, and—in the case of one nurse—perform cardiopulmonary resuscitation.

In some ways the consciousness experienced by the dream actor is similar to that of waking life. "I'm wondering where I am, what is happening, and looking for answers. In this manner I am myself," one woman said. However, like other informants, she tends to feel more dazed, bewildered, and uneasy in dreams than she does in actual experience. Another informant nicely described this quality of dream consciousness. "In reality I am—or act—controlled, confident, and humorous. In my dreams my sense of humor is totally absent. I am nervous, hysterical . . . in a desperate hurry. It is difficult for me to accomplish things in my dreams—I often have a difficult time running, expressing myself, or thinking clearly." This inability to think clearly is characteristic of dream experience. "My thoughts are incoherent and confused, my speech fumbled, erratic and irrational. I cannot take control of situations in my dreams, as I can in reality, by simply thinking things through." As this comment implies, a basic problem in dream thinking is the inability to step back from the immediate situation and analyze it logically.

When I'm dreaming, my brain can't seem to function properly. I'll have a problem and I can't seem to resolve it, or if I do find a solution I will stick to that even if it doesn't work. For example, when I broke away from the thugs [who were attacking her family], I wasted time trying to tell what happened to my neighbors instead of running . . . to call the police immediately. . . . When I woke up, I actually got mad at myself for being so dumb.

It is true that vivid forms of recall and anticipation sometimes occur.

Standing on a city street corner, I hear a radio news announcement: "A rapist and thief has pursued a woman into an apartment building but he has been locked out and is standing outside in old clothes. Apprehend him if you can before the police arrive." I had walked past this apartment just minutes earlier and while doing so I saw what I now realize was the criminal. I remember—that is, visualize—what he looked like as the broadcast is played. He is in his late forties with white hair and an unshaven face. He is wearing dirty, baggy pants and a loose shirt.

As the broadcast asks for help in apprehending the criminal, I begin to anticipate. I picture myself (in slow motion) tackling the man around the legs as he walks off down the street. I feel myself crashing him down onto the cement. All this is anticipation. I am still standing a few blocks away. I am thinking what I *might* do. . . .

Now I start to walk back up the street toward the scene of the crime. On the way, I see Frank and his Mexican wife (whom I have never met) working on his green Corvette. I stop to talk with them, forgetting all about the criminal, and the dream goes off in that direction.

Such vivid recall and anticipation is actually very rare in most dreams, including those of the informant quoted above. For the most part, the dream self is only dimly able to recall and anticipate. "When I am awake . . . I daydream (about the future) and deliberate. In my dreams I don't do these things. I make decisions instantaneously and don't stop to consider alternatives. In a way the dream just carries me along with it." This characteristic style of dream thinking ordinarily traps the dream self in the midst of present circumstances, and it seems to account, to a large extent, for the prevalence in dream consciousness of immediate coping strategies and the dominance of situationally derived emotions.

The dream self, like the waking self, experiences a flow of emotions. These emotions are similar to those of waking consciousness; they seem even closer to waking life than the cognitive processes. People easily describe their dream feelings with the vocabulary of waking life—"anxiety," "fear," "lust," "anger," "euphoria," "pleasure," "joy"—and they often report experiencing the physiological sensations that accompany such emotions—the anxious sweat, the pounding heart, the flow of adrenalin, sexual arousal, the churning stomach. Most of these emotional states are also similar to waking life in that they are systematically linked to the situations in which the dream self is enmeshed—one experiences fear in what the dream self defines as "dangerous" situations.

The dominant emotion seems to vary from dream to dream. Most informants can readily characterize a given dream as happy, neutral, unpleasant, or terrifying. For the latter we even have a special word, "nightmare" (derived from a Middle English term referring to an evil spirit who was believed to oppress people in their sleep). There seems to be a considerable variation, from individual to individual, in the prevalence of one or another type of emotionally tinged dream. A few people characterize their dreams as pleasant and agreeable. "Generally my dreams are happy, and if they are sad they usually have happy endings." In America, however, this is rare. The vast majority of my informants regularly experience unpleasant dreams, and for many this is the dominant mode. "In my dreams I am usually hostile, worried, frightened, incompetent—rather unhappy to say the least. . . . The situations I'm in are usually unpleasant and the people are usually negative. My dream world is not a cheerful place." As this informant implies, the negative emotional tone is usually linked to the situation in which the dreamer is entangled. Occasionally the dream self moves alone through empty buildings or deserted landscapes. Far more commonly he encounters other beings and engages in social interactions. A crucial and striking characteristic of American dreams is the prevalence of social interactions. In my sample of dreams, over 97 percent involved social encounters.[20]

As in actual experience, almost always there are other people. The dream world, like the world of the media, is an imaginary *social* world.

Dream beings range from hunchbacked monsters to familiar friends. From an analytic perspective they are phantasmagorical puppets, figments of our own imaginations, mere imaginary beings. We play ourselves in dreams, and we play all the other parts as well. And yet, within the dream, we experience these imaginary beings as compellingly real. They smile, laugh, and sneer; they speak, flirt, and attack. They are very "realistic" in the sense that they appear to the dream self as independent actors over whom he has no personal control. The seemingly real quality of these dream beings is an impressive testament to our ability to deceive ourselves into emotional entanglements with imaginary beings.

There are several distinct types of dream beings. First there are the strange, nonhuman dream figures. Here we find "hump-backed, hairy beings," "witches," "moongirls," "animate computers," "big, slimy, terrifying snakes," "large man-eating rats," "walking pinball machines," "malicious tornadoes," "large talking rabbits," "prehistoric animals," "zombies," "gargoyles," "vampires," and other assorted monsters. The nature and origin of these creatures is an intriguing question. Those given to psychoanalytic interpretations have had a field day speculating on the symbolic significance of such beings. Some of these interpretations are plausible and a few are convincing, but there is an aspect to their origin which has not been properly appreciated. Symbolic analyses have been based on the assumption that such dream figures are not part of the individual's waking experience and therefore must emerge out of the personal depths of the dreamer's subconscious self. This assumption is erroneous.

Whatever their symbolic significance, these strange dream figures can often be connected to the dreamer's waking experience—not to his actual experience but to his imaginary waking experience, that is, to the contents of the media he has consumed. Many people resist this interpretation, partly out of loyalty to psychoanalytic assumptions. One informant argued as follows: "The media doesn't affect my dreams because media experience just isn't deep enough to affect my subconscious." This is not true in general, and it turned out not to be true of this informant. The dominant motif in his most frequently recurring dream came from a movie he had seen as a child.

Similar parallels can be drawn for most of the "strange" dream figures mentioned above. Zombies, vampires, prehistoric animals, animate computers, blob monsters, and talking rabbits are not to be found in the real social world, but they abound in the fictional worlds of the American media. The presence of such beings in the dream world may tell us more about the individual's media socialization than it does about his subconscious self.

The media origin of strange dream figures is supported by other evidence. As noted earlier, dream settings sometimes involve exotic otherworldly scenes outside the dreamer's actual experience. However, one can find significant correspondences between these settings and the dreamer's media experience. Often there are direct connections. The futuristic white hallway turns out to be similar to one in *2001: A Space Odyssey*; the African jungle river appears after reading *Heart of Darkness*; and the strange undersea landscape was straight from *The Poseidon Adventure*. The situation is similar with many strange dream figures. Sometimes these figures resemble media beings; often they are identical. Describing the beings encountered, the informant often makes this connection explicit. It is not just a witch *like* that from the *Wizard of Oz*, it *is* the Wicked Witch of the West.

This leads to a consideration of a second major class of dream beings, the media figures. Just as unmet media figures play important roles in the individual's waking imaginary experience, so too do they often figure prominently in his dream experience. The media figures who appear in my sample of dreams include celebrities such as Walter Cronkite and Hugh Hefner; political figures such as Ronald Reagan, Franklin Roosevelt, and John F. Kennedy; sports figures such as Jim Palmer, Lefty Driesell, and Bill Walton; television stars such as Jaclyn Smith, Diana Taylor, and J R ("complete with cowboy hat"); popular musicians such as Elvis Presley, the Beatles, and Bruce Springsteen; and movie stars such as Jack Nicholson, Goldie Hawn, and Woody Allen. The presence of these media figures puts firmly to rest any misguided notion that media experience is not deep enough to affect our dreams.[21] Woody Allen dreams are now so prevalent in American sleep worlds that Dee Burton of the New School for Social Research is writing a book about them.[22]

A third group of dream figures are human beings who are unknown to the subject in his waking life. Some of these beings are probably dimly remembered media figures. Others may represent actual beings such as forgotten strangers glimpsed on a bus. Still others appear to be purely imaginary creations. In any case they are, typically, more or less plausible American types. They look like Americans, wear American hairdos and clothes, and speak American English.

The fourth, and most common, class of dream figures consists of imaginary replicas of known others: dream versions of one's acquaintances, kinsmen, and friends. These "doubles" have a vivid seemingly real quality—they not only look like the originals; they move, touch, and talk like them. Typically, they are fully accepted by the dream self as the real other.

The figures who inhabit our dream worlds do not just appear and pass by. They approach us, they say things to us—and we to them. Dream beings engage us in social interactions. The dream world is an imaginary social world not only because it is full of dream beings, but also because we are entangled in *social relationships* with these beings.

The structure of dream interactions is complex, but several points are clear. Occasionally dream interactions seem bizarre or meaningless, but more often they make at least some sense both within the dream and in waking retrospect. This is because these interactions are meaningfully patterned by the dreamer's enculturation into a particular system of knowledge. Dream others, like the dream self, seem to have internalized American social structural expectations and rules. Consider the following dream excerpts:

I am sitting in my Phil 400 class in my usual front seat. The professor is discussing Hohfield's concept of rights.

I am walking into a nightclub. A doorman walks up and asks if I have identification.

A sea of faces surround me as Dad and I walk arm in arm down the aisle. Mother is sitting up in the front pew.

I was watching "Nova" on television when the phone rang. It was a friend of mine that I had seen earlier that day. She wanted to get together for dinner that evening. We decided to meet at her place, then go to the restaurant.

As such examples demonstrate, interactions in the dream world are often directly structured by the cultural rules of American social roles. Role interactions played in my dream sample include brother to sister, husband to wife, parent to child, student to teacher, friend to friend, lover to lover, salesman to customer, waitress to customer, employee to boss, job applicant to employer, jogger to jogger, nurse to patient, dentist's assistant to dentist, accused to judge, and policeman to criminal. Where known figures are involved, they most often play the same role to the dream self that they do in waking life. Where they do not, they usually assume some other standard American role. (The secretary's boss appears to her not as executive but as salesman, spouse, or teacher.)

Similar considerations apply to media figures. Very occasionally media figures appear in the role of "celebrity."

I was sitting in a bowling alley with my friend Sam. There was a long line of people. . . . We were waiting to get autographs from Jim Palmer, who was in another room. It was soon our turn, so we walked through a small door where Jim Palmer was sitting at a small square table. I said "Hi" and he said "Hi" and then I handed him a piece of paper.

But even when the interaction begins as that of celebrity to fan, the dream relationship is likely to develop into a more familiar form of interaction.

I find myself at the Cheverly Swim and Racquet Club. There is a cocktail party going on, and it's apparent that there are some prestigious people around. I walk down to the pool, almost invisible to the crowd. When I'm poolside, I glance up at the clock, then I look to the other side of the pool. There, to my amazement, is John F. Kennedy standing in a small group, chatting. It becomes very important for me to talk with him immediately. I dive into the pool and swim over toward him. I get out of the pool, walk over to him, and say, "Hello." We chat for a while, just the two of us. I think that he is the most articulate man I've ever heard.

Most commonly the media figure assumes some intimate social role, often one corresponding to the individual's waking fantasy relationship with him or her. Frequently, the figure appears as colleague, relative, friend, or lover, as is evident in the following examples.

At first, I'm standing outside behind a window looking into the White House. . . . Suddenly a shift! I am now walking down the hall. Directly to my right, the President—Jimmy Carter, about one foot from my shoulder. He's a little shorter than me, and grinning. To his right is another man walking with us (I think he's Cyrus Vance, but I'm not sure). Both men have white-grey hair and are wearing impeccable dark grey suits. We are chatting, making small talk. I feel dignified, calm, poised. *I belong!* I've done this before, and I'll do it again. It's part of my job. We're going to a meeting.

The night before the concert, I had a dream about meeting Roger Daltrey. I was sitting backstage while the Who played their songs. After the concert was over, Roger came back and started talking to me. He asked me if I'd like to come with him on the rest of their U.S. tour. I, of course, said yes.

I am jogging in Golden Gate Park. It is a nice sunny day and lots of people are out. I see a little kid fall off of his bike. I stop to help. Then his mother comes over. She's pretty, a blonde. I've seen her before—on TV or in the movies. I'm not sure but it looks like Goldie Hawn. It is. I'm not very excited. I stay cool. She's just like an ordinary person. She thanks me for helping her kid. Then she invites me to her house nearby. It's huge, overlooking the ocean, made of dark brown wood, with many big windows. Inside, everything is brown and red and black and very rich-looking. There is a loft overlooking the living room. She takes me up there. The kids have vanished. We talk and make love.

The dream self is socially motivated by concerns that parallel actual social interaction. The dream self wishes to achieve desirable objects and experiences, wants to help certain people and harm others, and seeks to protect its own interests. Much of what seems to motivate the dream self—and dream others—appears to be specific motives and values associated with particular American roles.[23] In the role of "waitress" the dream self wishes to properly serve the customers, earn tips, please the employer, and take a vacation. In the role of "student," the dream self wishes to get the proper assignment, wake up in time for the final exam, and get a good grade. Even when an unrealistic combination of roles occurs, culturally constituted role knowledge and motivation is typically evident.

I was on campus with my sister and we were walking up the hill towards Tydings Hall. We were searching for something but neither of us knew exactly what it was. It was late in the afternoon, the sky was dark, and the wind was blowing so hard that our capes were flapping around uncontrollably. Finally we decided to go to my history class and went into Francis Scott Key Building. When we found my history teacher, Mr. Weaver, I was relieved. He said that he couldn't teach class unless he had a sandwich. At this point Sally was no longer in the dream and I was in another room which had a refrigerator exactly like the one in the cheese store where I work. I looked inside it and realized that I didn't know what Weaver wanted to eat so I went back to his office and he told me he wanted Italian salami with American cheese on white. He also asked me to serve it on "————." (I don't remember the word he used. It sounded French and in the dream it meant either a doily or paper plate.) I went back to make his sandwich and found everything inside the fridge to be a mess. . . . I tried to make Weaver's sandwich for an hour and was motivated by a desire to get an A if I did a good job. Unfortunately the sandwich was never finished.

Neither the dream self nor dream others necessarily conform to the cultural rules governing the roles they assume. On the contrary, cultural expectations and obligations are often violated. But this is true of the actual social world as well. In actual interactions, people often do more for us than we expect—or less. Furthermore, as in the actual social world, it is the tension between cultural expectations and individual behavior that provides much of the *drama* of dream experience. This applies, for example, in relationships with media figures. "My sister and I are in charge of Ronald Reagan for the evening. We are going to a show in Georgetown. On the way we stop at a liquor store. We leave Ronnie in the car. When we return he is gone. We spend the evening looking for

Ronnie." It applies to relations with other dream figures as well. In the following dream a young woman dreamed she was a man.

I am living down at the ocean. I am so pleased to be a man, I'm smiling to myself. Then I'm in bed with a woman, a young blonde. Shortly I am right on top of her and before long I have an outrageous orgasm. I feel great, but then I realize my partner does not. She is pissed . . . but I don't care. She calls me an insensitive bastard.

The same principle applies even more strongly in dreams in which the individual assumes familiar roles. While operating in occupational roles, the dream self may engage in anxious efforts to justify or cover up lapses in role performance and to avoid the punishment of occupational authority figures. An airline steward describes the following dream:

The passenger seating area looks like the coach section of a Boeing 747. I am working the flight. There is a supervisor watching me doing the bar service. She is very complimentary. With these good vibrations, I loosen up and take off my tie. My uniform vest and pants are tattered and worn. I had forgotten to shave off the beard I'd grown during vacation. Suddenly, I see my personal supervisor. I freeze up. I am so nervous now that I say something rude to a passenger. My supervisor hears this and is critical but cool. She keeps smiling. She doesn't seem to realize that I have a beard. I know that my beard is not regulation. I have to get rid of it before she notices. This becomes all-important. I tell the woman I am working with on the bar cart that I have to go to my room. When my supervisor sees me leaving work, she starts coming toward me. I run into the elevator.

In waking life our social roles are heavily influenced by the "grammar" through which our culture orders social relationships. This is true of our dream life as well.

Some dream interactions almost exactly mirror waking role play. This is one reason people sometimes have difficulty deciding whether they "really" did something or just dreamed it. But in many cases, dream interactions are systematically different from those of waking life. Often the mirror is cracked and darkened. From the perspective of waking life, strange distortions appear. If one compares the drama of the dream world to that of waking life, one interesting difference is the frequent experience of negative emotional states exaggerated beyond those characteristic of daily life. Often the dream world is "not a cheerful place" because the dream self regularly experiences anxiety, confusion, jealousy, frustration, humiliation, terror, and pain. The negative quality of American dreams often involves the exaggerated realization of fears directly linked to waking social roles. More than a dozen of my informants have worked as waitresses. Most of them report dreams like the following: "When I came out with the cocktails, the entire room was filled with customers. . . . I felt a streak of panic since all at once all the customers started calling for me to give them service. I frantically ran into the kitchen to get help but found no one there."

Another factor in the negative ethos of many American dreams is the prevalence of aggression and violence. Social aggression—situations involving arguments, conflict, and the violation of obligations—occurs in 58 percent of my dream sample. Physical violence occurs in 25 percent.[24] Sometimes the strange dream beings—the gargoyles, zombies, and computers—are friendly and supportive. Much more often they are threatening and aggressive, as in these two examples:

I heard a drum beat in the distance and was surrounded by the hags in a matter of seconds. I asked one of them what I had done and she said, "You know . . ." in a voice that sounded like the Wicked Witch of the West. The hags continued to chant. I woke up trembling.

When we left the room, he told me I was being arrested for killing my best friend, Anita. I told him that I would never do a thing like that and started crying. He gave me an icy cold stare and said there was one way to find out for sure. Next thing I knew I was in this room with computers around me. He sat at a terminal for what seemed like forever and finally the computer said, "You are guilty." I began pleading. . . .

Media figures, too, are often hostile. This is true of media villains, such as Nazi soldiers from World War II movies.

Between the ages of eight and twelve, I had a recurrent dream. . . . I am sitting with my family in the living room of our house. There is a loud banging at the front door (as if someone were trying to break it down). Soldiers with German uniforms and accents are shouting, "Let us in! We're coming in!" On the radio there is news that the Germans have invaded the U.S., and I realize that these soldiers have marched from Washington—I imagine them coming up the hill to our house. My family starts to go upstairs, but I implore them to come with me downstairs. . . . I feel such high anxiety that I could cry.

But even neutral or friendly media figures may appear as antagonists or bloodthirsty murderers.

My heart missed a beat when I saw a male figure coming from my room. When I saw it was only Doc from "Love Boat," I felt relieved. He kept staring at me strangely and I began to get frightened, so I asked him if he was here to hurt me. This question really made him mad. I thought he looked like he wanted to kill me. He had a butter knife in his hand and started slashing the knife at me. He only scratched my legs with this. Next he pulled out a butcher's knife and said, "Now I'm gonna do this." He lifted the knife over his head and brought it down. I instinctively held out my hand to shield myself and the knife sliced into it, leaving my hand cut all the way open. Then he was holding a small axe and struck out at my face, gashing both sides. During the entire attack I stood immobilized before him. I suddenly remembered my feet, so I ran, not even thinking far ahead enough to know where I was going. I ran downstairs and screamed frantically for anyone to help me, but no one answered. I ran outside and he was right behind me, hacking at me as I ran. He caught up with me and whipped me around. I got the axe away from him. Then he pulled a gun on me.

Strangers can be just as vicious.

I am in my parents' neighborhood with Jean. We are down the block from their house, talking. I see a strange man looking at Jean, leering at her (the way many men do when we are out together). She does not see him coming up behind her to attack. I scream her name in a strained voice. I am terrified for her. He gets angry that I have interfered with his conquest and grabs my arm with a fierce look in his eye. I scream and struggle. . . .

I am lying in the center of a very dark, deserted street. There are a few buildings around but no streetlights, no lights at all, no people. It is very cold, rainy, and windy—a bad storm. I have been attacked, someone has bashed in my head with a sledgehammer. I am lying alone in the middle of the street, in the darkness and rain. Blood, pouring from my head, is being washed away by the rain. Then someone walks by, pauses, looks at me—then flags a taxi and leaves me alone again.

98

Often the dream self is violent as well.

Then suddenly a man came from around the corner! I immediately extended my right arm and struck the man in the left side of the chest. The
gargoyle man struck him also. Blood was rushing from his body. . . . He
staggered across the floor and fell in the middle of the floor of the empty
room. He attempted to get up. I picked up a club from the floor and hit
him a few times in the head.

I was walking out of a bar on Route 1 with three close girl friends. We
were all talking and laughing when this girl came from around the corner
and called out my name. I turned around quickly and all of a sudden I
was standing alone face-to-face with this girl. She drew out her gun from
a holster and shot at me. I saw the bullet going very slowly through the air
and moved out of its way. A girl came from behind me, but somehow I
knew she was there and turned around and shot her. Then I turned
around again and shot the first girl. My friends were all around me and
we began to walk away. . . .

As in the example above, violence by the dream self is often a
response to the social aggression of strangers.

We back up down the road and come to the group of kids who threw the
object. I jump out of the car—there are four guys ages seventeen or eighteen. I head for the biggest guy, who is about six feet two inches. I slam a
punch to his solar plexus and then a punch to his jaw; then I grab his arm
and twist it behind his back. I twirl him around and slam him face down
on to the back of the car. His friends approach me, but I say: "Come one
step further and I'll pop his arm right out of the socket. . . ."

As Paul began to write the combination down for me, some guy kept
looking over his shoulder trying to steal the combination. I told the man
to stop, but he still kept it up. I yelled at him and still he tried to look.
Eventually I beat the man up because he wouldn't leave me alone. I made
pretty handy work of him and finished him off in four or five crush-
ing blows.

But perhaps most striking of all is the extent to which dream
versions of close acquaintances, kinsmen, and friends appear in a
malicious and aggressive role.

I see myself looking at Susan, my fiancée, and her mother talking. They
do not see me. It is as if I were at the movies watching the characters on

the screen. I see them but they cannot see me. The two of them are standing in Susan's mother's kitchen and I picture it just the way it really is. The colors and placements of objects is exactly the same. Susan is very upset, crying. I hear her say, "But I simply will not live anywhere near his parents. I can't stand them. They make so many demands on us, our time." Her mother is trying to comfort her and says, "Now honey, everything will be okay. You must let him know how you feel. The boy always wants to be near his family, but he eventually realizes that he must be the one to change. Always." Susan feels better after hearing this. I *feel* this. She says, "You're right. If he doesn't give in then I won't marry him." Her mother hugs her and says, "Of course, honey. If he doesn't give in then there can't be a marriage. It won't work if he is so stubborn." At this point Susan's father comes in and asks why Susan is crying. Her mother explains the previous conversation. He says, "Your mother is right, Sue. If he doesn't give you your way then he is not for you." Susan is no longer crying now. She is relieved. I feel anger and want to run into the kitchen and tell her folks to butt out, tell them off. Instead, I decide to call Susan and confront her with what I heard.

When the dream began, I found myself lying down on a bed in an unfamiliar room. I was surrounded by a group of people on three sides of the bed. Some were friends; one, whom I remember most vividly, was from work. Suddenly, this girl (a short-haired, huskily built, unfeminine woman) leaned over from the bottom of the bed with a vicious smile on her face and produced a white strip of thick cloth, which she tied around my head as a blindfold. I heard a lot of snickering and laughing; I began to shake from the fear and trepidation that something terrible was about to happen.

Then someone grabbed my hands. I felt a cold, smooth cylindrical object being pressed into my hands. They took each individual finger and pressed it firmly onto the object's surface. There was a lot of giggling and whispering while this was occurring. I heard distinctly, amid the discussion, someone saying, "Yea, we're gonna fix your ass good now, Jonesie." In the next part of the dream, I was in someone's room at school. A girl came in and sat on the floor. I knew that she was one of the persons in the room before; I knew she knew what the "conspiracy" against me was. I began yelling at her to tell me, but she kept laughing about it, shaking her head in a teasing, sarcastic manner. I went wild. I jumped on top of her, screaming at her to tell me what was going on. Then, I began pulling at her hair and shaking her. Her hair felt soft and fuzzy; suddenly, it began falling out in clumps in my hands. I jumped up and ran out of the room, and down the hall into my friend Kim's room. She was sitting at her desk, smoking a cigarette and watching TV. I sat down on the bed, sobbing, jabbering about everything that had happened. I realized she wasn't listening very attentively, but merely glancing up at the TV and lighting another cigarette. I yelled, "Kim!" and she turned her head. I saw a slight smile on her face; she raised one eyebrow, flicked her cigarette ashes, and said, "Oh, really?" I realized that she was, in fact, the head of the conspiracy; I recalled times, recently, when I had seen her talking with a group of girls from another hall, whispering, laughing. Feeling totally used and ignorant, I slowly left the room.

A common form of social aggression involves jealousy dreams, in which the dream version of the individual's spouse or lover becomes openly involved with someone else. Often the pain of betrayal is intensified because the rival is a friend.

Sally and I made plans to play darts in the evening, but when I called her to see if she was ready, she said that she had to write a paper instead. I decided to surprise my boy friend Larry and visit him at his house. As I drove down Western Avenue, I saw Larry in his car with Sally. They were so busy kissing each other that I drove past them unnoticed. I was furious at both of them and felt betrayed. I drove to the Dart Drug in Bethesda and called my friends Jill and Marie, but neither of them was home, so I decided to drive around some more. While I was on Utah Avenue, I saw Larry in his car again. He was with Marie and this time she was lying down with her head in his lap while he had his hand up her shirt. I looked in the back seat and saw Sally and Jill. Jill was climbing over the seat so she could be with Larry. . . .

It was late at night and I was talking with Marie in her parents' Toyota. . . . I asked Marie to refuse to go out with Larry if he were ever to ask her out. She said that she was sorry, but that Larry asked her to the movies and she already said yes.

As in other dream relationships, the dream self may also treat close friends and relatives aggressively and sometimes violently. One middle-aged informant provided the following example.

I was in New York with my friend Dave. There were some black kids in the street with a wagon. We went up to the apartment. It was a kind of combination of my apartment in California and my apartment here.

There were shotguns in the apartment. Dave wanted to shoot one. I said no because I didn't want the black kids to come up and rip them off.

He didn't listen. He was talking about one of the guns to someone, showing it off, and he stuck it out the window.

"Don't shoot!" I warned him.

He shot it out the window anyhow. I walked up behind him with another shotgun, stuck it in his back, and pulled the trigger. I just blew him away.

In the next scene Laura was complaining about how messy the apartment was, with blood all over the walls.

"Is this how you keep your apartment?" she asked.

As these examples suggest, the level of aggression in American dream interactions is much higher than that in actual social interactions. In their waking life, none of my informants experience the kind of social aggression and physical violence characteristic of their dreams. How should we interpret this pattern? Here we must step back from the phenomenological level and seek to account for the intensity of dream aggression revealed by our ethnographic explorations.

It may well be that psychoanalytic interpretations can accurately account for some of these dream patterns, but social and cultural factors are also involved. The available cross-cultural evidence strongly indicates that dream aggression is culturally relative. The level of dream aggression apparently varies from society to society, as does the type of violence which occurs. In the Pacific island of Baiga, aggression dreams constitute only 30 percent of the sample; on Truk, aggression dreams account for 49 percent of the sample. Furthermore, on Baiga the dream self is always the *victim* of aggression while on Truk, as in America, the dream self plays the role of aggressor as well as victim.[25]

This shows that even if aggression should prove to be a universal feature in human dream life, its manifestation is subject to modification by the peculiarities of particular social and cultural contexts. What is there about American experience that might lead to a high level of dream aggression? If Americans do not ordinarily experience conspiracies, betrayals, gun battles, and axe fights in their actual social worlds, where do they derive such vivid imagery? Given the material discussed earlier, one source of influence seems apparent. The intense aggression of American dreams derives in part from American media consumption, from our extensive vicarious immersion in the extraordinarily violent worlds of the mass media.

A twenty-three-year-old informant's autobiographical text illustrates this connection. He kept a detailed dream log over a period of thirty-four days, and in the following accounts he reflects on the high level of dream aggression:

The most surprising results come from the nature of the social relations in my dreams. In the majority of my social dreams, both those in which I am a participant and those in which I only observe, aggressive interactions are involved. At first, this is difficult to explain. During this period, my awake interactions with people were overwhelmingly nonaggressive in nature. In fact, many of the very intensely aggressive interactions in my dreams have never been even closely approximated by ordinary awake experiences. I generally regard myself as a nonviolent type of person. I cannot remember myself being involved in any kind of physical fight since I was six or seven years old. I have never committed, observed, or been a victim of a violent crime. I have never in my awake experiences seen a gun or other lethal weapon being used in a violent or aggressive way. However, in seven of the eight aggressive dreams in which I was a participant, the use of guns, other lethal weapons, and/or violent physical force were involved. The following is a description of one of the more detailed aggressive dreams I recorded:

I'm driving down Route 1 with Jane in the car, headed toward Greenbelt. We go past the firehouse and stop at a traffic light in front of the university. I see a lady—a young blonde standing on the corner across the street. She is yelling at someone in a car stopped at the light going in the opposite direction. The guy she's yelling at is her husband. If he doesn't meet her demands, she threatens to shoot him. Finally she gets real angry and pulls out a gun. We duck and roll up the windows of the car. We hear many shots. I tell Jane to stay down; then I look up and see the lady shooting at several of the cars stopped at the light. Windows are breaking and people are screaming. I put the car in reverse to get away. I finally pull into the police station. (It's actually the firehouse.) An officer comes out of the station and I tell him what happened. He grabs his gun—like a pistol but with a very long barrel—and starts toward the scene. I see him drop his gun on the grass. He keeps running without it. I pick up the gun and decide to keep it for protection. I drive back to our apartment, just down the road—it looks like the house I lived in as a kid in upstate New York. I am afraid the lady followed us and is out to get me for telling the police. I go into the basement to hide. I decide to climb into a narrow crawl space in the rafters of the basement. . . . I get very anxious. I know she wants to shoot me. . . . Finally, I get into the crawl space. I hear someone coming. I fire a shot from the gun. It feels powerful and smooth in my hand. . . .

The types of social roles played by the main characters in this dream are typical of those in many of my other aggressive dreams. The central character, the lady, is playing the role of a violent criminal. She is out to get myself and the others, who are playing the roles of victims, or potential victims, of her criminal activities. The criminal is mean, aggressive, carries a weapon, and is mainly concerned with hurting people and destroying property. The rest of us are mainly concerned with avoiding being harmed by her. We run away to keep from being shot, and I eventually use a gun to defend myself. . . .

Since I have never actually been involved in social situations such as these, where did I learn about the proper behavior for characters assuming these types of roles? For example, where did I learn that criminals carry guns and like to shoot people, and that victims are to run away and hide and use guns in self-defense?

I must admit to being a full-fledged member of the "TV generation." I was raised from birth with a television always available, and usually on. The set often served as my baby-sitter. And a large part of the content of the shows I grew up with involved criminals and victims in violent social interactions. During the 1950s and early 1960s, westerns dominated the television schedule and were my favorite types of shows. Practically everyone in these shows carried a gun, and people were constantly being shot or beaten in barroom brawls. Violent struggles between outlaws and lawmen were central to the plots of westerns. From the late 1960s through the 1970s, the most popular shows on television were the cops and robbers series, involving private detectives, secret agents, and police in various conflicts with crooks. Again, lethal weapons and violent social interactions were in abundance.

In addition to these types of shows, I was exposed to a horde of violence on television news broadcasts. I grew up watching the Vietnam War being fought on television. One of the most unforgettable scenes I have ever experienced happened on television: I saw a South Vietnamese officer casually walk up to a handcuffed Vietcong soldier and shoot him through the head at point-blank range. . . . Clearly, these artificial experiences have provided me with the knowledge to reconstruct similar situations in my dreams.

104

We have aggressive dreams, at least in part, because we entertain ourselves with a peculiarly aggressive mass media.[26] As noted earlier, there are some societies in which the dream self never commits aggression. It is difficult to believe that such a peaceful orientation to others could be sustained in the face of American media enculturation in which we are taught to enjoy identifying with "heroes" who kill off other people by the score.

This is not to say that the media are solely responsible for dream violence. Given the close structural parallels between the details of media scripts and dream violence, it does seem clear that the media heighten, stimulate, foster, and structure dream violence. It also seems clear that dream violence would exist to a lesser degree quite apart from media exposure. If an inclination to dream aggression exists apart from media influence, where does it originate? Must we abandon social and cultural interpretations and seek the answer solely in psychological structures? Not necessarily, as Freud himself indicated. In *Civilization and Its Discontents*, Freud argued that civilization is inherently frustrating.[27] Because civilization requires cooperative, organized behavior, people must regularly suppress impulses toward the gratification of their immediate desires. Whether or not this includes the suppression of innate inclinations to aggression—as Freud believed—this self-control invariably results in frustration, discontent, and suppressed anger. This rather pessimistic view of the relationship between the individual and society has been indirectly supported by all subsequent anthropological ethnography. There are no completely free cultures. All societies are based on elaborate systems of unwritten but restrictive rules—role-structured systems of rights and duties that specify what individuals must do for others and limit what they can demand in return.[28] If social aggression proves to be a universal characteristic of human dreams, it may well be that these imaginary interactions connect to the frustrations of waking social interaction. But the structure of these social rules varies significantly from society to society. The patterns that seem to exist in the dream aggression of different societies probably reflect systematic differences in the frustrations imposed by particular systems of social organization.[29]

Contemporary American society, with its bureaucratic megastructures and its currently problematic nuclear family system, seems to breed its own special kinds of nightmares. It may also be that the frustrations and problems of particular American roles connect to particular kinds of aggressive dreams.[30] My own dream sample, including some of the dreams quoted above, suggests that this may be true. Certainly Americans in many different roles experience their waking life as frustrating because they cannot realize the values to which they aspire.[31]

Here again there may be an important media connection. The world of the media is better than reality; in the media, basic American values—grandiose career success, romantic and sexual fulfillment, warm family relationships, happy friendships, and material affluence—are intensely realized. This unrealistic vicarious fulfillment probably contributes to a sense of discontent with the more modest levels of satisfaction to be found in the actual social world. The frustration created by the gap between media fantasy and social reality may well contribute to the aggressive structure of American dreams.

This interpretation is largely speculative. We do not yet have sufficient understanding of the connections between dream relations and waking interactions to make such interpretations definitively. Among other things, we need better cross-cultural ethnographic data on the inner worlds of dreams. However, there are other connections betwen dreams and actual social relations that can be more clearly demonstrated. These have to do with the effects of dreams on waking life—with the ways in which dream interactions affect the conduct of waking social relationships.

Because of its vivid seemingly real quality, the imaginary dream world typically holds us fully in its sway while we are asleep—so much so that the individual typically mistakes the dream for "reality." A moment later, upon awakening, he finds himself in the world of everyday waking life. The disorientation that sometimes accompanies the transition between these realities can be usefully compared to "culture shock." One problem involves the transformation of identity—as shown in the classic passage by the Chinese Taoist Chuang Tzu.

Once Chuang Chou dreamt he was a butterfly, a butterfly flitting and fluttering around, happy with himself and doing as he pleased. He didn't know he was Chuang Chou. Suddenly he woke up and there he was, solid and unmistakable Chuang Chou. But he didn't know if he was Chuang Chou who had dreamt he was a butterfly, or a butterfly dreaming he was Chuang Chou.[32]

Sometimes, the dreamer "awakens" to what appears to be the waking world, only to find that this is a dream.

I was lying in bed in the night wondering why my husband was not there beside me. Then I heard him in the next room talking to a man with a black southern accent, and I realized that he was talking to [blues singer] Lightnin' Hopkins. "What's going on?" I wondered and then as I stirred in the bed I awoke. Then I realized that my husband was actually asleep beside me and that I had only been dreaming that I was awake.

Or consider an even more confusing experience:

I dreamed that I woke up and got out of bed. But something strange happened . . . and I realized I was still asleep. Then I woke up again, but this too was a dream. And then I really woke up and got out of bed. It happened three times before I actually woke up—and even then I kind of wondered.

Such an experience can be disturbing—"Will I wake up yet once more?"—but even more frightening is the experience of being asleep, realizing that one is dreaming, and being unable to awaken.

I dreamed that I was asleep and that I was trying to make a noise so my father would hear me and wake up and come and wake me up. I was trying to wake up. In the dream I finally woke up and walked to the door of my parents' room. Then I began to scream but I couldn't make any noise. Then I really woke up and I was sweating and scared.

At the other extreme are instances in which dream consciousness directly intrudes into waking life. Here the person physically wakes up and actually gets out of bed, but his or her interactions are still controlled by dream reality.[33]

After her meeting, my wife was resting in the bedroom and fell asleep. About an hour later our dog went into the room and flopped loudly down on the wooden floor next to the bed. The sound evidently awoke her. I was sitting in the next room and I heard her jumping out of bed. "Oh my God! What time is it?" she says, almost shouting.

I go into the bedroom. She is standing at the bureau looking at the clock, desperate and upset.

"What time is it?" she asks. "Our meeting?" She is moving about but her face is somehow distant as well as upset. I tell her gently that the meeting has already occurred, that it is OK. She looks at me again wildly, then seems to dissolve, and falls back onto the bed.

Another variant involves waking up into what *appears* to be a dream world. A college student fell asleep on his campus green and awoke to find himself surrounded by knights in armor. "I must be dreaming," he thought, only to realize a moment later that the "dream beings" were only college students in costume.

Despite occasional moments of confusion, Americans usually negotiate the transition between the dream world and waking life with rapidity and ease. At one moment one is entangled in the doings of the dream, the next moment one is awake and the dream is fading, drifting rapidly from consciousness, as one confronts the concerns of waking social life. The dream is now an "illusion," gone and forgotten; it has "evaporated" from consciousness.

Or has it? In fact, residues from the dream world often affect actual interactions long after the dreamer is awake.

Sometimes I may half consciously be unfriendly to a person who had done something mean to me in a dream the night before.

I dreamed that my boy friend slept with a girl from work. The next morning I was mad at him even though I knew it was a dream.

Another informant describes the aftereffect of a dream that portrayed his fiancée and her parents in a negative light.

At first [upon awakening] I felt hurt and anger and actually wanted to call Susan right away. I then realized that I had been dreaming, so I did not call her in the morning. I must confess that even though I knew it was a dream I harbored some resentment for Susan all day.

Here the individual's actual interactions are emotionally colored by the dream experience. We know that this happens only because we are sometimes able to recall that a sense of resentment came from a specific dream. However, given that most Americans remember few of their dreams, it is likely that this process occurs much more frequently than we realize. When we feel a vague aversion to one person or a vague attraction to another, this is probably often due to the forgotten interactions we have played out with them in our dreams.

Conversely, remembered dreams may be deliberately employed in such a way as to affect actual waking behavior. For example, it appears that dreams often feed into artistic productions. Many tribal myths seem to be the direct result of individual dreams. Modern media productions may also be affected by the author's dreams—as when a dream will suggest a new character or the solution to the plot of a story. Sometimes this connection between imaginary worlds is claimed to be clear and direct.

Samuel Taylor Coleridge reported that he composed substantial portions of the magnificent *Kubla Khan* effortlessly in his sleep. Robert Louis Stevenson was almost able to harness the creative energy of his dreams at will. The plot for *Dr. Jekyll and Mr. Hyde* was revealed to him in a dream, and he claimed that much of his literary material was constructed for him by the "little people" while he slept.[34]

Where this occurs, an individual's private dream may, through the medium of mass communications, be subsequently consumed— and in a sense "dreamed"—by millions of others. And this media experience may also subsequently affect the night dreams of the audience.

Remembered dreams can also affect actual social relationships through interpretations that the waking self places on them. Many cultures assign considerable significance to their dream experience, and often waking interpretations of such experience have important effects on actual social conduct. Among the Ashanti, a dream of adultery requires payment of a real adultery fine. Among the Iroquois, certain dreams had to be publicly acted out.

Nightmares of torture and personal loss were apparently not uncommon among warriors. In 1642 a Huron man dreamed that non-Huron Iroquois had taken him and burned him as a captive. As soon as he awoke, a council was held. "The ill fortune of such a Dream," said the chiefs, "must be averted." At once twelve or thirteen fires were lighted in the cabin where captives were burned, and torturers seized fire brands. The dreamer was burned; "he shrieked like a madman. When he avoided one fire, he at once fell into another." Naked, he stumbled around the fires three times, singed by one torch after another, while his friends repeated compassionately, "Courage, My Brother, it is thus that we have pity on thee." Finally he darted out of the ring, seized a dog held for him there, and paraded through the cabins with this dog on his shoulders, publicly offering it as a consecrated victim to the demon of war, "begging him to accept this semblance instead of the reality of this Dream." The dog was finally killed with a club, roasted in the flames, and eaten at a public feast, "in the same manner as they usually eat their captives."[35]

In contemporary America as well, dream interpretations often affect actual social relationships. The effects vary since modern Americans apply a surprisingly diverse set of folk interpretations to their dreams. Certain interpretations parallel—and are sometimes borrowed from—non-Western societies. The dream may be understood as having supernatural or quasi-magical significance. Informants involved in the occult sometimes claim to have "astral traveled" in their dreams and even to have had "real" sexual encounters during such experiences. A similar kind of interpretation is taken seriously by a twenty-five-year-old man with a scientific job at an urban hospital.

My father and mother died when I was an adolescent—my father was killed in Vietnam and my mother died of cancer three years later. However, I continue a relationship with them ten years later. Specifically, I have night dreams that are laden with symbols and imageries of them returning for a visit, during which we discuss a number of topics. . . . I try to prolong these visits since it is the only time I get to see them. They ask about how things are going, about things in Washington, about how the Redskins are doing. Then they say, "We have to go now," and leave.

A significant number of Americans see in their dreams evidence of previous incarnations. An even more common form of supernatural interpretation is to find in one's dreams premonitions or extrasensory perceptions. Even otherwise skeptical informants tend to be open to the possibility of such experiences, "Although I can't say I believe in premonitions, I have had some very vivid dreams that were similar to things that happened the next day." Believers not only accept such interpretations, they frequently act upon them. A group of friends were planning a vacation at a shore resort. The night before they left, one of them dreamed of a sailing accident in which a dream figure was hurt. After she told her friends, they decided not to rent a sailboat during the vacation.

110

Premonition theories often overlap with quasi-psychological folk interpretations. In some cases, the dream is interpreted, Jungian style, as a possibly valid message from the unconscious.

When I have a dream about someone I know, it affects me a lot. I wonder if what happens in the dream could happen in real life or if how people feel about me in the dream is how they really feel in reality.

If I have an erotic dream of someone I have always considered just a friend, I may take a second look at that person.

Often I have dreamed of someone I'd lost touch with . . . and the dream will prompt me to call them up.

Most Americans are also familiar with some watered-down version of "Freudian" dream interpretation, and they often apply such symbolic interpretations to their own dreams. In a text quoted above, a young woman dreamed that she was a man. This dream distressed her considerably because she was afraid that it revealed a culturally stigmatized identity attribute, unconscious homosexual inclinations. Turning to media advisers for help, she sought psychology books that would tell her what the dream "meant."

Similar kinds of disturbances in self/other orientations are probably *caused* by popular dream interpretation manuals, some of which offer arbitrary and potentially destructive information on the "real" meaning of dream symbols. A 1979 *Reader's Digest* dream manual offers the following encouraging advice for do-it-yourself dream interpreters:

As a dream animal, the rat indicates unfavorable and dangerous situations. The dreamer may have unproductive, gnawing doubts which stand in the way of a positive attitude to life. But the rat can also be the dream's way of providing early warning of serious and dangerous physical illness.

Should a theft occur, this indicates a loss threatened by lack of attention on the dreamer's part. It may indicate the dreamer's loss of contact with the world about him.

The horse is a dream symbol of great significance. Dream research has to some extent confirmed the popular superstition that the horse is a messenger of death.[36]

Here there occurs a three-way "conversation" among the dream, the waking self, and the media advisor. Sometimes this develops into an actual social relationship. Americans occasionally discuss their dreams in social gatherings. Sometimes a flirtation strategy is involved ("I had a dream about you last night"), sometimes the intention is merely to amuse or entertain, and sometimes the motive is a desire for help in interpretation.

One such example is private therapy in which the interaction of patient and therapist is based on discussion and interpretation of dreams. More complex gatherings are also structured by dreams, as in various self-help "dream workshops." An account by Ann Faraday shows how the metaphor of a "social relationship" between the waking self and the dream self can be carried to an extreme. Under the direction of the workshop leader, the dreamer first asks his dream a question, then assumes the role of a dream figure and provides an answer.

I still vividly recall my initial experience of the Gestalt approach when John, my husband, worked on one of his recent dreams at our very first encounter group in London. At the time, I knew nothing of Perls's dream theory, which maintains that all dream images are parts of the dreamer's own personality, and I was puzzled when the group leader, without discussion, asked John to take a seat on one of the two empty chairs facing each other and talk to the characters in his dream as if they were sitting opposite him. He was then asked to move over to the other chair and assume the roles of the various dream images, giving them each a voice, letting them "speak for themselves."

In John's brief dream he arrived home to find our house pulled down. I watched fascinated as John questioned the various dream characters— the house, me, the workmen, and so on—about the demolition, and could scarcely contain my excitement when I suddenly realized that in giving the "demolition foreman" a voice, John was speaking with the accent, gestures, sentiments, even posture of his own father, who always disclaimed responsibility for his actions by saying it was not his place to question the orders of those in authority. It was a total revelation of the fact that John was allowing our life to be broken up by his first wife, bemoaning the fact, yet doing nothing to stop it, because from childhood he had been conditioned by his working-class father's reiterated conviction that ordinary people are helpless victims of circumstance.[37]

The following example, from one of Faraday's protégés, shows how such an approach can affect the conduct of waking relationships.

I had just spent a lovely weekend with the current man in my life and so I asked dream power what I felt about him in my heart—that is, what do I feel about my own judgment in a love relationship at this time in my life?

I dreamed I was vomiting large maggots and that my eyes were being eaten by smaller maggots. My mother was standing by me during all of this, as I faced a mirror and vomited into the bathroom sink. My father was in a phone booth, wondering what on earth was wrong with me and phoning a doctor rather casually.

Well, the dream was terrifying, repulsive—but when I acted it in a small group of friends and students, I soon learned that dream power's imagery remained friendly. I talked to the large maggots first and the dialogue went like this:

Ann: Who are you and what are you doing inside me?

Large maggots: We are father maggots—derived from all the hurt and anger you felt about your father's rejection of you. . . .

Ann: Who are you and why are you eating my eye?

Small maggots: We are young maggots feeding on your "I." We are young because we haven't been around long, only as long as your divorce. We'll go away from your "I" eventually but we came to tell you that there are still some of us around, and you need to remember this and not fall in love too quickly. If you get yourself into a close relationship with another man at this time, we and the big maggots inside could spoil it, so be patient.

Ann: But what can I do to get rid of you? I don't like you eating my "I."

Small maggots: Oh, just keep doing what you are doing, sleeping with this current man, who is very good for you, but don't start thinking marriage yet. Just be natural and spontaneous about the whole thing and let it flow—this is healing to the "I."[38]

Whatever such dreams *really* mean remains unclear, but such an account shows that it is not just "primitive" tribes whose social interactions are structured by dream interpretations. The gathering itself exists for and is structured by ritualized dream interpretation. The dream provides the "characters" (her maggots) who are made to play an oraclelike role to the waking self. Finally, the interpretation so revealed provides guidelines for actual social interaction—here a rationalization for continuing a love relationship.

This kind of dream interpretation, like most traditional Western interpretations, usually involves working with the dream after it has occurred. The dream provides a text that is subsequently interpreted by the waking self or other actors. However, dreams are sometimes therapeutically approached through techniques designed to influence the text itself. One method involves seeking to influence dream contents prior to falling asleep. Some therapists tell their patients to make a list of problems—in the form of questions—and to repeat these mentally before going to sleep. The intention here is to lead the unconscious self to produce dreams that answer or "solve" the dreamer's waking problems.

Another method involves trying to influence the action of the dream during sleep. Most Americans occasionally experience dreams in which they are fully asleep, yet aware that what seems to be happening is a dream. In such "lucid dreams," the individual is often able partially or totally to control what happens, sending the dream off in ways that accord with his own motives.[39] In America, people experience such dreams occasionally. In certain other cultures, people have reportedly developed techniques that allow them to experience such dreams regularly.

The most famous account concerns the Senoi, a group of some 12,000 people who live in the central mountain area of the Malay peninsula who have been studied by anthropologist H. D. Noone and psychologist Kilton Stewart. Like a number of other "primitive" groups, the Senoi are remarkable for the advanced state of their social system. There is, according to Stewart, an almost complete absence of mental disorders, armed conflict, and violence. In this society there may have been no violent crime for as much as 200 years. Stewart argues that "they have arrived at this high state of social and physical cooperation and integration through the system of psychology which they discovered, invented, and developed."[40] The essential feature of their ethnopsychology is a system of dream therapy in which dream beings are seen as potentially destructive forces that connect to conflicts within the self or between the self and the environment. With the aid of dream therapy, the Senoi believe that these hostile dream images can be turned to the advantage of the individual and his group. The Senoi spend a great deal of time discussing their dreams: "Breakfast in the Senoi house is like a dream clinic, with the father and older brothers listening to and analyzing the dreams of all the children. At the end of the family clinic the male population gathers in the council at which the dreams of the older children and all the men in the community are reported, discussed and analyzed."[41]

But dream interpretation is only part of their procedure. An even more important part involves teaching children to take control of their dream imagery. The Senoi child is taught that he must learn to master the contents of his own dreams.

The simplest anxiety or terror dream I found among the Senoi was the falling dream. When the Senoi child reports a falling dream, the adult answers with enthusiasm, "That is a wonderful dream, one of the best dreams a man can have. Where did you fall to, and what did you discover?" He makes the same comment when the child reports a climbing, traveling, flying, or soaring dream. The child at first answers, as he would in our society, that it did not seem so wonderful, and that he was so frightened that he awoke before he had fallen anywhere.

"That was a mistake," answers the adult-authority. "Everything you do in a dream has a purpose, beyond your understanding while you are asleep. You must relax and enjoy yourself when you fall in a dream. Falling is the quickest way to get in contact with the powers of the spirit world, the powers laid open to you through your dreams. Soon, when you have a falling dream, you will remember what I am saying, and as you do, you will feel that you are traveling to the source of the power which has caused you to fall.

"The falling spirits love you. They are attracting you to their land, and you have but to relax and remain asleep in order to come to grips with them. When you meet them, you may be frightened of their terrific power, but go on. When you think you are dying in a dream, you are only receiving the powers of the other world, your own spiritual power which has been turned against you and which now wishes to become one with you if you will accept it. . . ."

The astonishing thing is that over a period of time, with this type of social interaction, praise or criticism, imperatives, and advice, the dream which starts out with fear of falling changes into the joy of flying. This happens to everyone in the Senoi society.[42]

This kind of dream control often leads to special kinds of culturally structured interactions with dream beings.

According to the Senoi, pleasurable dreams, such as of flying or sexual love, should be continued until they arrive at a resolution which, on awakening, leaves one with something of beauty or use to the group. For example, one should arrive somewhere when he flies, meeting the beings there, hear their music, see their designs, their dances, and learn their useful knowledge.

Dreams of sexual love should always move through orgasm, and the dreamer should then demand from his dream lover the poem, the song, the dance, the useful knowledge which will express the beauty of his spiritual lover to a group. If this is done, no dream man or woman can take the love which belongs to human beings.[43]

Such dream control leads indirectly to peaceful actual social interactions since it removes or reduces inner hostilities. Senoi dream interpretation also deals with potential problems in existing social relationships. It is believed that hostile dream characters can only appear in the guise of a known person if there is some problem between that person and the dreamer. When this occurs, efforts are made to heal the social relationship both in the dream world (as by having the dream self help the dream figure) and in the waking world (as by an actual exchange of gifts) before actual trouble develops. "Thus before aggression, selfishness, and jealousy can influence social behavior, the tensions expressed in the permissive dream state become the hub of social action in which they are discharged without being destructive."[44] Stewart concludes with a comparison between Senoi culture and Western civilization. "My data on the dream life of the various Senoi age groups would indicate that dreaming can and does become the deepest type of creative thought. Observing the lives of the Senoi it occurred to me that modern civilization may be sick because people have sloughed off, or failed to develop half their power to think. Perhaps the most important half."[45]

Through a process of media-based cultural diffusion, Senoi dream therapy methods have influenced certain American social relationships. One of Stewart's essays appeared in a widely circulated collection of psychological articles. The essay attracted the attention of a number of dream researchers who are attempting to carry out similar dream control experiments. In one study, explicitly based on Senoi methods, an attempt is being made to treat sixty recently divorced and seriously depressed women by teaching them to alter the plots of dreams about their former husbands.[46] In some cases, there is evidence that Senoi dream control methods are working.

Sleep has its own world. But the social interactions that pervade dream experience have important connections to the conduct of waking social relationships.

Chapter 4

Social Relations in the
Stream of Consciousness

Dreams may take us to other worlds, but upon awakening we return to reality—or so it would seem from most social science models of cognition. Social science accounts typically postulate a waking individual who is steadily oriented to the external world. They picture a person busily "interpreting experience" (classifying external events) and "generating social behavior" (mentally selecting and activating appropriate behavioral plans). This is not an adequate representation of human consciousness.

Consider Anthony F. C. Wallace's article "Driving to Work." This study consists of an introspective attempt to formulate the cognitive processes characteristically employed by an individual driving from his home to his office. Wallace discusses the use of the "mental map" that allows the driver to follow the familiar route, and he describes the perceptual "monitoring" with which the individual scans variable features of his course.

I constantly check the road for vehicles ahead, vehicles behind, vehicles approaching on the other lane. . . . I check for bicyclists, for pedestrians, for animals, and for obstructions like slow-moving vehicles, excavations, accidents, and so on. . . . I *monitor* the state of the road with respect to its width, the conditions of the surface (dry, wet, snow, ice, leaves).[1]

Classifying these and many other perceptions, the driver activates a complex set of plans in order to appropriately maneuver the car.

Wallace's account is accurate, but only as far as it goes. He has described the cultural knowledge an American must learn, maintain, and use to drive a familiar route. But he has not described what such driving is like *cognitively* for a member of this society. This is because he has not described the forms of consciousness that accompany this activity.

In our society, at least, when an individual's attention is not fully taken up by demanding tasks or engrossing actual experience, his or her attention characteristically shifts inward to a curious subjective world of silent language and inner imagery. As Erving Goffman notes, "While outwardly participating in an activity within a social situation, an individual can allow his attention to turn from what he and everyone else considers the real or serious world, and give himself up for a time to a playlike world in which he alone participates. This kind of inward emigration . . . may be called 'away.'"[2] Driving to work alone is a classic situation in which an American is likely to be "away" in the "playlike world." Because the route is familiar and the operations routine, the individual rarely needs to devote much conscious attention to the task of monitoring traffic conditions and selecting appropriate behavioral responses. As Wallace notes, we feel as if we could drive to work in our sleep—and in a sense we do. Informants often report the experience of "waking up" while driving and realizing that for the past several minutes they have been driving, as it were, on automatic pilot, only dimly aware of the external world through which they have just passed. The solitary individual has been engrossed in the inner world, remembering a pleasant scene from the past, trying out a portion of the day's work, or arguing with the boss. The blank look of the solitary commuter does not mean that his or her mind is blank.

This area of inner experience, "daydreaming" or the "stream of consciousness," is a pervasive dimension of human experience, but it has been largely ignored by social science. This is unfortunate. The stream of consciousness should not be a matter of interest only to psychologists,[3] for the inner world holds considerable ethnographic interest, and it also has important connections both to cultural knowledge and to social conduct. Before exploring these connections, it is essential to consider what the stream of consciousness is like as experience.

The cultural study of the stream of consciousness is hampered by the lack of satisfactory descriptive accounts. One looks in vain through the literature of the social sciences for attempts to render it accurately. Even in psychology, descriptive reports are rare.[4] Instead of attempting phenomenological descriptions, psychologists typically generalize about the stream of consciousness in terms of their analytical frame of reference. The most vivid descriptive accounts are to be found not in the social sciences or psychology but in literature. The following is an excerpt from James Joyce's classic rendering of Molly Bloom's stream of consciousness in *Ulysses*, with an explanatory commentary in parentheses by the critic Robert Humphrey.

Quarter after (a clock has impinged on Molly's consciousness to remind her of the time) what an unearthly hour I suppose they're just getting up in China now combing out their pigtails for the day (her imagination has slipped off to China, still under the stimulus of the striking clock) . . . the alarm clock next door at cockshout clattering the brains out of itself (she anticipates an annoying occurrence of the mornings and again becomes anxious about losing sleep) let me see if I can doze off 1 2 3 4 5 (the anticipation of the neighbor's early alarm stimulates her to exert her will and she tries to count herself to sleep) . . . I love flowers I'd love to have the whole place swimming in roses (the renewed idea of a flower shop stimulates her imagination) God of heaven there's nothing like nature (from flowers to nature in general) the wild mountains then the sea and the waves rushing then the beautiful country with fields of oats and wheat and all kinds of things . . . and lakes and flowers all sorts of shapes and smells . . . primroses and violets nature it is (with a rush of images she defines her connotations of nature).[5]

While Joyce's description powerfully illustrates several features of the stream of consciousness, fictional portraits have certain limitations for culture studies. Many literary accounts are based on careful self-observation, but they are stylized rather than literal renderings. They are concerned with literary effects, not accurate description, and the social and cultural dimensions of the process are usually ignored. In order to conduct a cultural explanation of the stream of consciousness, we need ethnographic accounts from actual subjects in which the primary purpose is accurate description. During field work in Pakistan, I collected some com-

121

parative cross-cultural information. However, most of my data comes from some 400 American informants, including myself, and I will begin with that.

Initial interviews showed that the ethnographic study of the stream of consciousness is complicated by several problems. Like dreams, the stream is elusive. There seems to be a general amnesia for stream experience unless a production is strikingly unusual or repeated frequently. Linguistic conventions also obscure its content. Thus you may say, when asked about your "thoughts," that you were "remembering a visit to Los Angeles," or "thinking about someone" without bothering to reflect on the process or specify exactly what it was like as experience. Most people vaguely recognize that they "daydream a lot," but few pay much attention to these processes or can give much in the way of detailed descriptions. Conventional ethnographic interviewing is of little use. Direct monitoring is also unsatisfactory. One cannot simply sit down, pencil in hand, and ask one's mind to drift away into a natural stream-of-consciousness production. The mind refuses to cooperate. It balks, goes blank, or insists on thinking about this unreasonable task. For the same reason—and also because of the unnatural social context—one cannot ask informants to "stream" on request. Neither in the interview situation, nor in the psychology laboratory, nor on the psychiatrist's couch can one expect to generate natural stream segments. However, alternative ethnographic methods can be employed instead.[6]

As with dreams, it is possible to obtain better results if the subjects are asked to engage in retrospective observations in natural social settings just after a stream has spontaneously occurred. In the technique I use, informants are asked to try and "catch themselves" during routine moments of the day (commuting to work, performing ordinary daily tasks) and to try and identify what they have just been thinking about. They then write down as complete a record as they can, tracing the sequence back as far as possible. Using this technique, most people can produce detailed accounts of their reverie.

The following fleeting experience occurred while the subject was caught one fall afternoon in a traffic jam on the Washington, D.C., Beltway. At one moment he was looking out the window at the stalled traffic, at the next he was "away," that is, "remembering" a traffic jam during a snowy evening the previous winter on Georgia Avenue.

Suddenly I was stuck in the middle of Georgia Avenue just watching the cars standing still and the snow piling up. I felt myself sitting in my car, watching my windshield wipers go back and forth in a never ending battle to clear my windshield of snow. I hear the wipers making their swishing sound and hear the patter of frozen snow hitting my car. I could feel all the emotions I felt that day—I am scared, I feel great anxiety. . . . I see nothing but red brake lights in the distance standing out in contrast to the dark sky.

This segment illustrates one of the primary components of the stream of consciousness. The subject is "remembering," that is, having a memory, but this does not consist of some deliberate, abstract, linguistically mediated recall ("I was in a traffic jam last year. . . ."); it is rather a fleeting, spontaneously imaginative *re-experiencing* of the past event. Objectively the subject is sitting in his car on the Beltway. Experientially he is transported to a snowstorm on Georgia Avenue, or rather to an imaginary version of that other time and place. As he enters this inner world, he leaves the present and takes on the self of a year earlier. Assuming that persona, he sees and feels and senses from that actor's perspective. The experience is vividly meaningful because—like night dreaming—it is composed of pseudo imagery, sensations, sounds, and emotions. Often the individual experiences a memory from two different perspectives—partly from the experience of the previous self undergoing the experience, but also from the perspective of a kind of observer self watching an image of the previous self perform its actions.

The following account shows the transition from "observer" to "participant." A married woman visiting her parents' house is reminded of a trip she had made long ago.

I saw my mother, brother, and myself at the airport. They were telling my image goodbye. I was leaving for Arizona. My mind zoomed in on the image of myself, and I no longer saw the image, I had *become* the image. I was reliving my past experience. I felt all the anticipation, doubt, and excitement. . . . I was walking toward the tunnel that leads to the transport van.

Such an experience can be as vivid and powerful as a dream, but it is more realistic. It is also more subject to voluntary control and reflectiveness. One does not deliberately choose to "stream"; once underway, the stream seems to flow of its own accord—but the experience can be stopped, replayed, and otherwise deliberately modified. Also, the subject is aware that the illusion is an illusion. The Beltway driver was cognizant of the fact that he was *actually* on the Beltway, not Georgia Avenue: he was dimly tuned in to his actual surroundings. In response to changing traffic conditions, he maneuvered his car appropriately despite the fact that he was experientially elsewhere.

Spontaneous replays of past experience represent but one facet of the stream of consciousness. The following account introduces two other important aspects. The subject is walking to work.

While walking, a song was playing in my mind (I had heard the song several times the night before). While repeating the song over and over again in my mind, I started to think about a way of doing some work. "No good," I muttered to myself.

As I continued to walk, several images popped into my mind. I heard a bird overhead and looked up to see it, but the sunshine blocked my vision. However, it did silhouette a tree, giving it an ominous black look. An image of a similar tree I had seen in a movie flashed into my mind.

I passed the railroad crossing and saw a train in the distance. I had several "flashes" of train rides taken as a teenager. I saw myself staring out the window at the fast moving countryside. An image of myself sitting in a train car going over the Sierra Nevada Mountains about ten years later immediately followed that image.

I was almost halfway to work. (It's a good one and a half mile walk). While continuing my walk I began thinking about a girl I know. I thought about calling her up on the phone as soon as I arrived at work. I imagined myself sitting at my desk, my dialing the numbers, and the phone ringing in her dorm (I was familiar with all three images so it was not difficult). I began wondering whether she would answer the phone while it was ringing. I thought she might be in class. I imagined the phone ringing in her dorm and her answering it. She seemed surprised that I called her. I *saw* her clearly talking to me. We began to talk some more. "Are you going to stay in College Park this evening?" I asked. She said she was going to go home. Then I asked her if it was difficult to go to Washington, D.C. from her parents' house in Potomac. "No problem," she said. Then I sketched out my plans for spending a day in D.C. I mentioned the possibility of seeing a movie called *The Black Stallion*. The ad for the movie flashed into my mind. A snatch of conversation which we had earlier concerning horses came into my mind. I imagine the date. We enjoy the movie tremendously. Afterward we are walking through D.C. hand in hand (ah, young love) and I feel euphoric.

By then I had passed a yard where my company's vehicles are stored. A van was pulling out of the yard. It broke my concentration or whatever and I looked to see who it was.

Here again the subject's pseudo experience includes recreated versions of the past, but mixed in with the memories are "anticipations," imaginative renderings of expected future experience. These imaginary futures are constructed in part from memory elements, such as his familiarity with certain scenes and the appearance of the girl. Some of them involve only minor forms of imaginative work—as when he pictures something he has already experienced, such as seeing the girl answer her phone. Other scenes, such as walking hand-in-hand with her down the Washington street, are more purely imaginative. Here the individual departs from the objective present. "Teleported," as it were, into a possible future, he participates in a rich version of an anticipated scene. He becomes a future self and sees, speaks, and feels in that role. The event has not previously occurred—it may never occur —but he feels the euphoria of walking with the girl as vividly as if he were replaying a memory.

Another important element here is the use of language. First, there is the song. He "hears" the words silently in his mind much the same way he hears them when he is actually listening to a record. Secondly, there is the imaginary conversation. He imagines saying things to the girl and she "answers." Finally, there is a brief conversation with himself—the individual silently talks to himself and says, "No good." This dimension of the stream is more pervasive than the above account suggests. Often, as in the following text, it provides a dominant motif. Again, the subject is driving to work.

Shit. I'm late for work again. I've got to start getting up earlier. . . . I hope I don't get stuck at the light (an incredibly long light at Route 1 and Guilford Road). . . . Damn! (I caught the light, now waiting.) Boy, did I get ripped last night and that nut I met. (Remembering.) . . . Come on, light! (out loud) . . . It's about time. They really ought to do something about that light. I mean it's getting ridiculous. . . . I hope Alice (my boss) is in a good mood (anticipation). . . . better yet, I hope she's not there yet.

Here the individual characteristically talks to himself or herself much the way he or she might talk to someone else, except that the words are silent, both in the sense that they are not (usually) spoken aloud and in the sense that one does not "hear" one's tone of voice. (Say "I'm tired" to yourself without moving your lips, and you will recognize the quality of this inner voice.)

While self-talk sometimes dominates a given segment of the stream of consciousness, it is commonly mixed in with the images, emotions, and sensations of memories and anticipations.

"I'm hungry"—Memory images: of the white ice cream truck usually parked outside, the fat smiling man selling someone an ice cream; "I need to lose weight, though"—Anticipations: of myself in a bathing suit looking slim;—Memories: of the beach last summer; Images and sensations: hot/relaxing/sand sticking to wet skin/radio/beach ball/jogging; "I wish I could go to Florida at Christmas"—Images: of my grandmother's house in Daytona/sun/hot/beach/grandfather/long drive/car/sweating; "I wonder if it would be hot in December?"

Self-talk typically includes verbalized reflections about current, past, and future situations ("That was awful," "I'm hungry," "Won't that be nice?") as well as various directives and coping plans ("I've got to get up earlier," "I need to lose weight," "Don't forget to . . ."). This self-talk serves as a running commentary—a kind of Greek chorus—to the series of imagined scenes through which the stream self passes.

As the above examples suggest, the inner playlike world is experienced as a kind of "drift" or "stream" of experiences. This aspect of the process may be further illustrated by summarizing the connections in another informant's account. The sequence began with the subject looking out his window and then "reseeing," in a vivid but jumbled fashion, a scene he had observed on the same street the afternoon before, a truck driving full speed into a snow-drift. This was accompanied by a simultaneous refeeling of the wave of amusement the original perception had evoked. This dissolved into a remembered fragment of a phone conversation that had occurred just after the perception, and this led to a memory of a passage in a newsletter concerning the caller, followed by the silent question, "I wonder how that got in there?", which dissolved into a vivid memory of a scene in the university lounge where the newsletter is assembled, as seen from the place the subject had been sitting. This somewhat darkened imagery was accompanied by fragments of remembered conversation, leading from a speculation about the situation of one of the people there to a fragment of a story that person had once told. This developed into a painful memory of something similar the subject had experienced that he might have, but did not, speak about—including an imagined version of how he might have told about it. This in turn dissolved into further self-discussion about how the painful situation had come about, accompanied by vivid images of a night scene on a Detroit street. At this point the subject "awoke" and began retracing the sequence.

The stream of consciousness typically flows from topic to topic by chains of association. It is often possible to trace a given segment back over several distinct stages of association, sometimes to whatever started it off, such as an environmental perception. The logic of association is typically quite direct; an element in one topic suggests the next topic, and so forth. Here the actual perception of a scene evoked a recent memory image of the same scene. This suggested a phone conversation with which the perception was temporally linked. This in turn suggested a question about the caller, and so forth. Without regard for barriers of space or time, the stream follows its own logic, shifting rapidly from a memory scene to an anticipation and back again. Often the sequence runs on until some outside stimulus calls the individual back to his actual circumstances.

The following account nicely summarizes the basic elements of the stream of consciousness. The sequence began when the subject, a young woman, glimpsed from the train window a brick building similar to her Catholic elementary school.

Images of Saint Anthony's, a red brick building with chain fence and black paved school yard. "I wonder what it is like now?" . . . images of the first

127

day of second grade . . . a refeeling of the panic. "What was her name? She had hair on her face?" . . . images of second-grade teacher's face and figure, pinched in her habit . . . "Aha, Sister Elizabeth" . . . feelings of jealousy . . . recall of her telling me she was giving the role of Virgin Mary to Donna . . . images of Donna asleep at Beverly's pajama party . . . our filling her hand with shaving cream, tickling her nose with a feather (so she'd throw the shaving cream in her own face) . . . images of moving from the old neighborhood and carrying *Alice in Wonderland* into my new house (it was the only book I had ever read that was long and did not have pictures, so it marked the beginning of a new era, just as our moving did) . . . recall of pride "I have a *house* and my *own* room" . . . "God! I have lived in Columbia for *eleven* years." "I wonder what it will be like when I move out? I'll need to buy a couch, a vacuum cleaner, new dishes" . . . "Where the hell am I going to get the money?" . . . images of winning the lottery (from the subscription my grandmother gave me for Christmas) . . . a check for $50,000 in the mail. "I'll buy a car and then furnish the apartment and then buy some Frye boots and a new stereo and then that ring in Bailey, Banks, and Biddle with the floating diamond" . . . (a voice intrudes) "Now entering Trennntonnn New Jersey-ah, please check the luggage racks above your head. . . ."

Such are the "playlike worlds" Americans visit outside the confines of objective social life. But, granting that it is possible to obtain reasonably accurate descriptions of stream-of-consciousness experience, why should we bother to do so? The social science literature usually gives no hint that the subject has any significant cultural dimensions. In fact, this omission is evidence of one of the many links between culture and the stream of consciousness. Our neglect of the subject is itself a product of the orientations of Western cultural systems.

All systems of cultural knowledge embody conceptualizations of the external world "out there"; they also include explicit and implicit conceptualizations of the worlds inside the human mind. Beliefs about psychological processes constitute an important aspect of a culture's ethnopsychology. The peoples of all societies have words and beliefs about internal experiences such as emotional states, but their orientations to such experiences differ significantly, and they often have important effects on how the psychological process is experienced. For example, where dreams are deemed communications from the supernatural, people will pay attention to dreams, and even cultivate them, to a much greater degree than they will in a society where dreams are considered insignificant.

The same principle applies to the stream of consciousness. It appears that people in all societies experience drifting sequences of memories, self-talk, and anticipations, but it also appears that people hold different beliefs about such experiences and that, to a degree, they may experience them differently. Our evidence for this is still slight because our own culture's conceptualization of the stream as trivial has not only led us to overlook the subject in studying our own society—it has also hindered the collection of cross-cultural data. There is a significant set of materials on non-Western dreams, but no comparable data exist for the stream of consciousness.[7] It seems hardly to have occurred to most anthropologists to ask their informants about the stream of consciousness or to record their answers in an ethnography.

We are not even sure that the elements of the stream of consciousness identified above are experienced similarly in other societies. My ethnographic data from Pakistan suggest that there, at least, the stream of consciousness has both significant similarities to and differences from that experienced by Americans.[8] Pakistani informants are quite aware of the stream of consciousness, and refer to it as "dreams of the day," "consciousness," and, more colloquially, as "counting stars in the daytime" or "cooking pulao in the mind." Segments of the stream collected indicate that the same basic elements described above are present, but that the imagery is drawn from Pakistani scenes and the self-talk is in Urdu or Punjabi or, with more educated informants, a mixture of Urdu and British English.

"Uncle and Aunty should tell everyone. It'll be too late soon. They probably didn't want to earlier—afraid of being shunned (image of Aunty) (anticipation of my telling Shihida) "Nothing like this ever happened in our family. . . ." (Shihida nodding) "But I don't know, perhaps not. . . ." (memory of Mummy speaking) "They were a tremendous help" (in Urdu) (image of Mummy with arm around Aunty while everyone else avoids them) . . . . "Could be—I don't know. . . ."

129

While many people in Pakistan pay no more attention to the stream of consciousness than do most Americans, others devote considerable attention to this inner process. Certainly this was the case among the band of Sufi fakirs I studied in the Margalla Hills. For them the stream of consciousness was significant in at least four different ways.

When a disciple joins the Sufi world, he separates himself from the worldly life of the villages and cities in order to pursue a path of spiritual development under the guidance of a spiritual master. Part of the disciple's conversion involves developing a new orientation toward his own consciousness; the disciple is supposed to "hold up a mirror to his consciousness," to become more aware of the thoughts that run through his mind. This is because much ordinary thinking is understood to include egotistical memories, desires, and anticipations. These forms of consciousness are similar to those in the stream-of-consciousness reports provided by American informants, although the specific contents are drawn from Pakistani value systems. In the Sufi's view, these forms of consciousness are produced by the individual's lower, "worldly" self (*nafs*) and both embody and foster undesirable attachments, resentments, and ambitions. This kind of consciousness is not just matter-of-factly accepted; on the contrary, it is felt to be undesirable and partially controllable. "You will never be able to improve in the fakir system unless you overcome your *man* ('desires'), *tan* ('consciousness') and *ghussa* ('anger') from inside you." The disciple here uses the "mirror of consciousness" to clear his mind of egotistical, grasping forms of consciousness.

The disciple is also supposed to begin taking control of his own consciousness by replacing worldly thoughts with prayers or images of his master. Thus he begins to effect modifications in the contents of his own stream of consciousness. As this work progresses, the individual must also pay attention to his stream because, it is believed, some of the elements that now appear spontaneously will come from the spirit of a saint or the soul of his master. The Sufis often interpret night dreams as messages from the saints. The same interpretation is made of certain daydream elements. Sometimes the saint will send an "inclination," a subtle impulse toward a certain course of action. In other cases he will send an "indication," a more explicit directive. In either case certain images or words that appear in the disciple's consciousness are to be read as messages from the saint or master. Finally, the disciple is supposed to learn to bring the stream of consciousness to a halt. By stopping ordinary consciousness and focusing on religious images, he learns to shift into trancelike spiritual states of mind. It is considered crucial to avoid lapsing into ordinary worldly thoughts during these meditation exercises, and various kinds of supernatural punishments may occur if this happens. Through these techniques, the disciple seeks to rid himself of worldly attachments. He seeks not merely to replace a secular system of knowledge with a religious belief system but to transform the inner forms of consciousness through which the former is maintained. Because of their conceptualizations of the stream of consciousness, the Sufis not only interpret the stream differently; they also effect certain modifications in its contents and thereby *experience* it differently than do members of other societies.

Why have Americans, and Westerners generally, paid so little attention to the stream of consciousness? Two cultural factors are probably involved.[9] As many observers have noted, Western cultures are more interested in the world of action and accomplishment than they are in internal explorations. People are supposed to "stop daydreaming and get to work." This orientation is even more prevalent in America than it is in Europe. In his typology of psychological types, Carl Jung saw the difference between "introversion" and "extroversion" as a natural, value-free difference. However, when this classification system was imported to America, the outward-turning, extroverted type was equated with goodness and psychological health, while the inward-turning, introverted type was equated with badness and pathology.[10] An individual who admitted that he "daydreamed frequently" was suspected of neurotic tendencies. Until recently, many psychologists have viewed the stream of consciousness not only as trivial but as quasi-pathological. Laymen have generally held the same view.

One reflection of this attitude is to be found in the cultural patterning of American autobiography. The contents of autobiographies can be used as evidence about experiences that are regarded as important in themselves or revealing about the nature of the self.[11] It is a culturally significant omission that American autobiographies rarely include descriptions of the stream-of-consciousness. Similarly, many of my informants are openly surprised when self-observation leads them to discover the vividness and prevalence of their own stream of consciousness. They have been "streaming" all along—they have just never paid any attention to the process.

There is nothing inevitable about our own orientation to the stream of consciousness. Our own inconsistent belief that the stream is trivial and pathological is a cultural myth or delusion. There are many important connections between culture and the stream of consciousness and between the stream and actual social interaction. As soon as one examines texts of the stream of consciousness from an ethnographic perspective, it is evident that cultural factors are intimately involved in the process. Any given individual's stream of consciousness will have something to do with general human psychology and individual personality, but it will also have a great deal to do with the cultural knowledge system with which the individual operates.

Inner imagery is structured by perceptual enculturation—by the way in which the person has been taught to perceive, classify, evaluate, and physically and emotionally relate to the elements of cultural scenes. The memory imagery of the Pacific islanders of Fáánakkar includes scenes of outrigger canoes on a blue lagoon, thatch-roofed shacks on a white, sandy beach, and rocky trails through green mountain brush—an imagery necessarily quite different from that of someone socialized to scenes involving cement streets, metal cars, Frye boots, and red brick schools in Baltimore. An individual's anticipations as well as memories will be firmly rooted in a particular culture's scenes. In a text quoted above, the woman imagines shopping she will do in Baltimore stores like Bailey, Banks, and Biddle. Even when her anticipations are located in more imaginative settings, as when she "visits" a city she has never been to or anticipates residing in the dream apartment she has not yet located, the settings will be constructed out of American cultural imagery.

In our society, such unvisited scenes are also likely to be affected by the American media. People who have never visited New

York or Dallas "in person" have been there many times via the media. In constructing anticipations of an expected visit, media material provides the imaginative building blocks. Of course, this material is likely to be distorted—one may conjure up an imaginary New York that is more dangerous and decayed than its actual counterpart—but whether accurate or inaccurate, such media influence provides another clear example of how anticipations are culturally constituted.

The cultural structuring of the stream of consciousness is also particularly evident in its social dimensions. Inner self-talk—which might seem the most personal and private of individual activities—is very much a cultural and social phenomenon. The individual not only talks to himself in terms of the particular language and concept systems he has acquired through enculturation in a particular human group, he talks to himself much the way he might talk to someone else. The stream talk is more dialogue than monologue. It has the structure of an inner conversation.

This is evident in the curious mixture of pronouns, names, and modes of address employed. Often an inner voice says "I" (as in "I have to get going") but at other times a voice says "You" (as in "You're going to be late again"). Often, a voice addresses the individual by first or last name ("Come on, John") or, when chiding, by a variety of epithets ("idiot," "dumb shit," and the like.) Generally a sequence of statements occurs, with the second statement constituting an appropriate follow-up to the first. One part of the self offers a statement, directive, or question, and another aspect responds with an "answer." As one informant aptly noted, this self-division sometimes echoes Western assumptions about spirit beings. "It's as if the devil was sitting on one shoulder encouraging me to do one thing and there is this angel on the other shoulder telling me not to." Transactional psychology, too, sees consciousness as an internal struggle between aspects of personality, often classified as the Parent (the responsible conscience), the Child (the playful, spontaneous, id-like self), and the Adult (the ego-like mediator).[12] Here stream self-talk can be understood as an inner debate in which aspects of the self—like a family sitting around the dining room table—argue over what to do next.

The transactional approach points to an important part of inner

experience that has been regularly ignored by many of the supposedly more sophisticated psycholinguistic approaches—most
of which are solely concerned with overt social communications.
A few informants—including some over thirty—actually report
hearing their father's voice, especially when they are contemplat-
ing some action viewed as "wrong." However, inner voices are too
complicated to fit neatly into this classification system. Some
voices take none of the three roles postulated, and others come
from different sources—among them the media. Americans often
report "hearing voices" from the media. A typical example involves popular songs.

I find myself mentally "hearing" music. I replay from memory songs, or
snatches of songs, I know well—as I heard them. It is not a mental image
"I" that sings, but the individual group whom I heard sing them. I may
find myself mouthing the words, but it is not me that I hear.

More ominously, the directives from radio and television commercials, particularly singing commercials, may repeat themselves again and again in the stream of consciousness.

I had been watching a lot of college basketball on TV, and they kept showing this one commercial for Roy Rogers Restaurants. It showed these
super clean-cut and cheerful kids fixing hamburgers, and smiling Roy
himself, all to the accompaniment of this song which kept repeating the
phrase "Say howdy to fresh food at Roy Rogers" . . . again and again. I
must have seen the commercial thirty times, and I found that even though
I depised it, the song, or rather that phrase, kept running through my
mind. . . . Yes, damn it, I did go to Roy Rogers during that period.

The topics of self-talk, within the stream of consciousness, are
often highly social as well. Much of what Americans talk to themselves about is their relationships with other people.

"I've got to call Sally" (image of Sally). "What a yo-yo. She's got as much
sense as a piece of shit. . . . silly, silly, silly . . . wonder if she's going to
work? I'll call her there" (image of my work place). "I don't feel like being
bothered by those folks, they're too full of shit too. . . . Maybe Billy will
stop by" (image of Billy). "Really cute, kind of makes work worth the
crap. I must be crazy, I need to see him." (Anticipation of dialogue). "I
wasn't upset, I just didn't have time to talk with you, I've been busy; Audrey and I studied all weekend." (Image of Audrey). "She's really, really

pissed at me. . . . I didn't show up yesterday. Oh, shit . . . she thinks I should move too. . . . Fuck it. . . . I'll see her tomorrow and talk. . . . Might have to miss a class, though. . . . Good, all I need to do is miss another day of class" (image of class yesterday). "Jim must really think I'm falling to pieces, I really looked bad when I came to class. . . . What a day. . . I fucked up that test too."

In this characteristic example, self-talk is focused entirely on the state of the individual's social world. Clearer evidence could hardly be found of the social nature of the stream of consciousness.

The stream of consciousness is also social in that the scenes of memory and anticipation are filled with imaginary social encounters. Erving Goffman suggests that the daydream world is a "world in which he [the individual] alone participates."[13] While Goffman is correct in suggesting that the individual himself *creates* this private world, in another sense the statement is misleading. When an individual drifts off into the stream world, he is unlikely to find himself "alone." Occasionally, to be sure, the individual recalls an event he experienced alone or anticipates some solitary activity. Far more commonly, however, he plays out social scenes, scenes heavily populated by images of other beings. The stream world, like the dream world, is very much an imaginary *social* world.

Whose images does one meet there? In the following example a waitress is walking to work.

"Only eight minutes, takes five to change. I've got to book [hurry]." Imagery: A disgustingly filthy locker room. Visions of me running from table to kitchen table. Sounds. Forks and knives scraping plates, customers yelling over each other. "I have to make money. At least it's not as bad as last summer." Memory imagery: A tiny, dumpy diner. Visions of me sweating. Sensations of being hot. Visions of thirty marines eating and drinking. Sounds: country music on a blaring juke box. "Miss, miss." "I'll be right there, just a minute, please." Sensations of burning my arms in the pizza oven. Visions of dropping glasses. Sounds: Glass breaking, manager yelling, marines cheering. "Oh God, get me out of here." Sensation: Cringe, humiliation. "I *hate* waitressing. Can't wait to graduate and get a decent job." Visions of a paneled, brightly carpeted office with scenic pictures and healthy plants. Visions of me fifteen pounds thinner in a new skirt suit from Lord and Taylor. A great-looking coworker is pouring us coffee. Sounds of a clock chiming five o'clock. "Sure, I'd love to go out Friday night."

This young woman's memory of the past summer brings her into dramatic social contact with vivid images of the marines and her diner manager. These human images look and act like their real counterparts; they sit at their tables and they shout, cheer, yell, and laugh. This is characteristic. Imaginary replicas of acquaintances, kinsmen, friends, colleagues, and lovers play dominant roles in the stream of consciousness. This is just as true of anticipations as it is of memories. One does not merely recall past interactions with known others; one pictures them in future scenes. The waitress experiences upcoming as well as past restaurant scenes. When she anticipates a possible argument with her current manager, the imaginary version of her boss plays his part so vividly that she temporarily forgets that it is she herself who creates and manipulates this image.

Anticipations bring the individual into contact with other kinds of beings as well. Looking ahead to her business career, the young woman anticipates "a great looking coworker" asking her out for a date. This person does not exist. She hopes for but does not yet experience a business career. But in anticipating, she conjures up an office setting and peoples it with an imaginary friend. In imagining future social scenes, the individual fills in blank roles with imagined individuals. Such individuals may bear no direct resemblance to anyone that the individual has actually met; in other cases they resemble known others or are composites of people met or glimpsed. Sometimes they clearly represent another class of beings—the media figures. In the case above, the individual is not sure where the coworker came from, but she acknowledges that he resembles the handsome businessmen of media shows and magazine advertisements.

Media figures play significant roles in both memories and anticipations. In memories, the individual often replays segments from past media productions he or she has witnessed. Fans often do this deliberately, and typically they can recall their favorite scenes in the most vivid detail. Most informants also regularly experience spontaneous stream-of-consciousness replays of past media scenes. Often an environmental perception will suggest a media image and lead the individual's consciousness inward into a recall of social scenes from a book, newspaper, or movie.

It was early on a clear, sunny morning, and I was walking past a row of trees. The sun was burning white behind these trees, and as I walked, beams of light shifted and flashed at me from among the branches. In the next moment I was no longer seeing the trees and light but was seeing and feeling scenes from the movie *A Man and a Woman*. I saw images of a car, a Mustang, driving an empty road at sunrise with beams of light flashing through the trees—very beautiful colored shots, similar to the one I had just experienced. Immediately following this, I saw connected scenes from the movie, the face of the dark-haired woman riding in the train and looking out the window. Then I saw and felt the conclusion of the sequence—the woman getting off the train to find, with happy surprise, the man there waiting for her.

At this point I noticed what I was experiencing and began wondering why I had been thinking of that movie, which I had not seen for perhaps ten years, and which I did not recall thinking about recently at all. Then I remembered that I had seen an advertisement that the movie was going to be shown on TV. Then I also realized, although I had not at first, that it was the sun through the trees that started my train of thought.

Media figures occasionally appear in anticipations as well, as when the fan imagines meeting the favorite celebrity and plays the meeting out as an expected future.

One day the big news came. Elton John was going to be appearing in town next month. This was my big chance. I just had to meet him while he was in town. But how? I know! I'll get tickets to the concert and then sneak backstage posing as his girlfriend, and well, there he would be all to myself. It would be great! It would be after the concert, after everyone had left, and there would just be him and me. Oh, I was so thrilled, I could just picture the whole thing. He would whisper how he heard about me and was so glad that I was there, and then he would kiss me on the cheek.

As this example shows, in the social scenes of anticipation and memory, the self is often caught up in intense interactions with imagined beings. One does not merely picture other beings in memory or anticipated settings; one enters these settings and interacts with the imagined figures. Often the individual assumes a self much like the one he or she actually possesses, takes on an appropriately culturally constituted social role, and plays out culturally structured interactions. As in actual social relationships, the individual experiences a series of emotional states keyed to the way in which the inner drama is progressing. This depends directly on cultural expectations about the role relationships involved. In the example above, the fan is ecstatic that Elton treats her not as "fan" but as "lover." In the role of waitress, the young woman reexperiences a painful sense of humiliation as she once again drops her tray in the crowded diner. In the following text, a college student anticipates the sensation of returning home.

Looking at suitcases that will soon be packed, listening to the radio . . . (Image: my friend Alice and I have both just crossed the N.J. line in her car. We are near my house. We see my father's car. Feeling: anticipation.) "We finally made it—it's been almost two months." (Image: car pulls up to a stop right behind my father's car—he gets out.) "Wait until my mother sees what I have on and how long my hair has gotten." (Image: my mother's face when I walk in the door.) "Oh, Susan." (Feeling: It's great to be in my own house. Image: my father gets out of the car and I run over to him.)

"Pops, Pops!" "How are you, Suzie?" (Sensation: glaring lights, cool breeze—it's damp. Image: Alice is standing, grinning with arms crossed.) "Daddy, say hello to Alice." "Hello, Alice." (In a silly voice.) "Ooh, Ooh— Jesus, Suzie, how much did you bring home? What's in these, anyway?" "Oh, Daddy—you love it—your favorite daughter is home."

Another classic social anticipation is "the wedding." This informant has no idea whom she will actually marry, but the scene is clearly anticipated.

I will get married in a small but beautiful church in Tennessee. It will have many steps leading into the church with a beautiful stained glass window above the doors which open up into the church. It will be a spring wedding, early in the morning around 10 a.m. The day will be warm, and smell of wild flowers and spring. The birds will be out and singing their sweet wedding song.

The air about the church will be cheerful and exciting. All my relatives from Tennessee will be there, all of them! All of the new baby cousins will be there, and most of all my parents, and, God willing, my grandparents also. While the air at church is cheerful, there will be a somewhat sad, sentimental air at home, while everyone is rushed with the last-minute preparations of a wedding. My dad will come into my room and have his last father-daughter talk. Big tears!

The wedding will be the usual Baptist wedding. My father will give me away at the altar. I know I'll be a crying mess, but I guess I won't be alone. The wedding will be short as we exit down the long flight of stairs in front of the church into the navy blue limo and go to the reception.

This scene is elaborately structured by American cultural roles. Similarly, anticipated scenes of marriage occur in other cultures, but in terms of different settings, marital arrangements, wedding rituals, and marital roles. An important feature of Pakistani social organization is that marriages are arranged by the elder kinsmen of the girl, often to a distant cousin she has only briefly met or never seen at all. This aspect of social structure is reflected in Pakistani stream-of-consciousness anticipations. In the case below, a young woman who has been recently engaged—and feels ambivalent about it—anticipates discussing the situation with a favorite female cousin.

> Scene: Lahore, my uncle's house. A summer evening, various members of the family floating in and out of the house, many sitting in the garden lawn in front of a fan. Children walking about, Sofia and I walking. The others can't hear us. Conversation in a mixture of Urdu and English.
> Me: "I'm not sure about anything at all. I don't like the way everyone looks me over as though I were the prize heifer at an auction."
> Sofia: "Don't be daft. You always let your imagination run . . . at least it's someone you know. At least you aren't marrying a total stranger.
> Flashes of the past; Sofia, Navida, and I have a walking race; climbing the Tarbella Mountains; at the rest house . . . a phrase from an Urdu song.
> Me: "But Sofia—"
> Sofia: "Oh, shut up."

At other points in a marriage, other kinds of socially structured imaginings are likely to occur. Since the young Pakistani couple traditionally lives in a patrilineal household with the boy's parents, and since the household activities are frequently sexually segregated, the young wife typically finds herself working under the strict authority of her husband's mother. Dissatisfaction with this situation often engenders anticipations of the household scenes after the mother-in-law's death, when the woman will be free of this control, and can assume similar control over her son's wives.

Just as people conduct their actual social relations in terms of scenes, role, values, and rules of conduct given by their culture, so

139

too do they conduct memory and anticipation relations. The stream of consciousness is not merely a matter of individual psychology. It is also, to a very large degree, a culturally structured experience.

But granting that the stream of consciousness is a culturally patterned social experience, is it not a trivial, fleeting, inner phenomenon of little social significance? On the contrary. An ethnographic approach to the stream of consciousness shows that it has important connections to the maintenance of culturally organized social systems and to the functioning of individuals within such systems. Its significance can be seen through an examination of some of its effects on actual social conduct.

It is true, as our culture tells us, that the stream has certain detrimental effects, but these are much more significant than is usually realized. It is not enough to dismiss the stream of consciousness as a form of self-indulgence. Since all Americans spend considerable time "streaming," its negative effects are pervasive. Our folk and media mythology often portray an extremely "absentminded" individual whose daydreams interfere with his ability to accomplish minor external tasks. This is a very common phenomenon. A student may stare at the page of a boring text, even follow the line of print, but instead of absorbing the information he sees and experiences other imagined scenes.[14] He is lost in the stream world. He may drag his attention back, but then it drifts away again. This characteristic of consciousness can interfere with all kinds of social activities. As one informant observed, "I daydream to the point that it overwhelms everything I do." The "overwhelming" aspect of the stream is well illustrated in the following example:

Just before I left the house, the mailman delivered the mail. There was a postcard for me. I read the card as I walked down the street toward the shopping center. Much to my surprise, I discovered the postcard was from Jim, a very good male friend of mine. It was at the moment when I read the signature that I lost all touch with reality, and I began to slip into a faraway land. . . . I became unaware of the fact that it was freezing cold outside. I'm not really quite sure how I got to the shopping center, because I honestly don't remember the walk, since I was in such a daze. At that moment I had somehow, temporarily, forgotten my desired goals and my mind became possessed by ideas and dreams about Jim, my friend, and Joe, my boy friend. Both guys know of one another, but have never had occasion to meet. I suppose I must dread the idea of such an encounter. My mind, in this stream of consciousness, saw what could happen. In my daydream Jim and I were out on a date. We were walking down a street arm and arm, laughing, when out of the blue, Joe appears. Naturally my arm slipped from Jim's hold and I became quite nervous, to say the least. The dream came to a standstill. All I remember is the three of us staring blankly at one another. Then I began to cry and neither Joe nor Jim would console me.

When I got to the shopping center, I had quite a glum expression on my face. However, I went to the bank and filled out the appropriate deposit slips and proceeded to stand in line. Again, while standing in line, my attention wandered. This time I envisioned the three of us—Joe, Jim and myself—all accepting the situation and happy about it. I could not help but break into a smile. When the bank teller said for the second time, "Your bank book please," I said, "Excuse me, ma'am?" She replied, "Don't you want to make a deposit or withdrawal?"

Such absorption in the stream world is involved in many of the minor mistakes and slips that commonly occur during routine role performance—as when a person salts his coffee instead of his soup. The following examples are drawn from Donald Norman's psychological study of 200 cases.

I was in a hotel restaurant when the check came. I signed my name to it, but couldn't remember the number of my hotel room. So I looked at my watch.

As I was leaving the bathroom this morning, it suddenly struck me that I couldn't remember whether or not I had shaved. I had to feel my chin to establish that I had.

In getting ready for a party, one person carefully prepared a cake and a salad, then put the cake in the refrigerator and the salad in the oven.[15]

Such cognitive errors seem amusing and insignificant until one realizes that the same process interferes with more serious role performance, including mechanical control tasks such as driving a car. When the driver of a familiar route drifts off into the stream of consciousness, he or she may wake up to the screech of brakes and the smashing of glass and metal. Air traffic controllers, airline pilots, long-distance truckers, surgeons, and the operators of nuclear power plant controls are all subject to involuntary "daydreaming" in the midst of performing routine but highly dangerous activities. To the extent that this interferes with their ability to perform adequately, this form of consciousness constitutes a serious *social* problem.

Stream of consciousness processes interfere with real conduct in other ways as well. Most informants spontaneously experience painful memories, as when the waitress recalled dropping a tray in a crowded diner to the accompaniment of her boss's yelling and the customers' cheering. Like nightmares, these imaginary scenes are often accompanied by a vivid reexperience of shame, and they often lead to critical self-talk ("How could you be so stupid?" "What's wrong with me?") and humiliation. Such experiences are linked to both ordinary and clinical forms of depression.[16] Not only does depression foster the recurrence of painful memories, but such spontaneous memories also foster and sustain depression. Sometimes there is a direct connection between the social situation and the painful memory. One aspiring actress said that her vivid memories of past failures not only damage her confidence in auditions, but they also sometimes lead her to skip auditions completely.

Similarly, anticipations of failure can spoil performance. In the jargon of American sports this is called "choking." Forced to shoot a foul shot with the game on the line, a basketball player's desire to succeed, coupled with fearful images of failure, may engender such tension that the routine shot becomes difficult. Here the superior player may be the one who has learned to "concentrate" by blocking out imaginative interference.

Erroneous rehearsals of future social situations may also lead to the construction of maladaptive scripts for real conduct. One problem here is interference from fantasy—letting one's images of how one would like things to be distort one's expectation of how they are actually likely to be. The media provide a significant source of difficulties here. One of the latent functions of the American media is to socialize people into behaving "appropriately" in situations in which they have had little or no prior experience. Whether it be getting mugged or getting married, going to jail or going to war, there are few experiences for which we have not already been vicariously socialized. Since media portrayals are often distorted, such enculturation is often maladaptive.

Media beings like Baretta, Mary Tyler Moore, and John Wayne may be fun to identify with, but they do not necessarily provide appropriate role models for future conduct. As Lloyd Lewis has shown, the American male's media indoctrination into forms of heroic war behavior—particularly through fictional war movies —produced characteristic fantasies such as heroic charges against hordes of cooperatively death-prone enemies. This fantasy, the so-called John Wayne wet dream, sometimes inspired American soldiers to forms of behavior that proved suicidal in Vietnam.[17]

In a similar if less serious way, erroneous anticipations can foster depression. People are often "disappointed" in actual events because they do not match their glowing, media-derived anticipations. This kind of systematic mis-imaging seems to be characteristic of the vacation anticipation, the career change anticipation, the retirement anticipation, and the romantic love and marriage anticipation. That Americans often bring media-derived, grandiose images of true love and marital bliss to actual marriages may be one reason so many of them currently end in divorce.

Stream-of-consciousness processes pose certain problems and threats to the individual's social functioning and to the stability of the social order. However, to view stream-of-consciousness material exclusively from this perspective is to fall victim to our culture's traditionally negative orientation to these experiences— as if they were forms of "pathology." While some aspects pose threats, others make complex contributions to the individual's social adjustments and to the stability of the social order.

Imaginary anticipation provides a good example.

Consider how an ordinary day is put together. You awaken, and as you lie in bed, or perhaps as you move slowly about in a protective shell of morning habits, you think about what the day will be like—it will be hot, it will be cold; there is too much to do, there is nothing to fill the time; you promised to see him, she may be there again today. . . . You *imagine* what your day is going to be and you make *plans* to cope with it.[18]

As George Miller and his colleagues here suggest, we "imagine" what our day will be like. More specifically, we half-consciously talk to ourselves about what may happen ("Maybe she will be there today"), we picture scenes in our minds, and we imaginatively play out the action—as in the following example:

Looking through my high school yearbook, I came across a picture of my Spanish teacher from the eleventh and twelfth grades. I remembered how much she helped me emotionally during these years. . . . "She helped me . . . she cared about me. . . ." This led to a feeling of the infatuation I used to have for her. This was so real that I even felt myself regress, and I began to feel as I did when I was sixteen or seventeen.

It was so real that my perception of reality around me felt distorted. I was momentarily confused, like I was not really in the here and now. My awareness of sitting in my apartment felt strange.

"I want to go back to school to thank her. No, that's not good enough— I need a better excuse."

I visualize Dr. S. teaching class (I see her teaching class before I actually come into it.) She looks exactly like she did. . . . Nonchalantly I walk into class. It is a surprise to her. (I am taking on the feeling that she would normally have.) She acknowledges me with a smile—the smile that was so familiar, that meant so much. . . . It gives me a feeling of comfort and relief. "I miss her, I want to see her."

"What's a good excuse for going back to school besides 'just being in the neighborhood'?"

If people did not have this capacity, if we could not run through expected social interactions beforehand, we could not act as appropriately as we do, and the social order would be much less stable and predictable than it actually is.

A great deal of decision making is accomplished through stream-of-consciousness productions. Some of this is done through self-conversation, as one engages in an inner debate over alternative plans, but much of it includes an imaginative preview of the given possibilities. One pictures and *feels* oneself doing something one way and then another, and the difference between these imaginary experiences leads one to choose a given course of action.

Miller and his colleagues suggest that rough, rule-of-thumb anticipations are usually sufficient, and they imply that this is all that people ordinarily employ. It is evident from my own data that very

144

specific, detailed, graphic anticipations are common as well. In these detailed rehearsals, possible forms of conduct are imaginatively tried out, rejected, and refined. Characteristically, the individual strategically scripts out his or her own behavior and speech vis-à-vis imagined versions of real others.

After talking to a woman on the phone about buying her patio window drapes, my mind drifted off. I started to think about the drapes. Anticipating the encounter I and my roomate, Sam, would have at 1:00 p.m. with this woman, I pictured us walking up Cherrywood Lane to the prospective apartment. Since I had gotten the "daughter ran off to Florida leaving mother to sell stuff left in the apartment" story from the woman on the phone, my mind tried to picture what this woman would be like. I envisioned a gray-haired elderly woman, sort of short and stocky and buxom, wearing horn-rimmed glasses and a pale blue polyester dress, standing in this abandoned apartment with royal blue drapes hanging in the background. Then I asked myself, "Who should pay for the drapes?" "Let Sam pay for them, because you'll be moving out in the spring, so you can't even split it half and half." "No," I continued to myself, "you pay for them—$15 is a good buy and you'll most likely stay. You'll also have one up on Sam 'cause he's always saying at opportune moments how this is his and that is his and 'What do *you* contribute to this apartment?' So, you'll have the living room furniture and the drapes that you can say are yours." Next, I imagine myself carrying out the conversation with him. "Sam, I'll pay for the drapes," I say to him in a sort of do-I-have-to tone. Then he says, "No, I'll buy them." Then I see him say to himself, "Hmm, this is a good deal. I don't want to miss out on this, especially since she'll be moving out." "Oh, I hope he doesn't see that!" I say to myself.

Stream-of-consciousness anticipations sometimes have a social control function. Anticipated courses of action are typically rejected or modified in terms of imaginative renderings of the possible reactions of others.[19] Imaginary negative reactions often lead people to choose "socially responsible" forms of actual conduct. Several informants reported fleeting "worries" about the possible harm that might befall children they were watching over when they were tempted to relax their vigilance. Such imaginings involved altruistic concern for the children, but also included selfish fears about the imagined reactions of others (images of the child's angry parents). This is one way in which "social control" actually operates. Here the stream of consciousness, infused with cultural expectations embodied in the form of imagined others, serves as a self-socialization mechanism.

The stream of consciousness also supports the social order because it plays an important part in maintaining the culturally constituted definition of reality that lies at the heart of every society. All cultures include, and are based on, a set of beliefs and assumptions about the nature of the world—about what is true and false, possible and impossible, good and bad. However, knowledge about reality is both relative and precarious. It varies from society to society, and it is subject to disintegration and change. Cultures change their realities over time, and so may individuals, as when individuals or groups convert from one religion to another. How then do societies ordinarily hold their members to a given reality? In *The Social Construction of Reality*, Peter Berger and Thomas Luckmann point to the crucial role of language in "realizing," that is, apprehending, producing, and fixing a given definition of reality.

The most important vehicle of reality-maintenance is conversation. . . . Most conversation does not in so many words define the nature of the world. Rather it takes place against the background of a world that is silently taken for granted. Thus an exchange such as, "Well, it's time for me to get to the station," and "Fine, darling, have a good day at the office" implies an entire world within which these apparently simple propositions make sense. By virtue of this implication the exchange confirms the subjective reality of this world.[20]

Berger and Luckmann here refer to actual conversations between people who share a given definition of reality. These are important, but imaginary "conversations" also maintain reality. By rehearsing expected conversations, by recalling past conversations, and by silently talking to ourselves, we also bind ourselves tightly within a given culturally constructed framework. These inner conversations may be just as important as actual conversations. Through them, certainly, we are able to maintain a given reality—at least for a time—even when we are completely denied access to conversations with like-minded others. An example occurs in the American anthropologist Laura Bohannan's account of her fieldwork in an African village: "Publicly, I lived in the midst of a noisy and alien life. If I wanted conversation in my own language, I had to hold it with myself. . . . I could escape my cultural isolation only by being alone for a while every day with my books and my thoughts. It was the one means of hanging on to myself, of regaining my balance, of keeping my purpose in being out here before me, and of retaining my own values."[21] Ethnographic work on the stream of consciousness shows that under ordinary conditions as well, inner conversations help us to keep our purposes before us and to retain a sense of values. Far from being insignificant, the stream of consciousness is fundamental to the maintenance of basic cultural realities.

The reality-maintaining function of the stream of consciousness includes connections between world view and self-conception. As Bohannon notes, her inner conversations not only enabled her to maintain an American world view in an alien setting; they also allowed her to "hang on to" herself—to maintain a set of American self-conceptions consonant with that world view.

An important feature of this process involves memory. As Peter Berger shows, a shift in world view typically necessitates changing one's conception of one's past. "As we remember the past, we reconstruct it in accordance with our present ideas of what is important and what is not. This is what the psychologists call 'selective perception,' except that they usually apply this concept to the present."[22] As an example he discusses the "amazing transformation in identity" that take place during social migrations such as moving from Kansas to Greenwich Village.

Obviously going through such a transformation involves a reinterpretation of one's past, and a radical one at that. One now realizes that the great emotional upheavals of the past were but puerile titillations, that those whom one thought important people in one's life were but limited provincials all along. The events of which one used to be proud are now embarrassing episodes in one's pre-history. . . . We go through life refashioning our calendar of holy days.[23]

Sometimes we restructure our past deliberately, but more often, as Berger notes, we do so half-consciously. But how? It appears that much of this restructuring is accomplished through the stream of consciousness. Instead of deliberate recall, we experience fleeting spontaneous replays of the past as we drift in and out of the stream of consciousness.

Memories in this sense are full of self-concern. It is not merely that the individual replays past experiences he has witnessed or participated in; rather the self is the focus. The texts I have collected display an almost obsessive preoccupation with egotistical "successes" and "failures," especially the latter—with a particular emphasis on "hurts," slights, humiliations, mistakes, and embarrassments. It is possible that this degree of self-preoccupation is in itself a culturally constituted process. People of less individualistic, more communally oriented societies may experience less self-involved memories.

But why do American memories feature unpleasant social experiences? Does this not seem destructive to the sense of positive self-regard, so often held to be necessary to adequate social functioning? If one looks at such memories in the context of a stream sequence, one typically finds that the sequence does not end with the negative memory but leads onward to rationalizing self-talk. An interesting, if somewhat unusual, example is provided by the stream texts of a waitress at an urban bar. This role involved a steady series of identity-damaging social experiences, and she was often depressed afterwards.[24] Long before I met her, she had developed the habit of sitting down and scrawling, stream-of-consciousness style, the flood of negative images that disturbed her after an evening's work. Through this she gained "perspective" on the events, dismissed insults, separated herself from the people she encountered there, and distanced herself from the role. "After I finished," she said, "I felt much better. The experience was cleansing and directive. . . . It was like therapy."

Spontaneous memories often involve the breakup of love affairs and marriages. These actual experiences seem to require a particularly intensive amount of inner identity work. A typical segment from one informant (she was jogging at the time) began with memories of her latest lost lover, an imaginary conversation with him ("Oh, Dave why did you leave?"), a memory of other similar breakups, and the culminating accusatory self-appraisal, "What's wrong with me?" But the sequence did not stop here. She went on to assess her personal attributes and, drawing on other kinds of experiences and remembered testimonials, was able to list to herself a number of favorable identity attributes. She went on to lower the status of her departed lover and to attribute the breakup not to personal flaws but to unavoidable external circumstances. Through inner conversation, the threat to the self was overcome.

In other cases, the person imaginatively *recreates* the past, either through playing a heavily edited version of what actually happened or through creating and imaginatively living through a modified pseudo version of the past.

Driving on Beltway to Silver Spring. Nighttime. Lights of cars behind me. Lights on Beltway. A light rain on windshield. Bob Dylan, on tape, laments, "I love you more than. . . ."

"I wonder what happened to Liz" (old girlfriend). "I still don't know why she left me for Jack. Funny, it still hurts two years later." (Liz appears. Thin, pretty, flowing brown hair, big brown eyes. I miss her. A lot.) "She looks good to me, still." (Scene of breakup, still vivid: her room, she crying, me holding back tears. She means it this time.)

I switch lanes, having caught up to the car ahead of me. I realize that I have been speeding. Going 65. Now, back to 55. . . . "If we'd met again I bet she'd have confessed that she still loved me. She would have asked me to see her again. I would have played it smart, though. I'd revel in her display of affection but never let her have me again. . . .

My apartment, home turf. Knock on door. Is expected. Heart racing. Liz walks in. Looking sleek, sexy as ever. Indian shirt. No bra. Jeans. Sneakers. Big brown eyes I know are saying, "Kiss me." Me? Aroused. I don't look bad either. Sweater, sneakers, clean shaven. "But I always loved you, Mike. It's just that I needed time to realize it. Jack was nothing to me. Just a temporary diversion from the problems we were having. Can't we start seeing each other again?"

Honking horn. I realize that I have been talking out loud. I catch myself saying "we." I am only going 45. More honking.

This completely imaginary, fantasy-tinged "memory" helps the individual to repair the identity damage inflicted by the actual past.

Recreation of the past may extend to the imaginative bringing to life of persons who have died and the construction of encounters with them. Here a woman basketball player "remembers" an imaginary past.

There I was standing in my driveway. "Your wrist has got to follow through. . . . You have a good range from eighteen feet in, now will you just follow through on your free throws?" There was my father standing to the left of the free throw line giving instruction after instruction as to the form of my shot. He was wearing a typical grey sweatshirt with the letters COACH spelled across the chest. Then there was me standing on the charity stripe shooting one shot after another. ". . . 46/53 . . . 47/54 . . . 48/55 . . . ." The next one hit the front of the rim and rolled off. "Dammit! Sue, all that is, is a mental lapse. . . . Now let's get with it" once again came the instructions. "Once you shoot your 100 free throws, go back to your hooks, 25 to the right, 25 to the left. . . . Well, don't just stand there; we still have lots to cover. . . ."

The tape blared on, the train jolted me back to reality, and I was on the Metroliner from New York to Washington. Then once again I drifted off into my own world. There we were at the table. Once again there were my father and I, and once again there was conversation. "I really can't understand why you became a vegetarian. . . . Your training would be so complete if you only ate the diet I recommended. . . ." He no longer wore his COACH sweat shirt; he had on a blue alligator shirt. "I felt a lot better after dropping meat off my diet," I retorted. "Do you really think I'd do something stupid like not eat right?"

The tape player was buzzing in my lap. And once again I was on the Metroliner from New York to Washington.

This is a self-created "memory." The young woman's father died eleven years before and he never coached her in basketball.

Such dramatic creations of a fictional past suggest how minor transformations are accomplished. The individual half-consciously reinterprets the past through the stream of consciousness by constructing and imaginatively living out modified versions of what occurred. Sometimes these fictional versions are gradually accepted, and then remembered, as the real past. Thus two different individuals may hold dramatically different versions of an experience they shared together.

Sometimes such stream-of-consciousness interactions directly spill over into actual conduct. In Freudian therapy, the patient may be asked to "free associate." Here we have a specialized, culturally constituted role relationship in which the actual interactions of curer and client are structured by a stream-of-consciousness production—in the disclosure itself, in the subsequent psychological interpretation, and in the discussion of implications for actual decision making.

Other forms of American therapy and counseling also make use of the stream of consciousness. Guided imagery involves an actual situation in which the therapist seeks to induce a "daydream" in the client and then directs him through it by verbal instructions and questions. For example, James Morgan and Thomas Skovholt use guided anticipation in counseling Americans on the dilemma of career choice. The first step is to get the clients to relax, and to this end the lights are lowered and the participants are asked to assume a comfortable position. Next the therapist advises the clients to "let their imaginations take over" in response to a script that is spoken aloud by the psychologist.

Let your imagination take you 10 years into your future. As I talk, just let any images come that will. Don't answer my questions aloud. Just let the images form. (pause) . . . You are just awakening from a good night's sleep. You lie in bed just a minute longer before getting up and doing the things you usually do before going to breakfast. (pause)

On your way to breakfast now, look around you to see where you are—what this place is like. . . . Perhaps you can begin to sense things now. See if there is anyone with you. Eat your breakfast now and notice how you experience it. (pause) It is nearly time to go to work. . . .

You are approaching where you work. What do you notice? What do you feel as you enter and start about doing your work? Who else is there? What are they doing? Complete your morning's work right up to your lunch time. (pause)

It is lunch time now. Do you stay in or go out? What do you have to eat? Taste it. Smell it. Are you alone or with someone? Is this lunch like your usual one? (pause)

Return to work now and finish the workday. See if anything is different or if it stays the same. Notice what the last thing is that you do before you get ready to quit work for the day. (pause)

Leave your work place and go to where you live.

After your meal do what you do during the evening before going to bed. (pause)

Go to bed now. Just before dropping off to sleep, review your day. Was it a good day? What pleased you in particular?

Go to sleep now. I'll help you awaken in a moment. (pause)

You're awakening now . . . but not in your bed . . . in (this place). Open your eyes when you're ready, and just sit quietly for a minute.[25]

This method, the authors report, is highly effective in inducing vivid daydreams in their clients. Probably because of the intense gratification of imagined career success, American clients are sometimes reluctant to return to conventional reality. When this occurs, the therapist tells the clients, in a louder voice, "Finish it now and return to the room."

These psychologists use several other guided imagery scripts. In one, the client is asked to imagine growing up as a member of the opposite sex and to consider the career choices that might be made in that situation. In the "award ceremony" script, the client imagines receiving a special award at a banquet. Each of these scripts is intended to increase the client's understanding of his or her feelings about career choice through an imaginary experiencing of alternative social situations. The opposite-sex script, partially intended to combat cultural conditioning, is intended to "help participants examine occupational choices they may naturally rule out because of their own sex role socialization." The award ceremony script—more conventionally oriented—is designed to "help the participants crystallize their own goals and think about their motivations." After guiding the clients in and out of these imaginary social worlds, the clients and therapist discuss the results through actual interaction in a *group* therapy session.[26]

Such guided imagery techniques suggest that systematic "daydreaming" may deepen self-insight and increase the astuteness of major decision making. These sessions also show that such innovative methods can be readily assimilated into the American value system. Like traditional therapy, this new therapy can function to rationalize and maintain traditional American values and to uphold the conventional American social order. Finally, these sessions provide another classic example of how actual social relationships—here the interactions of therapist and client—can be explicitly organized around imaginary social relationships.

An even more dramatic therapeutic example involves actual situations in which people play out imaginary scenes, as when people reenact the past in "psychodrama."[27] One informant had been institutionalized in a private psychiatric hospital after attempting suicide over the breakup of an intense love affair. The daily routine of the hospital included psychodrama. There were fifteen patients in her group, and they took turns reenacting scenes from their past. The patient would play his or her past self, and the psychologist-leader would take the other major part. They would work out the script beforehand and then play it out before the rest of the group. The memories dramatized were often extremely powerful. In her first session, the informant witnessed the reenactment of an incestuous rape. "I didn't know what was going on. It scared me so much I wanted to leave the hospital."

Eventually she worked up the courage to play the most painful scene from her own memory, the confrontation in which her lover rejected her. "The psychologist played my boyfriend. It was like the real thing. He was so mean when we started fighting. He called me a 'screwy bitch' and said he didn't want to see me anymore." But like the creative memory of the stream of consciousness, psychodrama does not simply reenact the past. An effort is made to *restructure* the past with the intention of repairing the damaged self.

Where the real scene stopped the psychologist kept going. He called me every name in the book . . . and then I attacked him and hit him and hit him. They put this plastic stuff [like boxing gloves] on my hands and I hit him really hard. "Go ahead and hit me, you slut," he'd say and I'd say, "Fuck you," and hit him again and again.

Yes, it went further than the [real] action. It felt good. I'd wanted to beat the shit out of him and I did. I got those feelings out. I was laughing and crying at the same time. Before [in reality] he'd kind of won.

In psychodrama, imaginary memory relations dramatically affect actual social interactions. Such therapeutic cases are rather specialized and relatively rare, but they do point to processes that are common in ordinary social interactions. In everyday life people are often involved simultaneously in both an inner and an outer experience. In the midst of an actual social interaction, people may be simultaneously "away" in the imaginary social worlds of memory, anticipation, and self-talk. Sometimes these run counter to actual relations, as when a person is only half listening to another's words because he or she is simultaneously experiencing an anticipated meeting with someone else. Sometimes the inner experience so thoroughly overwhelms the individual that—assuming the telltale blank look—he fails to respond to the actual other's words or inappropriately smiles because of something that is transpiring within. In other instances, similar to the therapeutic examples given above, the inner stream of consciousness runs with, rather than against, the actual conversation. Sometimes a running stream of self-talk may accompany the actual conversation, as when the speaker silently talks to himself about what he should say next or speculates about the real motives of the other. Inner imagery may also be tuned to the actual interaction, as when associates simultaneously converse and mentally picture imaginary versions of future relations together. One informant described how she and her friends were swept away together by a combination of conversation and inner imagery while talking about their anticipated life together as apartment-sharing career women in New York.

A similar process occurs when friends simultaneously remember and converse about images of their shared past ("Remember the time we . . ."). This process sometimes brings out disagreements because of the differences in the contents of the imaginary replays accompanying such conversations. This is particularly true when the participants are no longer friends, and it often seems to result directly from the process examined earlier—the way in which memory is creatively reconstructed to fit with the individual's current images of self.

The following example involved four young adults who had all been students together several years earlier at a special educational project in the Southwest. They were gathered together for a reunion at a restaurant in Maryland.

Instead of catching up on what had been happening to us in the interim between then and now, Joe and Al began a "remember when" conversation. The trouble was, I could remember when, but I could also remember enough to know that Joe didn't remember anything with any admirable degree of accuracy. Here's my recollection of what he said:

"Remember that time Dr. Jones was giving us a lot of flak about not being cooperative, and I stood up and told her that if she was doing her job she'd treat us less like inmates and we'd be happy to cooperate with her ideas and even contribute a few of our own? No one could believe I told her off! So then we all went down to La Plata, and Win and I kept buying pitchers of beer and peanuts all night long. What a riot! We kept talking about how blown away she was that one of her students talked back to her. And everyone in the bar kept looking over at the whole bunch of us and laughing because we were having such a great time singing and all . . . and then to top it off we tried to pick up the waitress (much laughter here); she thought we were pretty funny. . . . God, what a good time!"

I wish it had been a good time. I thought it was the pits. Here's *my* recollection of what really happened:

Dr. Jones said our low grades on the interactive aspect of the semester were due to our unwillingness to cooperate with her instructions. Then she left. Then Joe said to the few people around him that if she treated us less like inmates, things would be a lot better. Only Al, Dave, and I heard him. Then Al, Dave, Joe, Rob, and I went to La Plata—and we *all* bought pitchers of beer and peanuts for the five of us. We talked about how blown away *we* were that she would have such a negative opinion of the group. Then the guys started talking louder and louder, and saying really silly things. Everyone in the bar was looking at us because they wished we would be quiet; the waitress was totally uncharmed by these egotistical, unappealing guys, and I was totally bummed (and embarrassed) that the four of them were going to ask her for her phone number and make a play for her while I was there.

Yeah, Joe was supposed to be *my* boy friend. So I left, walked home through downtown by myself, and cried myself to sleep that it had been such a crummy time.

If the participants choose to challenge each other, such divergent images of the past may lead to open conflict. Since their own self-conceptions are intimately involved in the disagreement, compromise is difficult and, as in divorce, the disagreement may contribute to the dissolution of the actual social relationship. Here again imaginary social relations directly affect actual social interactions.

We do not live only in the external world. We also pass much of our time drifting in and out of the playlike worlds of the stream of

155

consciousness. We do not simply use our cultural knowledge to classify and respond to the objects, events, and people around us. Again and again throughout the day, we depart from the external world and enter the culturally constituted imaginative worlds of memory, anticipation, and self-talk. These social experiences are neither trivial nor pathological. They have a complex inner structure as well as important connections to the organization of actual social relationships.

Chapter 5

Social Relations in Fantasy

What is fantasy? In popular American usage the term is sometimes equated with imaginary sexual activity, sometimes with visionary fancy, and sometimes with fictions about life on Mars. Even where "fantasy" is restricted to mental processes, many different meanings are employed, often with pejorative connotations.[1]

In the technical literature of psychiatry, fantasy is sometimes used very broadly, as "daydreaming," "woolgathering," "imagination,"[2] and, more narrowly, as "an imagined sequence of events or mental images" that "serves to express *unconscious conflicts*, to gratify the unconscious wishes, or to prepare for anticipated future events."[3] Frequently it is defined as a quasi-pathological "defense mechanism": "If . . . the gratifications of reality are insufficient, thinking may not be controlled by the demands of reality but may serve as a regressive or substitute satisfaction. Such musing is known as fantasy. . . . The psychotic patient may live simultaneously in two unrelated worlds—one of fantasy and one of reality."[4] Such definitions point to some basic characteristics of fantasy. They also offer problems because they suggest that fantasy is unnatural and pathological. This is erroneous. All my informants report fantasizing regularly. Like psychotics, normal people characteristically live simultaneously in two different worlds, one of fantasy and one of reality. The definitions above are also too broad since they fail to differentiate fantasy from other kinds of mental processes such as anticipations. If fantasy is understood as a sequence of mental images that occur when attention drifts away from focused rational thought, how does one distinguish fantasy from other drifting forms of consciousness?

Consider the following text, a young woman's musings as she drives the Washington Beltway.

"Now let's see, what do I have to do next—God, I have to take the Graduate Record Exam in October or maybe December or maybe I could put it off till January." Images of words like "peregrinate," of analogies, real numbers, lines, planes, X's and Y's. "Gotta talk to someone in the department. Wonder who the best person would be?" Images of faces, voices, memories of conversations and feelings. "I don't want to talk to Dr. Smith, cold asshole! But, I'd better talk to someone soon. Next week, I'll make an appointment. . . . I need to get those credits transferred and then see how many A's I have to get for a 3.0." I hear a friend's voice: "It's really tough to get into graduate school here. You have to have a 3.5 and 900's on the GRE." "Goddamn ridiculous! Nothing but A's and goddamn math and verbal ability. Goddamn crazy. Academia . . . wipe you out along the way. Is it worth it?"

"Probably be a lot happier in Alaska somewhere living in the wilderness, farming or hunting. . . . I'd learn to do all kinds of practical things, be creative, self-sufficient, and *happy*." Image of me in cotton blouse and jeans standing under a warm sun by a stream, reverently and deeply inhaling the fresh breeze, which is heavily scented with the fumes arising from heated pine and wild flowers. Not far behind me, near the crest of a green, treeless, gently rising hill, is a modest log house, complete with smoking chimney. I feel utterly content, satisfied, even smug. I stand there a long time thinking over what my next task should be. . . . "It would be great! A simple existence. I could have a *baby* . . . be a family.

This is a stream-of-consciousness experience, but one portion, the Alaska segment, is what I will here explore as "fantasy."[5] Her Alaska experience can be clearly differentiated from "memory" in that it hasn't happened; she has not been to Alaska. It can also be differentiated from "anticipation." She does not expect to go to Alaska and she knows that if she does it will not be like her imaginary Alaska. As she later remarked (switching to anticipation), "If I really did go to Alaska it would be cold, there would be loneliness, and nothing exciting like plays and movies. It wouldn't be this nice."

Fantasy is "unrealistic" because it is impossibly, or at least improbably, gratifying. As Freud put it, "The pleasure-principle triumphs over the reality-principle."[6] Fantasy is an escape from reality; it is also an escape from thinking about reality, from coping with it through self-talk, memory, or anticipation. In the passage above, the woman first thinks of what she "has to do." Breaking to the Alaska fantasy, she escapes from those thoughts. However, as we shall see, there are important ways in which fantasy is *not* escape.

Psychoanalytic interpreters typically define fantasy as a "mechanism" for the fulfillment of unconscious wishes and the resolution of unconscious conflict. They explain the gratification of fantasy in terms of their models of unconscious individual personality dynamics, that is, in terms of instinctual drives, appetite dynamics, and primary (id) processes. However, it is also possible to explore the phenomenological experience of fantasy for cultural answers to why it is gratifying.

Fantasy is more than a defense mechanism. Like memory and anticipation, it is a form of subjective *experience*. One is separated from reality, but one is transported to another world; one finds oneself as actor-participant in another reality. To understand the nature of fantasy, including its gratifications, it is necessary to explore this alternate world ethnographically and to consider how it differs not only from actual experience but also from the quasi-realistic experiences of memory and anticipation. Three characteristics seem particularly important: the nature of the fantasy setting, the nature of fantasy beings, and the nature of the fantasy self. The following text introduces all three aspects.

I am on a luxurious cruise ship in the Atlantic Ocean, headed for Bermuda. It is late afternoon, and the sun is beginning to set amidst a soft sky of pale peach, rose pink, and baby blue. The sun is a glowing orange ball whose warmth is sinking into my bronzed skin. I have a gorgeous, refined man standing by my side as we share this wonder of nature together. He pulls me close to him, and soon we are lost in a deep passionate kiss.

The absolutely gorgeous man has a fantastic body (six feet two inches, 200 pounds), black hair, and sparkling blue eyes. This man is sensitive, intelligent, humorous, responsible, mature, wealthy, and tan, but best of all, he is modest. He is perfection.

As for me, I have a slender, shapely figure on which I put the most classic of clothes. I never go out of style, and I always have the perfect outfit for the occasion. I am a multifaceted woman. I am also consistently beautiful from the time I wake up to the time I go to bed. My makeup always looks fresh, and my energy is boundless. I am a wonderful lover for my wonderful lover, and I understand his every gesture and mood, but I am a career woman, always aware of local and world events. What more can I say? I, too, am perfect.

My lover and I are on our way to Bermuda for a perpetual vacation. Once we arrive, the weather is always perfect, the beach always has pure blue water and glistening white sand (*no* rocks or shells to step on), and we never run out of money.

This fantasy world contrasts dramatically with the individual's actual environment: "Real life is College Park, Maryland, . . . a broken-up relationship, a two-bedroom apartment with my sister, a difficult job, and no vacation for three years. Life is boring, pressured, and stagnant compared to my fantasy." And yet, fantasy settings are not completely fantastic. The informant above is not on a cruise ship in outer space, she is on a cruise in the Atlantic Ocean heading for Bermuda. A few informants report visits to other planets or historic periods (the antebellum South, the American frontier, eighteenth-century England), but most American fantasies I have collected are set in recognizable versions of twentieth-century places, usually in the United States. Familiar settings are standard: "at a beach," "on a golf course," "in a bedroom," "at a law firm," "in a bar." Often the exact location is fixed; it is not just any bar, it is "Harry's Lounge." Typically the setting is recognizable and quasi-realistic. Its details correspond approximately to those of its real or media counterpart. To the fantasy self the setting appears lifelike, the elements are all in place. And yet the crucial feature of the fantasy setting is that it is different from its actual counterpart. In the fantasy setting, negative elements are magically erased and positive elements are heightened and magnified. In fantasy Bermuda, money abounds, the sun always shines, and the beach is free of stones. The setting is more beautiful, comfortable, amusing, and trouble-free than its real counterpart, and neither space nor time is an obstacle; both work to the subject's liking. At one moment she can be swimming in Bermuda, the next skiing in

Aspen. Boring and difficult moments are skipped over, as time flows backwards and forwards from highlight to highlight. The fantasy setting represents a radically superior version of its actual conterpart; it is "perfect."

Good as the fantasy world is as an accommodating place, it has another even stronger appeal. Entry into a fantasy world involves not only a transformation of setting, but also a transformation of self. Occasionally people borrow someone else's identity, as with informants who "turn into" their favorite media figure. However, in the majority of the fantasies I have collected, the individual remains someone he recognizes as himself. This is explicit in statements about fantasies ("I am me") and it is implicit in the way in which people report fantasy experience ("I am on a cruise ship to . . ." or "I like to imagine myself in a cozy bar" or "I am leaving my office.") But even here the fantasy identity is significantly different because the self is modified in various ways. Appearance is often enhanced. "I look the same, but with no fat, no blemishes— a perfect figure." Physical prowess is also perfected. The fantasy self is stronger, quicker, and more coordinated than the real self, can perform mundane tasks readily ("I answer letters quickly"), and can accomplish difficult tasks with equal ease ("Anything you can think, you can do").

Psychologically the self is also improved. Mental powers may be extraordinary; one can tell what others are thinking or foretell the future. Emotional life is also purified: "I am a much more carefree and easygoing individual." Typically the fantasy self feels satisfied: "My emotions are never negative such as jealousy, anger, or depression. I just experience romance." Poise and self-control are perfected: "The best part is my amazing ability to control my emotions." Sometimes, to be sure, negative traits, such as selfishness, are released. As one man noted, "My fantasy self is not like me in that he terrorizes women more. . . . He is carefree and uncaring towards others . . . an opposite of me in this reality. There is a Dr. Jekyll/Mr. Hyde type of difference between my fantasy self and me." In general, though, the fantasy personality is greatly improved: "My good points are all exaggerated while my bad points are almost nonexistent."

A third enticing feature of the fantasy world is the nature of the beings one meets there. Like other imaginary worlds we have considered, the fantasy world is a conspicuously social world. It is true that individuals sometimes place themselves in isolated natural settings such as an Alaskan wilderness or a desert island. However, in virtually all cases (100 percent in my sample), it is not long before other people make their appearance. A woman alone in a tropical jungle soon meets her green-eyed Tarzan. A shipwrecked man exploring his desert island sees a beautiful, English-speaking woman climbing down from a tree house. One does not just find that other beings are present in the fantasy world, one engages them in social interactions and establishes relationships with them.

There are several different kinds of fantasy people. Some are imaginary ideal types ("Mr. Right," "Prince Charming"). Others are idealized versions of real people. A third group consists of imaginary versions of admired or beloved media figures. All these imaginary beings have certain common characteristics. They look like solid real human beings, but they are better than their real world counterparts. Recall my informant's Bermuda companion. Not only is he "absolutely gorgeous." He is also "sensitive, intelligent, humorous, responsible, mature, wealthy."

Fantasy others are fully appreciative of the excellent qualities of the fantasy self. "I am acclaimed for my natural and unique style and appearance, commended for my intelligence, and admired for my sense of humor." Another informant summed it up this way: "Everybody adores me." Fantasy beings are also highly cooperative. Enthusiastically, reliably, and untiringly, they always do just what the fantasy self wants. Of course, there are rivals as well, and some fantasy beings provide fierce competition. But they are easily outshone by the fantasy self. As a fantasy basketball player said, "I can cover the court in seconds, I manage to outrun, outrebound, and outscore everyone else on the court." Fantasy villains are vanquished with ease: "Bad things do exist but they are always overcome. I always get what I want. I am always the victor."

The appeal of the fantasy world is clear. One enters a perfect setting, assumes a perfect self, and interacts with perfect others. As one informant said, "The only thing wrong with my fantasy world is that I have to return to reality."

162

Social Relations in Fantasy

Fantasy is often considered a particularly personal process, both because it is a private experience that takes place within the individual's mind, and because it is the product of the individual's psychological needs. Much work on fantasy both begins and ends with this assumption. Certainly fantasy is satisfying precisely because it is exquisitely tuned to the selfish wishes and personal desires of the individual self. And yet to focus exclusively on fantasy as a product of individual psychology is to overlook much of what it is about. To an important extent, fantasy is a cultural phenomenon. It reflects individual desires, but only as these have been shaped, twisted, and structured by social and cultural forces.

It appears likely, first of all, that fantasies connect to patterns characterizing particular *types* of cultures. People of societies with a cooperative, harmonious, group-oriented ethos may have less directly egotistical fantasies than people of more individualistic societies. More narrowly, fantasies seem to connect to the individual's social situation and social roles. Certain fantasies reflect particular stages within a given role, such as the steps of a particular career.

Most clearly of all, however, fantasies can be linked to the cultures of particular societies or subgroups. Despite the fact that fantasies are experienced privately and rarely communicated to others, there are strikingly similar patterns in the fantasies of people within a given culturally organized group. We have already seen that the settings, selves, and social relations of American fantasies are very American—they are constructed out of the categories and rules of American systems of knowledge. Fantasies also directly connect to the values of particular cultures. The fantasy world is "perfect," but by what system of standards? Perfect in terms of conceptions of the desirable embodied in American value systems. Noting that her fantasy gives her "an almost perfect self," one informant observed that what she becomes is the "all-American girl."

The fantasy material to be reviewed below was selected from over 400 Americans who varied considerably in age, subcultural background, and social roles. While there are variations that correlate with these differences, the overall American pattern is striking. The same kinds of topics appear again and again in the recurrent fantasies of these subjects. Taken together, they provide a direct index to widely shared American values; reflect the inner world of the American dream.

The first set of fantasies revolves around the ideal of occupational achievement and success. This value, widely acknowledged to have an important effect on actual American behavior, is also pervasive in American fantasy life. There are several kinds of fantasies. The first involves imaginary scenes that portray the fantasy self as spectacularly successful within the individual's chosen career. Often the gratifications imagined are tightly packaged in one vivid scene.

It's an early fall morning and I'm walking out the door of my Village apartment on the way to work. I have my master's from NYU and am working on my thesis. My physical appearance is a cross between the "Charlie" model, Lauren Hutton, and a Brooks Brothers' window display. I've got the job of my dreams: director of outpatient-inpatient services at Bellevue Hospital, and naturally I've done more in a few months than the old director did in years. Looking like the perfect career girl, I'm also bettering a forlorn social condition—and it's all been done while smiling.

In other cases, the individual fantasizes the stages of a whole career, as with a man who obtains a fellowship to Stanford Business School, graduates with honors, accepts a lucrative Wall Street job offer, and finally settles into a business school professorship with "a prosperous outside consulting career." Often, however, the fantasy is focused on a position on the career ladder a step or two ahead of where the individual is now. A recent college graduate has the following fantasy about continuing her academic career:

I picture myself being financially able to withdraw from the working world and able to go to graduate school full-time. I skip completely over the hard course work that must be done. I just go right into what it would be like to act like a graduate T.A.—to teach an introductory class, have an office where students can visit about problems with grades, etc. I talk often with the professor that I work for, and we go to lunch off campus. I dress very nice yet fit for the part of a grad student. I get along with the students in my classes, and my grades go well. I even picture exactly what my office looks like, how my books are arranged, and personal items in the office (a funny sign, a poster, etc.). I drink coffee from the department's coffee machine, and I often go out to lunch with other grad students as well. I am well liked and seem to be very, very happy. And then I picture myself going home each evening to a beautiful, well-kept home, to a happy and helpful husband. And when he and I go out socially everyone remarks on how well they think I am doing, and they all admire me for continuing my education. I must be a "real academic person," they all say. And through this I smile and smile.

Having experienced the reality of this social situation, graduate students *never* have this fantasy. Instead, their imaginary successes are focused on their first job as an instructor or as an assistant professor.

Such fantasies, like most occupation versions, include a gratifying sense of mastery and personal satisfaction. But there is another major theme as well—the social confirmation of self-worth. This theme is conspicuous in the following text. This informant, who has recently abandoned her career as a nurse to attend law school, pictures herself as a future lawyer.

I am sharply dressed. Sometimes I see myself wearing a wool suit, but always the look is tailored and very sophisticated. I am working with bright people for an environmental law firm. . . .

The job is very exciting. I am involved in research and writing and also have a lot of contact with various publics in the course of my duties. I articulate clearly, coherently, and succinctly and have distinguished myself as an authority on environmental issues. I meet with politicians to discuss legislation and also meet informally with concerned citizens. I am asked to be a speaker at forums relating to environmental problems. Frequently these lectures take me out of town. I have been asked to write for respected journals in the field because of my expertise on this subject. I am respected by other lawyers and am acknowledged and praised for my accomplishments. . . .

The environment of the lawyer I imagine myself to be in my fantasy is greatly different than my immediate reality. In dress, as a lawyer, I must always be conscious of my attire as I deal with clients. In my real world as a night nurse, my dress is much more casual. Also, my relationship to coworkers varies. As a nurse, there is very little respect for my ideas from doctors, but in my fantasy I am a noted authority and write for prestigious journals. My opinions are highly regarded, and I am often asked to lecture on my subject.

At least fifteen times in this text the individual sees herself winning the "regard," "acclaim," "acknowledgment," "praise," "recognition," and "respect" of others. Such fantasies reflect the peculiarly American ideology that personal worth is determined by achieved occupational position—the taken-for-granted assumptions that a lawyer is "better" than a nurse.

Another basic feature of these occupational fantasies is the notion that career success is the essential key to "the good life" generally. The following fantasy is experienced "at least once a day" by a graduate student in communications:

I envision myself as a successful radio personality having a three-hour talk show five days per week at a station in San Diego. I own a very comfortable home complete with tennis court and swimming pool.

I often eat breakfast on my outdoor patio overlooking a breathtaking view of the Pacific as it crashes upon the rocky coast. After my daily ten-mile jog along the beach, I shower and make myself comfortable on the patio—reading the newspapers in order to keep abreast of the issues and current affairs . . . to be discussed on the radio program. I enjoy freshly squeezed, tree-ripened fruit juices, a particular favorite being guava nectar.

As midday approaches, I leave the house to go to the garage, where my metallic grey Mercedes convertible waits to take me to the station. The show, of course, is extremely successful, as my guest and I are swamped with calls, etc. . . . I then return to my house for some late afternoon tennis. . . . Then it's off to poolside to join some "intimate" friends for a late-night dip and a few drinks. The people are all intelligent, professional types of one sort or another. Some guests leave, a few come inside. I light the fireplace, a little lovemaking ensues, then it's off to bed to rest up for tomorrow's program.

Given such intensely imagined gratifications, it is not surprising that these fantasies often motivate actual behavior.

High achievement within the individual's own field constitutes the most direct manifestation of the value placed on career and success. However, there are two other sets of fantasies linked to it.

The first is one of the most powerful and recurrent forms of American fantasizing. In this imaginary experience, the individual separates himself from his actual work field and enters an imaginary

166

version of an alternate American career, typically one for which he has little or no actual aptitude. There, by means of his improved self, he achieves spectacular success. What roles are selected? Virtually all of them involve becoming a media figure: a best-selling novelist, a famous politician, a successful artist, a sought-after model. The most popular imaginary careers are sports star, movie star, or rock star. What gratification does the individual receive from these fantasies? Part of the appeal is connected to the pleasure and excitement of masterfully performing the basic work activity, usually defined in fantasy as glamorous and fun in itself. In a typical sports fantasy, the informant vividly imagines himself going "head to head" against Jack Nicklaus in the Masters Tournament. "Before I hit my tee shot, Jack and I shook hands and both wished each other luck. I hit my tee shot about 250 yards out and Jack followed with a shot fifteen yards past mine." Typically, the individual also experiences the enjoyment of the material rewards that success in these fields brings. However, once again a key element in these fantasies is social recognition, acclaim, and adulation. In the golf fantasy above, the individual eventually edges out Jack Nicklaus in the Masters and experiences the award ceremony that follows. American fantasizers win an enormous number of Olympic gold medals, Pulitzer Prizes, Emmy Awards, gold records, and Academy Awards. In her autobiographical account, Caryl Rivers provides a classic example of the movie star version of these alternate career fantasies.

Now and then Life magazine would run a feature on a Movie Star Coming Home (Elaine Stewart Returns to New Jersey) and I would sit on the glider on our porch with Life on my knees, imagining how sweet it must be to be Elaine Stewart coming home . . .

I imagined Me, coming home.

There would be a motorcade, of course, and it would pass under a huge banner: SILVER SPRING WELCOMES CARYL RIVERS. The Life caption would read, "Caryl Rivers, the slender, beautiful blonde who is the hottest thing to hit Hollywood in years, waves to fellow citizens of Silver Spring, Md. She is the winner of this year's Academy Award for her role as a nun with amnesia stranded on a desert island with an American flier. Her big scene, when she has fallen in love with the flier and finally remembers that she is a Sister of Charity, brought out handkerchiefs all across the nation. With Miss Rivers in the limousine is her co-star and fiance, Grant

Trueheart. The couple, both Catholics, will be married in the Vatican next week in a ceremony that has been billed as The Wedding of the Century."[7]

Basic to such fantasies is "the Great American Vice, the appetite for media recognition."[8] A standard variant in my sample includes the appearance of the fantasy self on television talk shows.

In this fantasy, I am a young, newly discovered actress who has received stupendous acclaim for a supporting role in a new dramatic film. The fantasy opens with me walking through the heavy curtains of the Tonight Show stage to the enthusiastic applause of a rowdy, Friday audience. . . . I am conscious to smile to the crowd and greet a standing Johnny Carson, who offers me a friendly handshake, a smile, and a wink for encouragement. Sharply dressed in a tan suit, he motions to the guest chair and we begin a conversation. . . .

We talk for a time about my newness in the business. Johnny Carson asks me if I like Hollywood, how I am adapting. A few satirical remarks are made about Washington (since I am from there in my fantasies). He brings up my background, my law aspirations, etc. This point is very impressive to Johnny and his audience. I am witty, confident, and gracious on stage, interjecting stories of how I was discovered, humorous events which occurred while filming, etc. I am asked what it was like to work with a particular distinguished and handsome leading man, and what my plans for the future are. Later, I am asked to set up a film clip from the movie; it is of me, in a dramatic scene with the star, ending with me in a highly emotional state, smashing a bat through the windshield of a sports car. The audience roars, applauds. Break for commercial.

The individual departs from the real social world, where he or she is average and recognition is slight and grudging, enters a "glamorous" and media-glorified career field, and becomes the best. The individual becomes "somebody," "a god to millions," through the mass recognition of others. Recognition is offered by the general public, by imaginary versions of superstar members of the opposite sex, and by various media commentators implicitly assumed to be the ultimate arbiters of human worth. In the following fantasy, the informant imagines himself as the new manager of the Boston Red Sox hearing an evaluation of himself in the media.

Hello again, everybody, this is Howard Cosell and "Speaking of Sports." The Red Sox did it again last night; they won their seventh straight game, downing the Orioles 2–1. Manager Bob Black must be in ecstasy over his Red Sox. Every critic who laughed when Black was hired has already swallowed his words. Last night was no exception. With the score tied 1–1 in the ninth, Black had Carlton Fisk squeeze in Rick Burleson with a bunt to win it. The surprise was that nobody expected what Black claimed in that situation should be obvious. Well, the critics may be silent for yet another day, and the Red Sox, under the direction of young Black, have taken a firm four-game lead over the second-place Birds of Baltimore. Well, it just proves that managers come from just about anywhere. Those who thought Black to be a joke are no longer laughing. In fact, they are choking on their own words. This is Howard Cosell.

Indirectly this acclaim can often be interpreted as an implicit winning of respect from those in the individual's actual social world. Sometimes this aspect is explicit. The star's family and friends are pictured cheering in the stands. Often present also are those who have offered rejection in the past: parents, former teachers, ex-spouses, and critics of any kind. One not only gets the pleasure of their acclaim; in addition, past social failures are magically transcended and avenged. Caryl Rivers comments on her fantasy of triumphant return to Silver Spring as follows: "It was the ultimate vengeance. It would erase every snub, every social gaffe. Who would remember that your underpants showed at a party in the fifth grade or that you wore braces and stepped on boys' toes when you danced? No one could fault a movie star. No one could say a movie star hadn't made it. . . ."[9] Through her undeniable achievement she forces former critics to recognize what they had previously failed to acknowledge—her spectacular worth as a person.

My informants have usually experienced success in several of the fantasy careers described above, but most people have one favorite role to which they return again and again. Among younger informants this is often the role of popular musician or rock star. The following fantasy is frequently experienced by a young woman who, like most of the informants quoted below, is almost completely lacking in actual musical expertise. "I have never even picked up an electric guitar," she admits. "I can barely even play the [acoustical] guitar." She pictures herself sitting in a nightclub audience.

I am with a group of friends, drinking beer at a table. The band that is playing are old friends of mine from NYC. One of them mentions that they have a friend in the audience whom they want to come up and join them in the next number. I act pissed off about being put on the spot and forced to go up there, but I do. I do, much to the surprise of all of my friends at the table (they had absolutely no knowledge of my talent). I get up there and wail like Hendrix—no, better!

In my fantasy I am me at my best. I'm a great guitarist. I'm charismatic, funny, cool, wild, and surprising. I even fantasize that I'm ambidextrous. I experience things by being totally on top of them. Even though I am only being asked to play a number, I end up stealing the show and leading the band off in my own direction (but of course no one minds).

In other versions, she becomes a full-fledged star, goes on tour, and performs professionally. For most informants this is the standard fantasy.

A daydream I have frequently is that I am a famous singer in a rock group similar to Stevie Nicks of Fleetwood Mac or Linda Ronstadt. My character is always beautiful, slim, and sexy. Of course, my voice is fantastic, and all my songs and albums are on the top of the charts. In my daydreams I create the most beautiful costumes for my character to perform in. Most of the time the costume is a white, flowing dress a bit see-through and much more risque than what I would normally wear. The lead singer, who is a handsome male, is also my boy friend. He usually has dark curly hair, on the longer side, a dark beard, dark brown eyes, and wears an earring. He plays the guitar while I play the piano. The male singer and I put on a fantastic show, sing our hearts out, and the concert always ends with wild applause and many encores.

Obvious in these fantasies is the theme of extreme social acclaim. A concert hall full of hundreds or even thousands of adoring fans represents a most intense form of recognition.

"Ladies and gentlemen, Miss Anne Jones!" Clap, clap, applause; the crowd is going wild, almost like a Bruce Springsteen concert. I come out on stage, pick up the microphone and tell the boys in my band to start playing. This is a special performance and my fans are going nuts.

Also clearly present is the gratification of powerfully affecting a mass audience. The individuals who have such fantasies are members of a generation that has been deeply influenced by rock music, and they want to achieve a communicative power and control over others. Sometimes this includes the idea of affecting people philosophically, "opening up their minds to new kinds of music," or promoting worthy causes. In many ways this fantasy is analogous to the "great novelist" fantasy so powerful in the imaginative life of an older, print-oriented generation. Tom Wolfe describes it as follows:

At this late date . . . it's hard to explain what an American dream the idea of writing a novel was in the 1940s, the 1950s, and right into the early 1960s. The Novel was no mere literary form. It was a psychological phenomenon. . . . It belonged in the glossary to *A General Introduction to Psychoanalysis*, somewhere between Narcissism and Obsessional Neuroses. In 1969 Seymour Krim wrote a strange confession for *Playboy* that began: "I was literally made, shaped, whetted and given a world with a purpose by the American realistic novel of the mid- to late-1930s. . . ." The piece turned into a confession because first Krim admitted that the idea of being a novelist had been the overwhelming passion of his life, his spiritual calling, in fact, the Pacemaker that kept his ego ticking through all the miserable humiliations of his young manhood—then he faced up to the fact that he was now in his forties and had never written a novel and more than likely never would. . . . After thinking it over, I realized that writers comprise but a fraction of the Americans who have experienced Krim's peculiar obsession. Not so long ago, I am willing to wager, half the people who went to work for publishing houses did so with the belief that their real destiny was to be novelists. Among people on what they call the creative side of advertising, those who actually dream up the ads, the percentage must have reached 90 percent. . . .[10]

Even more than the novel fantasy, the rock star fantasy includes the mythical life style presumed to accompany this career. Discussing her fantasy, one informant said, "I feel like I've seen it before in the movies, books or else on television." Even when he or she recognizes that the actual life of a rock star is far from what the media suggest, the individual may still be powerfully drawn to the mythical version, "a life of fun, physical pleasure, mental satisfaction, and money—who could want more?"

There is another important gratification as well. In many ways the mythical life style of the popular musician is the opposite of that which is required for even modest advancement in a conventional career. Instead of putting on a tie and working hard, one wears outrageous clothes and lives a life of fun and leisure. Instead of working from 8 A.M. to 5 P.M., one sleeps late and makes one's own hours. Instead of submitting obediently to authority, one follows a rebellious, irresponsible, destructive life style. Often one "freaks out" the bourgeoisie, as by destroying sacred American material culture. In the following fantasy scene, the individual has already attained standard rock star status.

In a short while we become famous and acquire enormous wealth and prestige. This allows us to do insane things, virtually whatever we want. For example, Dave and I go into Macy's department store and buy out the entire china shop. It's filled with delicate, imported glassware, and signs saying, "Please do not touch" and "Please do not handle" are everywhere. We clear the store of customers and enter with baseball bats. As we approach the first rack of dishes, I whisper to Dave, "Be sure not to break anything and whatever you do, don't do this!" With that I take a grand-slam swing and smash the display to bits. We then both scream like savages and proceed to destroy the entire department.

One rebels and yet one makes it big. No one can deny that a millionaire rock star has made it. The implicit appeal of the rock star fantasy is built on resolution of this conflict. One can be rebellious, unconventional, and destructive—and still attain the conventional society's definition of success. As with many fantasies, the appeal lies in resolving a cultural value conflict; one can have one's cake and eat it too.

A third set of standard fantasies consists of imaginary visits to scenes of peace, leisure, and simplicity in tranquil settings of natural beauty. Typical examples include the wilderness cabin, the houseboat, the desert island, the country farm, and the isolated, unspoiled beach.

I am camping with a close friend, a man, on a beach at Assateague Island. It is mid-May, still too early for the crowded summer tourist season on the Chesapeake Bay, and my beach is deserted. We've already pitched a tent on the sparse, sandy grass behind the dunes, about fifty feet beyond the high-tide watermark. At the time my daydream begins, it's early morning, and I and my friend are just awakening. It is a cool, clear, and breezy morning. We fix a simple breakfast, and while we're eating, we watch the seagulls ride the air currents. After breakfast, I play on a guitar for a little while. Later, with the guitar put aside, we explore the island, collecting shells and rocks that catch our eyes as we look for tidal pools. After our brief expedition, we return to our campsite, and together we carry our hang glider to one of the high dunes and, one at a time, we launch ourselves into the air. When my turn comes I position myself beneath the glider and, strapped in, I run until my feet meet with the air, and then I climb the sky. I soar. Finding a rising air current, I take it and ride it out; the only sound I hear is the sound of the wind whistling by my ears.

At first glance, such fantasies might seem to be completely unrelated to career and success. However, both their contents and interviews about them reveal a direct link to the American occupational achievement value. This link arises from the ambivalence many Americans have toward career striving. Fantasy visits to unspoiled natural settings constitute an escape from the world of work. They embody the positive opposites of the negative qualities associated with career roles: natural beauty vs. urban ugliness, cooperation vs. competition, peace and simplicity vs. pressure and complexity, inner harmony vs. tension and stress.

Informants often directly articulate the negative connection to career work. A business man whose job is centered in suburban shopping malls has the following recurrent fantasy: "My lifelong unfulfilled wish is to someday just walk away from it all and disappear into the mountains, where I would live off the land like Daniel Boone. It would be a life of peace within myself, living close to nature and the God who created it." Such fantasies are often derived from media experience. In his case the fantasy developed out of a childhood hero-worship of the TV version of Daniel Boone. In other cases, fantasies can be linked to nature writing or to novelistic portrayals such as Michener's *Chesapeake*. In any event, they echo a persistent theme in the American media—the attractiveness of a life close to nature.

These imaginary productions do not usually involve total isolation. It appears from the excerpt quoted above that the individual may be imagining a solitary, hermitlike existence. This is not the case.

In my fantasy, I'm friends with all the animals, and one with the forest around me. I have played the roles of . . . vengeful mountain man against all those intruders who would abuse nature and also the heroic guide who saves the lost travelers to whom nature has dealt a harsh blow.

Several intellectually inclined informants fantasized rural communes full of artist friends. One planned a whole city of such associates.

I have this fantasy of starting an artist's community in the wilds of Idaho. Here among the mountains, forests, rivers and streams, I, along with a small group of companions, would build a primitive city. From what we have learned from the "civilized" world we would know what mistakes to avoid (soft technology, no cars, ecologically sound) and would draw the best from all cultures, "primitive" as well as industrial.

Here would gather musicians, artists, writers, spiritual seekers, and freethinkers. Our years would be spent creating folk art, which would be utilitarian as well as aesthetically pleasing. Music would be heard—Folk music from the world round, classical, jazz. Artistic creations would be in abundance everywhere for the enjoyment of all, rather than locked up in a few buildings. Everyone would spend their time musing, meditating, engaging in stimulating conversation, smoking dope, drinking wine, and making love.

A life devoted to the aesthetic and the ephemeral rather than the practical. That which we delegate to our "space time" now would be spent doing all the time. The only work to be done would be that work that was necessary to make ourselves self-sufficient. Farming, building, growing dope, and making wine would be our work. . . . what else could one ask for? A garden of Eden.

What one escapes from here is not the social world but the social world of work and competition. These fantasies often seem to be initiated in the stream of consciousness when mental coping and aversion to work reach a certain negative threshold, as with the fantasy segment quoted at the beginning of this chapter. Sitting in one's office, one can yet teleport imaginatively to the Alaskan wilderness or the Idaho commune. Such excursions provide relief from work pressures. They also provide "role distance," a separation of the self from the identity implications of one's current job. These fantasies say to the self, as it were, "I could be happy at something else, I could make another kind of life, I am not just an assistant manager." This aspect is nicely brought out in the informant's comment on her Assateague beach fantasy.

Not only does this beach fantasy provide me with a brief respite, but also it reminds me of an easily overlooked truth: I always have options. This recurrent daydream powerfully demonstrates to me the alternative life style(s) that exist, given my personal nature. I realize that I can focus either on a socially valued system, such as climbing the socially acceptable career ladder, and/or on a more individual and personally valued status, such as successfully managing a hang glider.

Another set of American fantasies centers on material wealth. Some materialistic fantasies center on the acquisition of wealth— the individual wins the state lottery or breaks the bank at Las Vegas. Often they involve a social dimension in which the acquisition of wealth is due to the individual's display of self-worth. In many cases this comes about because of the fantasy self's spectacular success in an imaginary career.

The most dominant daydream that I have is that of having endless money. I like to be able to spend whenever I want to. This daydream is usually brought on when I want to buy something but cannot afford to get it. I sit back and think about a time when money would always be available. I usually place myself in a position such as a model. Everyone wants me to model for them. It starts out when a man (photographer) sees me in a store or something and asks me to do fashion modeling for him. The rest is history—everyone wants me. I become a success overnight. I have so much money that I don't know what to do with it. I take the money and invest it in stock and everything goes right in the stock market. As the movies go, I live happily ever after.

In other cases the individual does something noble for imaginary others and is suitably rewarded. One informant imagined receiving a massive fortune from an unknown relative because he was the first descendent to perform a "good deed." Another common variant is the rescue scenario: "I am in D.C. and I miraculously save the adult son of an Arabian oil baron from assassination. I am roughed up in the process but it turns out OK and the young man's father rewards me with a tidy, unmarked sum of $25,000."

Once wealth is obtained, the focus shifts to American forms of consumption. Many non-Western cultures can be aptly characterized as materialistic; like Americans the members of these groups are highly concerned with the acquisition, display, and enjoyment of material objects. However, the complex of knowledge involving the definition, evaluation and use of desirable objects varies from one materialistic society to another. Western Pacific cultures, with their cargo cults and Big Man syndromes, are often notoriously materialistic, but the objects of desire and status—outrigger canoes, taro patches, pigs, and dancing bracelets—are different from the objects Americans have been taught to love. One standard American fantasy involves the imaginative outfitting of the individual's ideal apartment or house. The following is a fairly restrained example:

A common daydream of mine involves my first "real" apartment. I enjoy walking through furniture stores, which is somewhat inconsistent, considering my allegedly liberal, antimaterialistic values, and picking out the furniture I would like to have. I particularly like Roche-Bobois and Scan, so the daydream usually begins with me walking into such a place with nary a care about such mundane details as cost or money. I wander through the store, in and out of all the model rooms and I just point. "I'll take that . . . and that . . . and two of those. . . ." I have all the rooms planned, and the floor plan is perfect. There is a beautiful old fireplace and a huge window filled with plants in the living room. The kitchen is fantastically modern, with wooden cabinets, with all the newest gadgets. It is sunny, bright, and enormous. The apartment is, of course, a duplex, so up the spiral stairs, in the bedroom, you can look down over the living and dining rooms. The bathroom has a huge sunken bathtub and a phone. There is a balcony with a small greenhouse and a glorious view.

The decorations throughout the apartment are magnificent. There is a mixture of modern and antique furniture. I would have an oak dresser and desk and a satin quilt. The living room furniture would be modern, with big brass lamps and glass tables. The chrome and glass dining room set would sit on deep, plush carpet. There would be beautiful paintings and pieces of art all around, and it would all be paid for.

A major influence here is media advertising, particularly magazine advertisements and television commercials that persuasively communicate the appeal of object possession. Fantasy descriptions of ideal houses often sound like commercials, and many can be traced directly to particular media productions (for example, a

California bachelor's pad to a layout in *Playboy*). Like their media counterparts, these mental commercials characteristically embody the intense, quasi-sexual gratification that supposedly can be had from possession of luxuries.

This imaginary gratification is understood to come in part from the ownership and use of "beautiful" objects. However, there is another dimension as well. As one woman observed about her fantasy, "I have fallen prey to the American notion that in some convoluted way, my personal worth in society can be measured by creature comforts." Partly such a notion involves direct self-enhancement: "I have all this, therefore I am somebody; I am worth $500,000." Often self-confirmation is received indirectly through imaginary others, as by winning their gratitude, admiration, or envy. This theme, incessantly employed in media advertisements, is regularly echoed in American fantasies. Thus, fantasies of the ideal house typically include showing the house to admiring others. As one informant put it, "The awe and respect and wonder of my guest are basic to every daydream about my house."

Another common American fantasy consists of imaginary violence. Typically this involves threatening social situations in which the fantasy self, insulted or attacked by imaginary villains, responds with justified aggression. Given the improved qualities of the fantasy self (newfound strength, coordination, karate prowess), this aggression is usually spectacularly and gratifyingly successful.

While sipping on my beer at the bar, I was rudely interrupted by a push on my backside. Recovering my balance, I turned and barked, "Excuse me, watch where you're going!" A large, well-built, pot-bellied man turned in disbelief and said, "What?" I returned, "Watch where you're going!" He then remarked, "Fuck you!" He walked a little closer to me. He had two friends, just as big, come to his aid. "This is where my karate can come into use," I remarked to myself. I jumped in the middle of the three and cried out, "Hoiwsaa!" By this time, the music had stopped and everyone had focused their attention on us. I began circling my arms while maintaining a back stance. The head guy threw a punch at me, but I immediately blocked it and proceeded to punch him out. Within a matter of milliseconds he was laying down flat on the beer-soaked floor. Quickly turning, I side kicked one of the other guys in the ribs. Two down and one to go. The third guy came at me with a bottle. He tried to hit me in the head, but I blocked his arm. I proceeded to do the following to him: roundhouse to the side, spin side kick to the stomach, and punch to the face. By the time he, too, hit the floor, the bouncers were there examining the situation.

Fantasy violence reflects the competitive ethos of our society, and it also connects to patterns in actual social behavior. America is a relatively violent society, and the possibility of being attacked by aggressive others is something everyone occasionally anticipates. Violence is also an American value; its successful application in what are seen as "justified" situations usually meets with approval. Yet most of my informants have relatively little direct experience of actual violence. Where, then, do they acquire their highly elaborate and detailed aggressive imagery? Once again, much of the fantasy imagery comes directly from portrayals in the mass media, sometimes from news reports of actual violence, more often from the lovingly detailed, glamorized violence of the fictional media. This influence is apparent, for example, in the text just cited. The informant also commented, "I was cool, like James Bond walking through Harlem. Nobody bothers me!"

Media images of glamorous violence are so pervasive that one might easily assume that it would be impossible to grow up consuming American media without experiencing fantasies of attacking and killing others. Virtually all male informants have fantasies in which they play the role of physical aggressor, but many women, including some who are highly aware of their own inner life, claim never to experience fantasies in which they commit violence against others. My data suggest that perhaps 30 percent lack such fantasies. When they do occur, womens' violent fantasies parallel those of men in that the violence is both justified and extreme.

I am leaving my office, walking to my car in the parking lot, it is twilight, and the lot is half empty. A man is walking toward me from a distance. Very soon I realize that he is heading directly toward me. My adrenalin starts pumping, my pulse rate skyrockets, but I maintain physical control. He comes up to me, obviously thinking that he can easily overpower me. He grabs my arm and tries to twist it behind my back. I turn in the direction he is twisting me and immediately kick him in the shin with my high

heel. He momentarily loosens his grip, and I seize the opportunity to become the attacker. I deliver a left jab to his stomach, followed immediately by an upper cut to his jaw.

By now this fellow is sorry that he ever set foot in the parking lot. He
tries to get away, but I'm not done yet. He is still partially bent over from
the blow to the stomach. I quickly apply my knee to his chin, causing him
to bite his tongue. He stands upright, holding his mouth and chin. I take
the opportunity to deal the final blow to his groin with my pointy-toed
shoe. Naturally he doubles over in excruciating agony. I cannot resist
shoving him over with one more kick.

Boys in American society learn to engage in a remarkable
amount of violent play. They play "soldiers" with toy figures, they
consume violent media enthusiastically, and in games of "guns,"
"war," "cops and robbers," and now "Star Wars," they playact
scenes of violence drawn from the mass media. These socialization games are eventually dropped, but the fantasies continue. In a
typical adolescent fantasy, a student saves his high school from attack by foreign invaders.

One of my favorite recurrent fantasies involves sitting in my high school
classroom when suddenly the school is under siege. I see friends being
shot down by soldiers in uniforms carrying machine guns. I quickly run
behind the door, and as one soldier enters the room, I smash him with a
chair. I take his machine gun and grenades and cautiously enter the hallway. Suddenly there are four soldiers in the hall. I step aside and mow
them down with my gun. I distribute the guns to my brave friends and
lead them out to the courtyard, where we engage in bloody combat. I
throw grenades and shoot until my gun is empty. Suddenly I am shot in
the arm. At this point the battle is nearly over. I receive instant recognition and my peers hold me in awe. I am in newspapers across the country
and receive distinguished awards.

By contrast, girls in our society have traditionally been socialized toward a less aggressive, nurturing, noncompetitive ideal.
Instead of playing "guns" or "war," they have played "dolls" and
"house." Women who do not commit imaginary aggression are
following modes of fantasy behavior consistent with traditional
American sex role enculturation. But what of women who do
experience fantasies of violent aggression? Presumably there are
a number of different factors involved, but one appears to be

cultural changes in sex roles. Many of the women reporting violent fantasy have either had nontraditional upbringings or have adopted feminist attitudes. The informant whose fantasy involved beating the would-be rapist put it as follows: "I view the fantasy as symbolic of myself as a woman breaking away from the old female stereotype and fully asserting myself in accordance with a new female image." Conversion to a new belief or value system may lead to changes in imaginary as well as actual social relations.

Since humans are highly sexed animals, erotic fantasies are probably part of the imaginary life of people in all societies. It might be supposed, then, that American sexual fantasies are not cultural at all but rather represent the expression of transcultural biological drives. On one level this may be true; however, a consideration of fantasy texts suggests that these imaginary productions are also subject to a great deal of cultural patterning.

By definition sexual fantasies are social. They consist of encounters between the fantasy self and imagined others. Most of my informants experience a variety of sexual relationship fantasies, but they can be classifed roughly into two different types. In one, sexual activity plays a central part in a relatively elaborate relationship. In the other, the focus is confined largely to a sexual encounter with little or no background elaboration as to how the relationship came about or how it will end. This is well illustrated in an informant's account of his relationship with a "five-foot-six, blue-eyed, sex-starved blonde female possessing a body that would shame any current media sex symbol."

My sexual encounter with the beautiful blonde normally begins after a relatively short introduction, which I usually skip in my daydream. We are already seated on a couch and within moments she has begun to slip into something more comfortable: skin. Wa-hoo! At this point I am sincerely lustful. As she undresses me, I prepare for a truly exhilarating experience. We frantically engage in . . . unprecedented sexual activities for a period of hours.

What is culturally determined about such imaginary sexual activity? In the first place, cultural factors influence the imaginary other who plays the role of lover. Whether this is an imaginary version of a real person or a totally imaginary construct, the lover's appearance in the fantasy world typically depends on his or her "attractiveness" to the fantasy self, a dimension largely determined by the standards of beauty that prevail in the individual's culture. In our society the media has become very important here. Not only does the media help to define attractiveness; it also provides many fantasy partners. Imaginary versions of glamorous media beings, such as figures from *Playboy* or current TV and movie stars, are commonly encountered in American fantasy worlds.

Fantasy sex is also culturally constituted because, like actual sexual behavior, it is strongly affected by cultural rules. First of all, the basic mode of sexual expression—heterosexual, homosexual, or bisexual—is affected by culture. In societies or subgroups where homosexuality is the norm, people not only engage in homosexual activity; they also fantasize homosexual encounters. Cultural techniques of sexual seduction and intercourse influence imaginary as well as actual sex. Some cultural taboos also apply quite rigidly in fantasy worlds. Thus, middle-class American restrictions on incest and homosexuality often, although not always, apply in the fantasy realm. In other cases, a cultural taboo indirectly determines a fantasy action precisely because the actual performance is disapproved. Fantasy sex is less restrained than its actual counterpart. As one informant said, "Fantasy gives me the freedom to do what I want to the other person—and sometimes that gets pretty demented." However, the particular lack of restraint is partly a product of whatever restrictions the particular culture puts on sexuality. In fantasy as well as in actual behavior, there are cultural guidelines for "unrestrained" behavior, "rules for breaking rules." For example, many American fantasies involve bondage and rape. This culture pattern possibly connects to rules against "letting go" sexually (if one is tied down one is not responsible or guilty; if the other is tied down she or he cannot resist). It would be interesting to know whether similar fantasies exist in societies with less restrictive forms of sexual socialization. In any event, a careful cross-cultural study of fantasy would almost certainly demonstrate that people are just as much cultural conformists in their sexual fantasies as they are in any other form of imaginary conduct.

Most informants also report romantic fantasies in which sexual activity is placed in the context of a dramatic story line. Because these fantasies are more elaborate, they are even more culturally structured as to settings, roles, dialogue, and background assumptions. For example, on Truk the taken-for-granted belief in the efficacy of love magic enters directly into fantasy life.

Similarly, a quasi-mythical belief in "romantic love" structures many American fantasies. In a typical fantasy, an informant finds that a casual acquaintance has suddenly been smitten by this magic. "She is beautiful, sexy, interested, impressed—and, best of all, madly in love with me." Standard scenes of love are characteristic in these sexual-romantic fantasies: nights of wine and candlelight and mornings of running slow motion through a field of daisies. Many of these scenes come directly from the media. "I see him [the imaginary lover] coming from a wealthy family. This man falls in love with me beyond words and all possible feeling. We play in the snow like Ali MacGraw and Ryan O'Neal in *Love Story*." Like their media prototypes, romantic fantasies often involve dramatic action that puts the lovers together, tears them apart, and finally brings them together again. One twenty-nine-year-old informant observed that her fantasies follow a distinctive "formula" analogous to that of popular novels. The romantic lead varies, but the plot remains the same.

This formula can be broken down into nine basic steps. First, since the person is unknown to me, a "scene" must be created wherein I can meet this person and interact with him. The scene is usually a routine, non-melodramatic occurrence; however, we each manage to "imprint" ourselves on the other's mind. In the second step the scene fades and we mundanely go our own ways. Third, something out of the ordinary happens and we are again thrown together (for example, he is in trouble and I rescue him, or I am in trouble and he rescues me; more specifically, I am fixing a flat tire on a little traveled road when I get mugged, and I am lying unconscious on the road when he finds me). In the fourth step, the rescuer has to take responsibility for the victim for a while (note: victim is loosely defined, as it could refer to being ill, physically harmed, slandered, hunted down by others, emotionally upset, and so on). In this example, the victim (myself in this version of the formula) is physically harmed by others. This responsibility may only refer to taking care of the victim, or it may involve the future confrontation, by the rescuer, with the villains (step six). Fifth, the interaction that occurs is platonic and even, at times, resented or performed under duress (for example, he may wish to go back to his journey, but there I am unconscious or barely living, so . . .). In the sixth step, another crisis occurs (the illness worsens, something intensifies the emotional upset to suicidal proportions or, as in the specific example, the villains, who perhaps have been threatened by the rescuer in step five, now retaliate by physically harming him or by physically harming me). Seven, in responding to the crisis, the relationship switches to a very high level of intensity, both physically and emotionally (if he has gotten himself beat up I, still barely alive myself, stagger out to help him; if I am being attacked again, he comes out to help me—in either situation, once the villains are vanquished, at great cost, then our own relationship flowers). Eight, this intensity continues for a time, often amid actions aimed at resolving the specific crisis in a given formula. Finally, in step nine, the relationship is resolved in some way and numerous possibilities might be acceptable as resolutions. For instance, the intensity for both of us wanes . . . or, the intensity dies down for me but not for him, so the parting involves him attempting to continue the relationship.

Among other gratifications, such fantasy relationships provide an intense vehicle for self-enhancement. In the glow of the other's sacrificial love, self-worth is confirmed.

Another standard set of American fantasies centers on blissful marriage.

I get married, of course to Mr. Perfect, the man of my dreams. We have a nice stone home in a residential area, two cars, two dogs, and two children. Naturally we are always happy—never a moment's despair.

In some variants, the whole course of a happy married life is envisioned. In others, the focus is on a highlight scene such as the proposal, the dream wedding, or the finding of a perfect house.

Jim and I are looking for a special piece of property, preferably located on a back road, surrounded by trees, with a little stream on it—a perfect place to build our dream house. The day is beautiful, so we decide to ride bikes. I guess we're in southern Maryland. After a while, we meet a farmer walking down his driveway. We stop to chat and ask the farmer if there is any land for sale in the area. He becomes wary and looks us over good (he fears developers). Jim senses this and assures the old man that we are merely looking for an acre to build our house on. He continues by telling him we are getting married in two months. At this remark the farmer seems pleased, and he invites us "up to the house" to meet his wife and have some lemonade. She is a pleasant old lady and is very pleased to meet us. They invite us back for lunch next week and he assures us he will look around for an acre.

The next week we join the old couple for lunch and have a wonderful time. She asks if we plan to have children. "Yes," I reply, "probably around three." At this she winks to her husband and he smiles. Later he says he has some land to show us. He drives about a mile and a half down the road and shows us a piece of land. It's perfect, of course, and he says he'll sell it for five thousand dollars. He winks at me and says that he knows it's probably worth more, but since he never planned on selling it, five thousand was more than he had bargained for. Jim and I are ecstatic because now we know our dream home can become a reality.

Other variants involve children: "I imagine telling my husband about my pregnancy as Barbra Streisand told Robert Redford in the movie 'The Way We Were.'" Or: "I am a good mother, loving, warm and caring—always there at their most vital times of growth and development." Occasionally troubles appear, but these are always handled well—that is, to the gratification of the fantasy self. "I imagine having a sexual affair and telling my husband and we understand each other so well he doesn't mind." Many people express cynicism on hearing fantasies of blissful marriage, but most people also admit experiencing them.

In our society fantasy has traditionally been viewed in one of two ways. First, like stream-of-consciousness processes generally, fantasy has often been seen as "woolgathering," an unrealistic, unimportant waste of time—and hence a trivial subject for research. Alternatively, it has often been viewed as quasi-pathological activity, a proper subject only for abnormal psychology and psychiatry.[11] In recent years both these assumptions have gradually been replaced by an increased recognition of fantasy as a normal experience, having important functions for the maintenance of psychological equilibrium.

Unfortunately, fantasy is still largely ignored in culture studies.[12] Aside from a few psychoanalytically oriented studies, ethnogra-

phers have paid scant attention to the fantasy worlds of their subjects. One looks in vain for attempts to explore ethnographically
the inner worlds of fantasy and to link such descriptions to cultural systems. Yet fantasy is highly social; it is pervaded by imaginary social relationships. It is also highly cultural; the structure of
fantasy relationships is directly or indirectly affected by systems of
cultural categories, rules, and plans. Moreover, fantasy relationships are organized around the values of a given culture. Despite
some systematic variation in social roles and subcultural affiliations, middle-class Americans seem to share a very similar fantasy
life.[13] The recurrent fantasies of my informants fall into only seven
major classes: career success, alternate career success, natural
world escape, material wealth, successful violence, sex-romance,
and blissful married life. Also, any given fantasy usually includes at
least one and often several of the other topics. Thus a fantasy
focused on blissful married life often includes material wealth,
natural world escape, and career fulfillment as well. In their "private" worlds, Americans regularly fantasize the same American
dreams. This has important implications for culture studies.

Values have been traditionally defined as mental constructs, that
is, as "conceptions of the desirable."[14] Despite such cognitive definitions, values have not usually been explored further as aspects
of consciousness. Having identified a conception of the desirable
(for example, "A sense of accomplishment" or "a comfortable
life"), the attempt is made to see how this value "influences" behavior. This procedure may account for some of the problems in
values research. The material explored above indicates that our
understanding of cultural values could be greatly increased by
careful attention to their manifestation in fantasy. Here one can
see the values dramatically rendered in pure form. Here one can
investigate the tacit assumptions out of which the value is constructed and explore the kinds of gratifications involved.

But fantasies do not merely reflect and express American values. They also help to maintain values. The most common interpretation of fantasies is that they constitute a form of "escape."
This view is regularly expressed by American informants.

The main thing that daydreams do for me is to allow an escape from
reality.

Fantasy is beneficial in that it is an escape—something each of us feels a need to do at times.

Why I would want to do this I don't know. I guess everyone wants to be something different than they are. . . . Plus it's good to escape. You can't be an accountant or a teacher twenty-four hours a day. You'd go crazy.

This is one of fantasy's important functions.[15] Fantasy removes the individual from direct coping thought and transports him or her to a more satisfying world where values can be realized. In the process, tension is released, gratification obtained, and the self repaired. Some fantasies are particularly susceptible to this interpretation, as when the harried businessman sitting at his desk mentally retreats for a few moments to his imaginary wilderness cabin. Such mental "trips" to imaginary worlds provide a psychic vacation.

And yet, from a cultural perspective, fantasy is not completely escape. First, the fantasy is partly determined by the particular cultural norms it attempts to transcend. Second, even anticultural fantasies are typically structured by cultural rules for breaking rules. Finally, such fantasy indirectly contributes to the social order. As long as the individual does not tarry too long in the other world, as long as he does not try and act out his fantasy, then it is beneficial to society. Once the businessman has had his forty-second wilderness vacation, he can return refreshed to cultural reality and put his nose once again to the occupational grindstone. It is good business for society to grant its workers such temporary breaks. Fantasy, like religion, is an inexpensive opium for the people.

But there is another important way in which many fantasies contribute to the maintenance of the social order. Consider the standard fantasy of achieving great material wealth. These fantasies vividly convey the exquisite pleasure and social acclaim to be realized in acquiring, possessing, and displaying "desirable" material objects. The consequence is typically not satiation but a renewed desire to work toward the acquisition of such objects. Such fantasies are not escapes from culture at all. They should be viewed as mental commercials for a materialistic value system. The same applies to other fantasies that focus on the pleasurable realization of American values. Career success fantasies provide powerful motivation for actual career work. Alternative career success fantasies may be impossible to realize, but they reaffirm the value of success. Dreams of a blissful married life are also powerfully motivating. In an era of high divorce, they are sometimes even stronger than reality—which may help to explain why, when a first marriage fails, most Americans marry again. In fantasy, one does not escape from American values, one internalizes them. The fantasy experience of the "perfect" gratification to be obtained through the achieving of American values renews the incentive to pursue them even harder in reality. In this sense fantasy is not a defense mechanism but an internal self-enculturation technique.

While much fantasy conforms to official reality, it can also be a powerful source of innovation. Here, the unconscious self produces imaginative solutions to the frustrations of current reality. Fantasy solutions are often unrealistic, but sometimes they can be partially realized in actual life. Dissatisfaction with a current job, coupled with persistent fantasies of some alternative life style, sometimes leads an individual to abandon a conventional career. On a larger level, fantasy sometimes provides the basis for social change. Fantasy solutions to negative aspects of current social arrangements provide the creative force behind utopian fiction. They also provide the visionary image in terms of which cultural reform movements—revolutionary movements, utopian movements, cult movements—seek to create a new society.[16] At the heart of all such "revitalization movements" is the visionary "goal culture." The image of the ideal social system typically comes directly from an individual's fantasy, a fantasy that not only solves personal problems but solves them in a way that appeals to other individuals suffering similar kinds of identity frustrations.

Sometimes fantasy leads the individual out of the current social order; more commonly it keeps him in conformity with it. Even when the individual knows that a complete fulfillment of the fantasy is impossible, it may still have an important motivating effect. An informant quoted earlier, the man with the grandiose California success fantasy, put it as follows: "The idea that I could someday realize even a small part of my fantasy provides a powerful incentive to struggle by on my present salary." The following text provides another good illustration of the motivating value of fantasy. When the informant wrote this text, her fantasy—of a dream house and a happy family life—had just dissolved. She had just broken up with her fiancé.

My fantasy had some positive aspects besides the simple escape from the everyday realities of life. It kind of gave me a purpose—like something to work for. It gave work a reason. Not only did I need spending money, I needed to save for the future. Basically my fantasy gave me purpose. Everything became important because it was bringing me closer to my goal. Time was finally on my side. I began meeting deadlines and attacking my work. I enjoyed life more because I had so much to look forward to. It was a goal I could strive for without any immediate failures to deal with.

Now that Andy is gone some of my purpose has diminished. Life seems dull and trivial. I'll have to find a new fantasy to cheer me up.

By providing purpose and meaning, fantasy has indirect but important effects on actual interactions.

One of the most interesting of these effects involves social situations in which one person communicates his or her fantasy material to another and sometimes ritually enacts it. In American society, people rarely disclose their fantasies. The evidence shows that most Americans experience vivid fantasies daily, but that they rarely talk about them to others. This taboo on disclosure is based, in part, on the cultural assumption that fantasy reveals "pathology." Even psychologists are susceptible to the anxiety that other people will interpret their fantasies this way. Prior to revealing some of his own fantasies, Jerome Singer cautions the diagnostically inclined reader as follows: "However idiosyncratic these experiences may appear to some readers, most of the phenomena have also been reported by other persons, sane and insane. Let me urge the hastily interpreting reader to take a fresh look at his own stream of thought and daydreams before casting the first diagnostic label." [17] In fact, his fantasies are not idiosyncratic at all— at least for someone of this society. The contents are directly derived from the American media, and the structures he describes represent typical manifestations of the grandiose alternate career success syndrome.

Since psychotherapy is one American social situation in which fantasy has been traditionally disclosed, patients may resent their therapists because of this. Nora Ephron expresses this resentment in an extreme way: "I never told anyone the exact details of my particular sex fantasy: it is my only secret and I am not going to divulge it here. I once told almost all of it to my former therapist; he died last year and when I saw his obituary I felt a great sense of relief; the only person in the world who almost knew how crazy I am was gone and I was safe." [18] This peculiar conceptualization of fantasy is, fortunately, no longer shared by many therapists and clients. Summarizing current work in the field, James Morgan and Thomas Skovholt write as follows: "Recent research indicates that fantasy and daydreaming can be and often are—positive, life-enriching, stress reducing, creativity-increasing human activities that should be encouraged in many instances." [19]

Outside therapy, fantasy is also sometimes directly communicated and enacted in the context of intimate social relationships such as those of sexual affairs and marriage. However, even in these American relationships, disclosures of fantasy have traditionally been rare. An interesting historical indicator of this pattern is found in the 1938 edition of Havelock Ellis's *Psychology of Sex*. In his discussion of daydreams, Ellis concludes that, for women, not only "erotic fantasy" but fantasy in general "frequently ceases with marriage." [20] This "finding," apparently based on interviews, contrasts strikingly with more recent research that indicates that married persons not only regularly experience sexual fantasy but that they often do so during sexual intercourse with each other. [21] What then of Ellis's findings? There are several possible cultural explanations. The most likely one is that his subjects, finding admission of fantasy incompatible with their public images as respectable married persons, simply lied to the investigator. It is also possible that cultural taboos of the time led people to repress their awareness of these experiences. Finally, it may be that there has been at least some shift in the nature of fantasy life as the culture has changed.

In *Open Marriage*, a 1972 volume considered sensational for its advocacy of freedom in marital relations, the authors discussed the possibilities of exchanging fantasies. Along with fantasies about obtaining a fur coat or a plane, the authors mention two examples of sexual fantasies—a husband who fantasizes group sex and a wife who imagines "sleeping with Paul Newman in technicolor detail." The authors consider the possibilities of husband and wife exchanging such fantasies, but they are very cautious. They warn that this is a "drastic method." "If you feel uneasy," they write, "don't even try it."[22] The reason is jealousy. One partner may resent the fact that his or her spouse enjoys fantasy sexual relations with imaginary beings. Disclosure here may parallel disclosures of "real" infidelities. Fantasy lovers are perceived as rivals, and imaginary social relationships become a cause for real anger.

While fantasies are still rarely disclosed, there are some couples who have gone beyond disclosure to the ritual enactment of their own sexual fantasies. In these bedroom interactions, people abandon or modify their own actual behavior in order to play-act imaginary social action that has originally occurred in sexual fantasy. Here the individual imitates his or her fantasy self. The process is interestingly analogous to role-modeling on media figures and, to the extent that the fantasy is media-influenced, the connection is closer than that of analogy.

Fantasy enactment seems to have attained the status of a minority culture pattern that ranges from mild play-acting to elaborate dramas. One report includes an account by a thirty-two-year-old woman who, with her partner of seven years, claims to play out such ritual enactment of fantasy in an extreme way.

I suppose we've been through every possible way that two people could meet and have sex together.

I can't remember all the things he's been, all the things I've been. Once we met at a train station, two separate people; he was a film director and I was trying to get a part in his film—a starlet—so he wasn't treating me very well. I've been raped, obviously. . . . He's been a dirty old tramp that I've picked up. I love dirty old tramps, and we play that one. He likes being a chick who seduces me—he dresses up as a chick.[23]

Despite such enactments, fantasy disclosure is not complete. "We're very open with each other, but I don't tell him everything . . . like he doesn't know half the fantasies that go on in me."[24] For another couple, difficulties with the bondage paraphernalia led from fantasy enactment to an actual encounter with firemen and police.

One night we were introducing into our play a pair of handcuffs bought in a toy shop. They had come with two keys, which up to that point had always worked perfectly. This time, however, first one key and then the other broke inside the locks. The result was one well-hand-cuffed wife. It was indeed lucky she was wearing a long evening gown, since visits to two local fire stations proved necessary, though abortive, and each time a fireman tried to open one of the cuffs, a ratchet would tighten a notch. Finally, we had recourse to the nearest police precinct. Beyond reminding us that the possession of handcuffs was locally illegal, the boys in blue couldn't have been more courteous; they had, however, to send out for a special car containing an expert in what was known, it seemed, as a "ring-job." Having first identified their make (Japanese), the officer opened up the cuffs easily enough. It was all accomplished in a spirit of pleasant banter; by an extraordinary coincidence it was Halloween.[25]

Beyond the marital bedroom, fantasy enactments have some-times been standard in certain American "houses of prostitution." In a house called Mae's, which operated in Los Angeles in the 1930s, a client could live out his fantasy of meeting and making love to his fantasy idol, that is, his favorite media actress. Movie director Garson Kanin reports meeting a variety of "stars" there.

In addition to "Barbara Stanwyck" and "Alice Faye," I met "Irene Dunne," "Joan Crawford," "Janet Gaynor," "Carole Lombard," "Marlene Dietrich," "Luise Rainer," "Myrna Loy," and "Ginger Rogers." But never, as has been earlier indicated, "Greta Garbo" or "Katharine Hepburn."

There were, needless to say, cast changes from time to time. Stars faded and fell away. New stars appeared. Novas. A stage star, say Margaret Sullavan, would come out, make a success and settle down. Before long, "she" could be seen at "Mae's."[26]

The stars of Mae's were, of course, not the originals but rather carefully made-up facsimiles. The girls were selected for their re-semblance to currently popular starlets and then carefully dressed and styled accordingly. They were provided with information about the real star's current life and background, and they imi-tated their conversational style and tone of voice. Kanin describes one example of enactment at Mae's which influenced the actual relationships of his working world.

I was directing *They Knew What They Wanted*, starring Carole Lombard and Charles Laughton.

I was a young Hollywood bachelor, and like everyone else who ever came into contact with Carole Lombard, I fell. The fact that she was married to Clark Gable did not seem to deter my fantasies. She was everything I had always wanted a girl to be: beautiful, funny, talented, imaginative, able, warm, dear, and no-nonsense.

I found myself touching her at every possible opportunity, and when those opportunities did not arise, I invented some. I was, to put it mildly, bedazzled by this golden girl—although I knew I was in a hopeless situation.

Then my brother married. His friends gave the customary prenuptial stag dinner. When it ended, part of the group, by prearrangement, repaired to "Mae's."

And in came "Carole." I took her aside and we talked for a long time. We discussed the stuff we had shot that day, and I explained what we were going to do the following day. She *loved* my ideas. We panned Laughton. She told me she was thinking of leaving Clark. A clash of careers. I told her I thought she was doing the wise—the only thing. She asked me if I was hungry. I said yes. She suggested we have supper up in her suite. I told her I thought that was a great idea. The rest is a Glorious Technicolor, out-of-focus, slow motion dream.

The next morning, I was the star of our little on-the-set ritual. Carole Lombard and Frank Fay and I had fallen into the habit of meeting in my trailer every morning right after the first shot for coffee and conversation. Our meetings soon developed a theme of sorts. We agreed that we would each tell—in precise, unsparing detail—what we had done the night before. Often, there was little to tell; more often, I suspected Frank of soaring invention; Carole and I usually played it straight.

I told of my visit to "Mae's," of my encounter with "Carole," leaving out nothing.

My account was punctuated by Carole screaming with laughter, "I'll die! I'll die. Wait till I tell Clark! Jesus, no, I better not. He'll go there! I'll die! I'll die!" [27]

There are many other social situations in which fantasy enactment occurs. Children often play games based on shared, often media-derived, fantasy. "You be Tonto and I'll be the Lone Ranger," or "You be Han Solo and I'll be Luke." Adults go to costume parties, perform in amateur theatricals, and engage in fantasy role-playing games. Perhaps the most striking contemporary example is the game of Dungeons and Dragons.

In Dungeons and Dragons, a group of several players create and enact a shared fantasy. The players begin by selecting a role from one of six standard alternatives, "elf," "dwarf," "thief," "warrior," "wizard," and "cleric." They roll dice to determine power attributes ("strength," "intelligence," "dexterity"), and they personally create others. One person, the Dungeon Master, creates the imaginary world (often a process of four or five hours) complete with map, history, environmental features, and imaginary beings (villains, monsters, dragons). Sitting together around a table the players assume their roles and use dice rolls and conversation to explore this fantasy world.

Once again, the media influence is significant. Published Dungeon Master scripts represent a specialized media form, and even when the Dungeon Master creates his "own" world he typically draws directly on fantasy fiction.

What I have done, and what most DM's have done, is use the imaginative creations of my favorite authors to map my worlds.

The adventurers step down through the apparently solid rock floor of the crater and see the jungle-filled valley deep below. . . . In the distance they hear the ominous beat of drums. Now, softly on the breeze, comes the sound of human voices, chanting.

My players, I am betting, have never read A. Merritt's *The Dwellers in the Mirage*. They do not know the terrible secrets of the worship of Khalk'ru the Dissolver, and they do not know the dreadful risks of invading his realm.

At other points in the game, my players have wandered through bits of Barsoom and Hyperborea, through worlds created by Edgar Rice Burroughs, Robert E. Howard, H. Rider Haggard, A. Merritt, H. P. Lovecraft, and Clark Ashton Smith. Sometimes they recognize where they are, sometimes they do not.[28]

Partly because of the media influence there is a great deal of aggressive interaction. "The level of violence in this make-believe world runs high. There is hardly a game in which the players do not indulge in murder, arson, torture, rape, or highway robbery. I have even had players tell me that their characters had stopped along the way to one of my underground dungeons to spray-paint graffiti on the walls!"[29]

While the game provides the raw materials, the players must deliberately fantasize in order to flesh it out. One regular described this explicitly. "The game isn't enjoyable for those people who can't get into fantasies. You have to really *become* your character and really experience what's going on to enjoy it." Assuming her fantasy identity, she introduces her own character as follows: "My name is Sasha. I am a female, human, fighting warrior. I wear chain-mail type armor and I have a shield for protection. The weapons I carry are a battle ax and a sword. I am tall, very strong, and have long, dark, wavy hair." Asked about the resemblance between her self and her fantasy character, this player answered, "She is more like myself than I am; she is my true self." Recognizing herself to be an aggressive person, she has felt restricted by the need to conform to her sex-role socialization. In the guise of "Sasha" she can become her "real" self and freely incorporate aggressiveness into her fantasy relationships.

Once I *become* Sasha I leave all the cultural-social pressures behind and I am one among my fellow companions. I fight like the others, I kill like the others. They don't say, "Oh, leave Sasha behind while we go into the room and fight some creatures. It's much too dangerous for a woman." No, I'm always right along with them, confronting the danger as they do. Hence, in this fantasy, I escape from the cultural values that are placed on me because of my gender.

The character has even become important to her outside the context of the game. She likes to fantasize about Sasha in a number of stressful social contexts. "I also like to engage in it [the Sasha fantasy] when I'm angry at someone. By taking myself out of reality and becoming Sasha, I can release my tensions and anger at the creature that I am fighting. Thus, when I return to reality I find that I am more relaxed and less angry."

Fantasy enactment also occurs at various public rituals, including the performances that occur in places like Disneyland and the Wild West shows. In Ocean City, Maryland—about as far east as you can get—you can visit Frontier Town and witness a staged version of a cowboy shootout. Again, the hired actors feel it necessary to really "get into" their roles. They do this through the assumption of a fantasy identity. As one actor informant told me, "You have to really feel the part, that you're really going to shoot them down—you have to have a 'Western' feel!" The media provide the model. This actor drew his inspiration from his own Wild West fantasies, but these were directly conditioned by his media experience.

You look for someone as a reference. I don't know any real cowboys, so I looked to actors who played it perfectly. Sometimes I thought of Clint Eastwood. I love a good Western. But mostly I looked to John Wayne as the example of the true cowboy. Most of my fellow "cowboys" saw him in that role. In my roles as various cowboys and outlaws I almost lived the part, as if I were a John Wayne figure—as if I were him. When I rode into town to rob the bank, I wanted to look every bit as mean and just as level-headed as John Wayne always was. I pictured him in my mind countless times as I shot down the McClowerys and the Clantons in the O.K. Corral.

Once again the fantasy identity spilled over into actual social relationships. After the performance, parents and their children would approach the "cowboys" for pictures and conversation. "We'd make up stories. We'd talk 'Western' even to the parents. Tell them we were from Denver, a cattle ranch in Denver. We'd see who could pull off the biggest stories. There was pressure from the other 'cowboys' to be a nut. We were only acting so it was totally acceptable." Even at night, when the "cowboys" visited the bars of Ocean City, the fantasy mixed into their actual social interactions.

When we went into town we dressed 'preppie' maybe three times the whole summer. The rest of the time we went Western—spurs, chaps, holsters, guns, hats. We lived that way all night. People loved it. I never met so many girls in my life. They'd be curious. When we walked in the door, people would look. Twenty minutes at most and we'd be talking to some girls.

This was two years before the "urban cowboy" fad, but the Ocean City girls, themselves raised on the cowboy-as-hero image, were suitably impressed.[30]

There are also several media productions in which fantasy is communicated, but in one media form where it might be expected, fantasy disclosure is unusual. American autobiography, with its emphasis on real world accomplishments and interactions, rarely includes much material on the individual's fantasy life. Here literary communications are probably structured by the cultural conventions that shape actual interactions. However, in another rather specialized form of print media, fantasies are directly communicated. In the 1970s a new genre appeared—the collection of sexual fantasies. Some of these were deliberately designed as erotic presentations, while others claimed a more serious approach.[31]

Such collections represent a curious if minor genre, but there is another extremely large set of American media productions in which fantasy is *indirectly* communicated. In disguised form, transformed by artistic conventions, fictional writing is a form of fantasy communication. As Freud noted long ago, fantasy provides the basis for fiction.[32] The process of creative writing involves tapping into standard personal fantasies or deliberately inducing new fantasies. Like other authors, television scriptwriters explicitly report "daydreaming" their characters' imaginary social interactions until the plot is far enough along to write out.

Given this perspective, television and film productions involve the enactment of an author's fantasy by a set of professional actors who temporarily "become" the author's imaginary characters. Finally, the successful act of communication typically depends on the individual members of the audience identifying with—that is, imaginatively transforming themselves into—these same characters. Here we arrive full circle. Media productions constitute formalized encodements of an author's culturally constituted fantasies. Media communications represent the mass consumption of such fantasy.

Chapter 6

Social Relations
in Hallucinations
and Delusions

A step beyond the realms of everyday imaginary experience lie the fantastic worlds of "madness." In our society, these hallucinatory and delusionary worlds are typically associated with various kinds of psychotics, particularly "paranoid schizophrenics." These abnormal imaginary systems have been traditionally interpreted through the psychiatric paradigm.

In American society, the basic test through which judgments of madness are made is the psychiatric interview or mental status examination.[1] The procedures followed on the ward I studied appear to be typical.[2] Here we find a special kind of social interaction in which a person in the role of psychiatrist questions a prospective patient. In some cases the patient has come voluntarily because of subjective distress. In most cases the prospective patient claims to be well, and arrives more or less unwillingly at the instigation of others such as relatives, neighbors, or the police. From a cultural perspective, people are brought to the ward because they have violated cultural rules about appropriate behavior. They have engaged in social deviance that has proved annoying to others. In a few cases people have threatened or attacked others. Much more often they have done nothing violent but have performed actions that strike other people as inappropriate or bizarre.

In the mental status examination, the psychiatrist seeks to determine if the person is mentally disturbed and to establish the proper diagnosis. If the psychiatrist suspects psychosis, he will be particularly concerned about whether the patient has hallucinations and delusions. The presence of these symptoms is often suggested by the patient's answers to standard questions, as when a patient responds to questions about his identity by claiming to be "the ambassador to Russia," or "a Jewish angel." The psychiatrist will also ask questions intended to elicit evidence of these symptoms.

"Do you ever see things?"
"Do you have any influential friends?"
"Have you had any special experiences?"
"Do you hear voices?"
"Have you ever been in contact with God?"
"Do you ever get the feeling the TV is watching you?"
"Have you ever hallucinated?"

Often such questions yield answers suggesting the presence of hallucinations and delusions.

But what exactly are such phenomena? A typical assessment defines "delusion" as a "firm belief opposed to reality but maintained in spite of strong evidence to the contrary," and "hallucination" as a "sense perception for which there is no appropriate external stimulus."[3] Such definitions assert that a delusion is a *false* belief and that a hallucination is a *false* perception. From the psychiatric point of view, this is a straightforward problem. If the person believes what is not true or sees what is not there, then he or she is obvious "psychotic" or "out of touch with reality." Such a person, often diagnosed as "paranoid schizophrenic," is consequently in need of institutionalization and therapy, that is, treatment intended to alleviate these destructive symptoms and to return the individual to reality.

From a cultural perspective, the question is more complex. As Berger and Luckmann observe, when judgments are made about whether or not a person is "in touch with reality," the appropriate question is "Which reality?" or "Whose reality?"[4] Reality is culturally constituted and relative. All societies are based on beliefs about what is true, possible, real, and perceivable. Experiences outside those boundaries will generally be seen as "false." However, what is a true belief or a valid perception in terms of one set of rules may be a delusion or hallucination in terms of another.

Sometimes this variation is cultural, and sometimes it is individual. This is evident in the mental status examination. From the patient's point of view, his beliefs and perceptions are valid; it is the psychiatrist and other ignorant "normals" who are deluded. One prospective patient explained that he was really two people, that he has a "double" whose experiences directly affect him. He concluded with the following statement: "I'm not confused, this is reality!" During his initial mental status examination, another "schizophrenic" said, "You're looking at me and thinking, 'What kind of a nut is he?'—I'm thinking the same thing about you." When the psychiatrist judges someone to be out of touch with reality, he is saying that the person is out of touch with the psychiatrist's version of contemporary, secular, middle-class American reality. From this perspective, therapy is a system of social control. It involves procedures designed to remove deviants from society and/or to bring deviants back into conformity with the current beliefs and perceptions of society.[5]

Adopting such a perspective suggests that the mental patient may be operating with a personal system of beliefs and perceptions that happen to be out of touch with, or contrary to, the cultural reality currently prevailing in his social surroundings. The crucial questions then become, "What is the subjective nature of mental disorder?" and "What are these systems like from the inside?"

Despite the voluminous literature on mental illness in general and schizophrenia in particular (over 5,000 research papers since 1920), there has been relatively little work addressed to the subjective reality of schizophrenia.[6] Instead of looking at the phenomenological inner world of the patient's beliefs and perceptions, researchers have been concerned with theorizing about mental illness in terms of their own outside concepts. Such literature tells us much more about the beliefs of psychiatrists than it does about the beliefs of schizophrenics.

One exception is Bert Kaplan's book, *The Inner World of Mental Illness*. This volume consists of commentary and edited excerpts from autobiographical accounts of people who have experienced so-called mental illness. In his introduction, Kaplan observes that the psychiatrist is typically not concerned with the patient's subjective reality. This is evident in the course of the mental status examination itself. If the patient claims that he is being tormented by Martians, the psychiatrist will not seek to elicit the patient's theories about the motives of Martians. Once he has satisfied himself that the patient is "deluded," he simply codes this in his own classification system (for example, "delusion of persecution") and employs it as evidence from which a diagnosis can be established. On the ward I studied, it was considered counterproductive to discuss the patient's delusions with him since this might reinforce them.

However, from an ethnographic perspective, we must look at these imaginary systems from the inside—that is, in terms of the patient's perspective and experience. Kaplan makes this point cogently:

From the point of view of the sickness, the subjective perspective, distorted though it may be, is the more relevant one. It is the psychiatrist's theory that is "outside" the phenomenon and which appears ridiculous and irrelevant. . . . If our concern is with understanding the illness, what is required is an empathy and even a sympathy with it which contrasts sharply with the psychiatrist's aim of destroying it and changing it into something else.[7]

In the traditional view, the patient's perspective is bizarre, meaningless, and absurd, but Kaplan goes on to argue that attention to the patient's perspective often reveals the presence of an intelligible, culturelike system of meaning. In becoming mentally ill, the individual has not abandoned meaning; he has undergone a shift in meaning. He has experienced what Anthony F. C. Wallace refers to as "mazeway resynthesis," a redefinition of his personal sense of reality, such that he now operates with perceptions and beliefs at odds with those around him. Often it is this shift in meaning that leads him to behave in ways that other people view as bizarre. Usually, however, this shift in reality is only partial. Typically, the American schizophrenic still operates with many basic aspects of American cultural knowledge. He has merely grafted onto standard American knowledge a significantly different, fantasylike system of meaning and perception.

Kaplan suggests that in "choosing" his own reality over that

200

of society, the individual is abandoning social relationships. "Through his psychosis the person renounces what is normally regarded as perhaps the most valuable and significant of all life's activities—participation in a social group and the possibility of positive relationship with other people."[8] Kaplan indicates that the individual may break with reality partly because he experiences his actual social situation as highly dissatisfying. Certainly the actual social worlds of many schizophrenics are highly negative, and this often seems to be an important factor in a person's abandonment of conventional reality. However, Kaplan is mistaken in implying that the inner world of mental illness is not "social" and in suggesting that the psychotic has in fact *renounced* "participation in a social group and that possibility of positive relationship with other people."

One of the most characteristic features of the inner world of hallucinatory and delusionary systems is their social nature. Although in entering another reality the individual may alter or even drop his actual social relations with others, he does not drop social relations in general. Far from it. On entering the psychotic world, the individual enters a social world, takes on a modified identity, meets others, and becomes entangled in complex systems of imaginary social interactions. The schizophrenic world, like the other imaginary worlds we have examined, is typically an imaginary *social* world. For a schizophrenic, as for the ordinary fantasizer, almost always there are other people. Let us consider an example.

In terms of the psychiatrist's outside perspective, L. Percy King is a psychotic suffering auditory hallucinations and delusions of persecution. The official diagnosis is "schizophrenia, paranoid type." Because of this diagnosis King has been hospitalized involuntarily for twenty-eight years. It is considered unlikely that he will ever be released.[9] However, from the inside, according to L. Percy King, the situation is very different. He is hospitalized, to be sure, but this is not due to insanity. On the contrary, not only is he fully sane, he has become an extremely important person. He is the brilliant discoverer of the "greatest psychological phenomena extant" and the heroic resister of an extraordinary and evil conspiracy. His institutionalization is due not to any personal psychological disorder but to the evil persecutions of his enemies, including his former employers and the psychiatric staff of the mental hospital. He hopes and expects soon to be freed from his captivity and triumphantly recognized as "the most wonderful person alive."[10]

In order to gain his freedom and to accomplish his victory over the conspiracy, King writes long letters to various unmet persons outside the institution. In these letters he explains the "real" causes of his institutionalization and the nature of the conspiracy he is fighting. One of these letters (some 20,000 words in length) reached the Harvard psychologist Robert White. As he observes, "The letters are of exceptional value, for they give us in detail and with feeling the inside story of a severe psychosis."[11]

By his own interpretation, both King's discoveries and his misfortunes involve social relationships; they have to do with his connections to a set of evil human beings with occult powers whom he calls "pursuers." His first encounter with these beings took place when he was visiting relatives in New York City.

Being a stranger I was surprised to hear someone exclaim twice: "Shoot him!", evidently meaning me, judging from the menacing talk which followed between the threatener and those with him. I tried to see who the threatener, and those with him were, but the street was so crowded, I could not. I guessed that they must be gangsters, who had mistaken me for another gangster, who I coincidentally happened to resemble. I thought one or more of them really intended to shoot me so I hastened from the scene as fast as I could walk. These unidentified persons, who had threatened to shoot me, pursued me. I knew they were pursuing me because I still heard their voices as close as ever, no matter how fast I walked. . . . Days later while in the Metropolis again, I was once more startled by those same pursuers, who had threatened me several days before. It was nighttime. As before, I could catch part of their talk, but, in the theatre crowd, I could see them nowhere. I heard one of them, a woman, say: "You can't get away from us; we'll lay for you, and get you after a while!" To add to the mystery, one of these "pursuers" repeated my thoughts aloud, verbatim.[12]

In seeking to make sense of these experiences, King considers various spirit explanations before discovering what he takes to be the correct scientific interpretation.

The question occurred to me: How could as many of these pursuers follow me as quickly unseen? Were they ghosts? Or was I in the process of developing into a spiritual medium? No! Among these pursuers, I was later to gradually discover by deduction, were evidently some brothers, and sisters, who had inherited from one of their parents, some astounding, unheard of, utterly unbelievable occult powers. Believe-it-or-not, some of them, besides being able to tell a person's thoughts, are also able to project their magnetic voices—commonly called "radio voices" around here—a distance of a few miles without talking loud, and without apparent effort, their voices sounding from that distance as tho heard thru a radio headset. . . . An uninitiated person would probably be very much startled over such phenomena. For example what would you think if you were on a level, desolate tract of land without any vegetation, or places of concealment upon it, and without a human being within miles, when you heart a mysterious, seemingly unearthly voice answer a question you were just thinking about? [13]

Because of their ability to read thoughts and speak to people at a distance, the pursuers often force people to do things against their will. Sometimes they pretend to be God or some spirit.

As a matter of fact, certain pursuers, who are sadistic, have had a lot of "fun" impersonating supernatural beings, and inducing and terrorizing certain gullible persons, into doing astonishing, terrible things. Certain pursuers have been able to get many persons to carry out their slightest wish, and these pursuers are evidently proud of their ability to do this. Being naturally, offensively domineering, they take delight in seeing what awful things they can get persons to do. [14]

In other cases, because of their ability to read thoughts and discover a person's secrets, they blackmail weak people into following their orders.

Suppose certain mindreading pursuers decide to boycott a merchant. Every time a customer is about to enter the merchant's establishment, he hears a mysterious radio voice whisper: "Don't trade here! The merchant across the street sells a better quality, cheaper." Suppose a certain customer answers: "Who are you anyway? I won't trade across the street. I'll trade where I please!" Then the radio voice might say: "You'll trade where I say. If you don't, I'll spread gossip around you have a lot of money hidden in your mattress, and tell your husband you stayed with another man in a house of ill-fame last night." [15]

The evil pursuers not only have the ability to read minds and speak to people over a mile away, they can also affect people's senses at a distance, as by causing a person to smell a certain scent or feel a tickling sensation. Sometimes they use these powers to engage in sexual interactions with their victims, who include some of the other patients at King's mental hospital.[16]

But why are the pursuers so intent on persecuting King and his fellow inmates? As White observes, "In his logical fashion King, too, has pondered this question, and has arrived at the following answer, which constitutes the most startling and original feature of his great discoveries."[17] It turns out that King has certain allies, the "soul sisters" who are mysteriously linked to him. Because the pursuers wish to gain control of these women, they are seeking to destroy L. Percy King. First they began to force people to act in ways which hurt King emotionally. "From the unseen distance by means of their 'radio voices,' certain pursuers, by force of example, and otherwise induced different ones [coworkers] to make vulgar, and sarcastic remarks of ridicule, and defamation in the nature of 'smart talk' about me to me, or in my presence to hurt my feelings."[18] They also began a campaign to force King out of his job.

By means of their "radio voices" pursuers induced one of my bosses to make things disagreeable for me. This boss became rather surly, ordering me to move heavy office appurtenances, and empty trash baskets with the colored porter. . . . In my new office I was discriminated against by being given the only poor typewriter I know of in the Division—an old-fashioned, "invisible" Remington with no Backspacer, and a worn ribbon. No one could have done very good, speedy work on it.[19]

King is fired, but even this is not enough for the pursuers. As White writes of this period, "Now he was completely miserable. Pursuers left him no peace of mind as he sat in his lodgings, murmurings in the street below told him all too plainly that his murderers were assembling. Voices on the stairs revealed that a lynching party was creeping toward his room, so that in panic he called upon a neighbor to protect him.[20] In despair, King attempts suicide and is taken to the state mental hospital. As White notes, the pursuers ensure his commitment. "During the psychiatric examination he was depressed and indifferent, speaking as little as possible. Later he realized that pursuers had forced this behavior upon him so that he would be judged insane."[21] But King's strength returns and he continues heroically to resist the pursuers. Through letters like the ones I have been quoting, he hopes to enlist the aid of allies and to obtain an eventual victory over the pursuers. On his release from the mental hospital, he expects to be showered with gifts and hailed as a hero.

What should we make of this? As White observes, we should resist the temptation to treat Kings' writings as meaningless ravings. "The outcome of his reasoning may be completely absurd to us, but he is obviously attempting to reason and to make some kind of sense out of his experience. His queer ideas are not random productions as if the machinery of thought had suddenly disintegrated. If we look closely we find consistent themes. . . ."[22] King's beliefs seem "fantastic" and "absurd" to us because they violate our definitions of reality. But King holds intelligible beliefs, and these fit together logically into a well-composed and coherent system of knowledge through which he interprets his experience and generates social behavior. Although King has a special system of meaning, he has not constructed a totally separate culture. In many respects he operates with basic aspects of American cultural knowledge. Even his deviant knowledge has cultural dimensions. His emphasis on logic, on the marshaling of evidence, and on scientific, mechanistic explanations is very American.

But what is the main theme of King's hallucinatory and delusionary system? The extracts quoted above demonstrate that King's world is pervaded by a set of special *social relationships*. King has not renounced social interactions. On the contrary, he has immersed himself in a tangled system of social interaction. The basis of his system is a set of imaginary beings—his allies, the soul sisters, and his enemies, the pursuers. A complex set of relationships with these beings dominates his experience. He is also caught up in sets of imaginatively structured actual social relationships. Both his earlier relationships with coworkers and his current relationships with patients and hospital staff involve actual interactions. However, these are imaginatively transformed by his belief that their behavior toward him is a result of their control by the pursuers. The center of King's madness is a system of imaginary social relationships.

King's theory of pursuers is his own original creation, but his meaning system is representative of American hallucinatory and delusionary systems in that it is based on imaginary social relationships. If we look at the inner world of paranoid schizophrenia, we find that imaginary social relationships dominate. Auditory hallucinations, the most frequent of American hallucinations, usually consist of hearing "voices"—hearing what appears to be communications from others. Delusions characteristically involve beliefs about a set of other beings that Norman Cameron has aptly characterized as the "paranoid pseudo community."

Paranoid schizophrenics may involve themselves with various strange imaginary figures who are something other than ordinary humans. This set of beings parallels a similar group of dream figures. Like King's "pursuers," they may be quasi-human beings with special powers or, they may consist of material objects endowed with human attributes and motives. One of the patients on the ward I studied was involved with an animate cigarette dispenser and a malicious electronic machine. Similar cases are often mentioned in the literature. Second, schizophrenics may fill their private worlds with beings drawn from traditional Western supernatural systems—God, Jesus, the Holy Ghost, angels, witches, the devil, and various other ghosts and spirits. A third group are the media figures. American movie stars, musicians, political figures, and other celebrities seem as important in schizophrenic imaginary systems as they are in ordinary American fantasy. The patients I knew had special relationships with Adolf Hitler, Henry Cabot Lodge, Cortez, Richard Nixon, Marlon Brando and J. Edgar Hoover. We have already considered the media relationships of Steinhagen, Chapman, and Hinckley.

A fourth group consists of imaginary human beings who are somehow connected to the patient. Sometimes the link is quasi-physical, as with the man who had a double whose actions and sufferings directly affected him. In other cases the link is social. Imaginary friends, spouses, and children are common. One woman claimed to have over 900 sons and daughters.

A fifth group of others is composed of transformed actual acquaintances. The schizophrenic's pseudo community does not involve just imaginary beings, spirits, and unmet celebrities; it also includes real individuals with whom the schizophrenic is actually in contact. However, as in ordinary fantasy and dreams, these individuals are imaginatively transformed, that is, assigned roles and attributes different from those they are generally understood to possess. Their new attributes often have to do with their connection to imaginary beings. Thus King's coworkers, like the hospital staff, were seen as conscious conspirators or dupes of the pursuers.

The schizophrenic develops various kinds of imaginary social relationships with these beings. In his classic account of the paranoid pseudo community, Cameron suggests that the patient characteristically finds himself involved in hostile relationships with a group of enemies. "The paranoid pseudo community is an imaginary organization composed of real and imagined persons whom the patient represents as united for the purpose of carrying out some action upon him."[23] And: "In form it usually corresponds to one or another of the common dangerous, hostile groups in contemporary society, real or fictional—gangs, dope and spy rings, secret police, and groups of political, racial, and religious fanatics."[24] Some of the patients I observed believed in similar plots by "lousy neighbors," spouses, siblings, doubles, employers, blacks, the CIA, the FBI, the electric company, Nazis, other patients, nurses, and psychiatrists.

While it is true that hostile beings are prevalent in these schizophrenic systems, enemies are far from the only beings involved. Noting that Cameron seems to suggest that the paranoid pseudo community is exclusively hostile, Milton Rokeach points out that sympathetic beings are also present. He illustrates this observation with reference to three "paranoid schizophrenics" whose delusionary systems he has studied in depth.

If real external, positive referents are missing in paranoid mental patients . . . this does not mean that these mental patients have no positive referents whatsoever. Again and again we were struck by the fact that the three men would mention certain referents to whom they obviously looked in a positive way. But these referents were either completely delusional or only quasi-real. Clyde for example frequently hallucinated and spoke warmly of someone called Gloria, a lifelong chum he had grown up with and gone to school with. . . . In the case of Leon, there was at first his wife the Blessed Virgin Mary, and his uncle George Bernard Brown, the reincarnation of the Archangel Michael. Later, of course, he transferred his affections to Mrs. R. I. Dung, or Madame Yeti Woman. In contrast to the negative things Leon had to say about all real human beings, he always spoke positively and warmly of his relations with these creatures of his imagination.[25]

L. Percy King not only had a positive relationship with his female soul sisters, he also expected to enlist the aid of prominent unmet persons from the outside world. In my sample of cases, paranoid schizophrenics claimed friendly relationships with the "top scientists in the country" and various political and religious figures. One woman spoke glowingly of Jesus Christ, with whom she used to walk along a New Jersey beach. Cameron himself indicates that the victim of an imaginary conspiracy may enlist the help of allies and, in another context, he describes "erotic delusions" in which psychotics develop imaginary love relationships. The examples Cameron mentions are already familiar.

There are paranoid delusions in which the patient believes that he is loved sexually by another person who, for one reason or another, does not make a direct avowal but does indicate his or her love in a thousand little indirect ways. . . . the individual selected as the delusional lover is usually of the opposite sex, and often a public figure—in politics, on the stage, in television, the movies, etc.[26]

The schizophrenic's pseudo interactions are not limited to enemies. They also include positive imaginary relationships with beings who play roles such as ally, friend, spouse, and lover.

Occasionally, imaginary schizophrenic systems may have little perceptible effect on the individual's actual social conduct. Kaplan's book includes an autobiographical account by Renee, who saw herself as the victim of a mysterious Persecutor who caused her to experience horrifying and painful hallucinations.

It seemed that my mouth was full of birds which I crunched between my teeth, and their feathers, their blood and broken bones were choking me. Or I saw people whom I had entombed in milk bottles, putrefying, and I was consuming their rotting cadavers. Or I was devouring the head of a cat which meanwhile gnawed at my vitals. It was ghastly, intolerable. In the midst of the horror and turbulence, I nonetheless carried on my work as secretary.[27]

Despite her persecution, she played her role so well that her office mates did not realize—at least for a considerable period of time—that anything was amiss.

Typically, however, paranoid schizophrenic systems not only structure interior consciousness but also affect the individual's actual social relationships. When the pseudo community is hostile, actual others are often seen as part of the conspiracy. Therefore, the individual may begin to treat these actual others not in terms of their ordinary roles and identities but in terms of the fantasy identities he has projected upon them. As it did with King, this leads to a break in the ordinary system of social conduct.

Cameron describes the case of a businessman who argued with his real bookies and then became (mistakenly) fearful that they had hired gangsters to do him in. Consequently, all kinds of people with whom he came in contact were perceived as gangsters.

He noticed a number of rough-looking strangers hanging around the hotel lobby. They seemed to be watching him closely and waving signals to one another. The patient became himself watchful and apprehensive. . . . They all seemed to be watching and shadowing him, wherever he went and whatever he did. There was no escape. He was convinced now that he was a man marked for execution, and in a near panic, he barricaded himself in his hotel room against surprise attack.[28]

In other cases, the delusionary relationships impel the individual not to hide or flee but to confront his enemies, as by accusation or physical attack. Such disruptive, seemingly, unwarranted, actions will not be welcomed by those in his actual social field. Often they respond with aggression. "To the patient this counter-aggression seems the final confirmation of his delusional expectation of assault. Thus, in the end he brings about a reality situation that corresponds to his psychotic reconstruction. The hostile world that he has built up in his imagination at last confronts him as external reality."[29]

Positive delusionary relationships may have similarly disruptive effects on actual social conduct, as when the individual approaches another on the basis of an imaginary love relationship. Of "erotic delusions" Cameron writes, "These delusions are responsible for a good many police actions, since paranoid and paranoid schizophrenic persons with such delusions may eventually take action. They pester the supposed lovers with letters, come to see them, or demand an avowal at a public meeting or performance."[30] The individual operating with an imaginary social system is likely to come into serious conflict with his actual social field. Because he is operating with an alien belief system, he is like an immigrant in a foreign society. Perceiving and acting in terms of his own reality leads him to violate the expectations of those around him.

In trying to account for paranoid imaginary systems, theorists have advanced a large variety of psychological explanations. For example, White interprets L. Percy King's psychosis as a problem in personal identity. "The Pursuer theory can be looked upon as a systematic hypothesis designed to account for all his experiences, and at the same time shield his self esteem."[31] More specifically, White sees a sexual problem as the root of his projections. "The basic underlying conflict in King's psychosis is between his self-confidence, arrogance, and ambition on one hand, and his effeminacy and sexual timidity on the other. . . ."[32]

While White does not force this interpretation, he here goes along, in part, with the controversial psychiatric theory that paranoid delusionary systems such as that of King represent a defense against homosexual tendencies. According to this theory, the individual loves men but feels forbidden to do so. Therefore, he unconsciously uses denial and reversal to reach the conclusion that men hate him.[33] Finding signs of such unconscious motives requires an arbitrary symbolic reading of King's account. And even if one were to accept the controversial theory of the homosexual origin of King's system, his problem would still be *cultural*. If King had grown up in a society that condoned homosexuality, he would have had no need to construct such an imaginary edifice. There would have been no pursuers, for there would have been no conflict between his homosexual tendencies and his social reality.

However, if we accept White's suggestion that King's system may be designed in part to protect his self-esteem, what problems other than sexual inadequacy might his system be seen as solving? One involves a conflict between King's "ambition" and his failure. King is preoccupied with his job difficulties. In terms of the American value of occupational achievement and success, he is a total failure. King's desire for achievement and recognition does not require a symbolic reading of his account; it is clear throughout the text. It is strikingly explicit in his fantasy anticipation of the events that will occur when he and his soul sisters obtain victory over the pursuers.

> When the public finds out that the writer in that respect is the most wonderful person alive, that no one has ever lived like him, his photo and write-up will be published in every important newspaper and magazine on earth. These helpless women and he will receive so many tons of fan mail that the post office will have to employ extra mail trucks to handle it. Throngs of people will crowd here on the grounds to get a peek at him, so that special police will have to be employed to keep them off the grounds. He and these helpless women will receive visits from world-famous scientists from everywhere and will receive offers to go on the air, into the movies, on the vaudeville stage. . . . These helpless women will be showered with so many presents from all over the world that the presents will have to be stored in a special building. He and they would be invited to appear before the State Assembly, in special session, and will be invited to the State House. He will be pensioned for life by the State and will go home in a special train and be met at the station by a band.[34]

This anticipation is not the product of some idiosyncratic psychological conflict, it is a classic rendering of the standard American fantasy of personal achievement, success, material reward, and celebrity style social recognition.

Such American value concerns are often apparent in schizophrenic worlds. It is sometimes asserted that psychosis involves a rejection of societal values—"perhaps the most extreme and complete form of negation that is possible."[35] Yet, like King, most of the patients on the ward I studied had not really negated American cultural values. On the contrary, they regularly expressed the desire to achieve love relationships, grandiose career success, and millionaire style material affluence. Their problem was that they had gotten nowhere in pursuing these goals. As we obtain a better understanding of the various components that go into schizophrenic imaginary worlds, we may find that one dimension involves a fantasylike attempt to imaginatively account for and to repair identity damage associated with a failure to realize cultural values.

Psychiatrists usually talk as if paranoid schizophrenics were vastly different from sane adults. However, their thinking is often considered similar to that of children and "primitives." Sometimes this comparison is implicit and metaphorical. But James Brussel directly equates the thinking of "the aborigine, the infant, and the psychotic."

The psychotic rejects this world and creates his own galaxy of associates. . . . Reverting to the behavior associated with the fabrications of childhood, he "sees" and "talks to" real but nonpresent, or fictitious beings (hallucinations). . . .

The similarity between infantile and psychotic behavior has another equivalent—primitive life. . . . Studies of aborigines reveal typical feral, childish, uninhibited practices."[36]

Brussel is correct in noting certain similarities between these three groups, but the differences, which are equally important, render the equation false. Anthropological studies have long since invalidated the ethnocentric notion that the thinking of non-Western tribal peoples is inferior, primitive, or childlike. Their thinking is just as developed, complex, and subtle as that of contemporary Americans—sometimes more so. The navigational systems of Micronesian sailors—which allowed them to reach distant tiny islands after sailing across hundreds of miles of open ocean—are so elaborate and complex that they have eluded the grasp of Westerners who have sought to study them. The important differences that do exist between non-Western and Western forms of thinking have to do with differences in styles of logic and in the concepts employed.

It is true, of course, that many non-Western peoples, like many Westerners, are involved with a special galaxy of spirit beings outside the boundaries of what Westerners may take to be objective reality. But on Fáánakkar, as elsewhere, spirit relationships are part of an elaborate, widely shared belief system understood to represent reality. People there believe in, see, and talk to spirit beings not because they are childlike or psychotic but because they have been enculturated in a society that views these beings as real and that provides implicit instruction in techniques for communicating with them. We are dealing here not with mental inferiority but cultural relativity. The evidence clearly indicates that where the cultural orientation is favorable and where instructional techniques are available, most humans can learn to have visionary experiences that American psychiatrists would characterize as hallucinations. All that is necessary is a minor shift in belief and a certain amount of concentration on ordinary fantasy imagery. The Sufi disciples I studied are taught to conjure up and concentrate on an interior image of their master's face. This, it is taught, will allow the master's spirit to visit by merging with the inner image. By cultivating inner imagery, disciples learn to "hallucinate" messages from their master's spirit. In more advanced Sufism, techniques to induce trance are developed and cultivated. Furthermore, people who display a special inclination toward nonordinary, "hallucinatory" modes of perception will be treated not as stigmatized deviants but as especially gifted and talented fakirs. The same is true on Fáánakkar. There, the medium role seems to serve as a haven for people especially inclined toward hallucinatory social relationships. However, it is not just specialists who see and talk to spirits. Most ordinary people also have such experiences. So-called primitives engage in what Brussel sees as hallucinatory social relationships not because their thinking is infantile or psychotic but because they are operating with a culturally constituted mode of perception and belief different from that currently in favor in contemporary middle-class America.

But what of the equation between children and psychotics? As Brussel observes, children in our society often "see" and "talk to" fictitious beings. The classic example is the imaginary friend relationship often present in American children between the ages of two and six. Typical imaginary companions include animals (a friendly tiger), animal-human figures (Mickey Mouse), supernatural creatures (elves), and imaginary children. Typically, the child does not merely recognize the existence of such a being but engages in elaborate social interactions with it. One informant recalled her relationships with an invisible boy-girl figure named James-Judy.

My imaginary friend would be invited to birthday parties, tea parties, doctor appointments and simply to play at my house when no "real" playmate was available. In being by my side, James-Judy became both a protector at doctor appointments and a companion. Unfortunately she/he could only talk to me and we conversed in a secret language.

Here, as in many such relationships, the child not only talks to the imaginary companion but "hears," that is "hallucinates," its voice.[37]

Again, such beings are often directly drawn from the media; from children's television ("Six Million Dollar Man," "Wonder Woman") from movies, and from children's books. One informant drew her companion from a picture on her living room wall.

According to my mother, my family's introduction to Saucy came when my mom and I (age two and a half years) were just leaving to go shopping. I had yelled, "Wait a minute!", jumped onto the living room couch, reached my hand up to the painted path in a picture of an old summer alpine chalet, took "something" down from the painting, and then had raced back to my mom, ready to go shopping with her.

"What have you got in your hand?" my mother asked me.

"Saucy."

"Who's Saucy?"

"She's somebody," was all I said.

It seemed that Saucy and I had a close friendship which was not to be shared beyond ourselves. I still do not know where the name Saucy came from, but I do know that I was nearly fanatical about taking her with me whenever I went out of the house. Being at most two inches high, Saucy slipped easily into my coat pocket and seemed perfectly satisfied with the snug accommodation.

I had "three-dimensionalized" that painting which hung above our couch. I used to stand very close to the painting, as close as I could possibly get, and I would enter into the world of the painting; I firmly believed that I was walking up the rocky dirt path which led to Saucy's door. I would knock on the door and ask if Saucy would come out to play. Although she seemed like my constant companion, she also had an independence of her own which I learned to respect, for she was not always available every time I wanted to be with her; that is, she too had her own life.

As I recall her, Saucy was older than I, she was about nine years old, dressed in what I can vaguely describe as layers of woolen cloth garments. Her hair was blond and worn in braids. She sounds a lot like Heidi of the Alps, but when I asked my parents whether I'd had any type of media exposure to Heidi, they said that my introduction to Heidi occurred after Saucy was already going strong. I wouldn't be surprised, however, if my parents were wrong in their response, for the parallels between Saucy and Heidi seem to be quite strong.

Another informant drew her imaginary companion from *Harvey*, a movie about imaginary companions. Harvey is a six-foot-tall rabbit, the invisible pooka (a Celtic spirit creature) companion of Elwood P. Dowd, played in the movie by Jimmy Stewart.

All of his [Jimmy Stewart's] relatives thought he had gone senile and should be committed. I believed he actually saw the rabbit because I saw the six-foot animal myself. I fantasized that the rabbit left Jimmy and came to live with me. I would talk to Harvey at the dinner table. . . . When my siblings were harassing me, I would give the threat that Harvey will beat them up.

Her young sister—perhaps out of envy as much as altruism—soon developed a similar imaginary companion of her own: "My younger sister, thinking Harvey might be lonely, introduced her invisible friend, Joe. Joe was a six-foot bear. Joe was just as real as Harvey to us. Harvey and Joe never got along, though, so they were constantly fighting. My sister and I spent much time separating them." Here, as in many other instances, imaginary companions may structure the child's actual interactions. As with the hallucinatory relationships of psychotics, these imaginary companions can affect the individual's actual social conduct.

There is a definite social dimension to these imaginary companions; they often fill a gap in the child's actual social world. Many children with imaginary companions are either first-born children or have no siblings near their own age. Thus the imaginary companion may often provide a kind of substitute sibling.[38] There is also a cultural dimension. Children have these relationships not only because they are "more imaginative" than adults but also because they are not yet fully enculturated. They have not fully learned—or learned to take fully seriously—the culturally constituted distinction between imagination and reality that older persons are not only expected but required to maintain and display.

Until quite recently, even childhood imaginary relationships were viewed negatively by many parents and psychologists. As Maya Pines writes, "Only a generation ago, children who reported imaginary companions of this sort were thought to be hallucinating and dangerously removed from reality. Their alarmed parents generally tried to cure them. 'The child is crazy. We must take him to a doctor.'"[39] Some psychologists continue to feel that imaginary companions are a dangerous symptom of insecurity, withdrawal, and latent mental disorder, but many now believe that childhood imaginary companions are not abnormal either statistically or in terms of their consequences for mental health. It now appears that a majority of American children have such companions (65 percent according to one study).[40] It is true that such children are different from those without imaginary companions, but they are different in a positive, not a negative way. "The children who had imaginary companions differed sharply from the rest; they were less aggressive and more cooperative; they smiled more; they were seldom bored; their language was richer and more advanced. . . ." Once again there was a media connection. "Another major difference was that the children with imaginary playmates watched far less television—only half as many hours per week. And even when they did watch the screen, their choice of programs was quite different; they were not interested in the cartoons and violent shows that the other group preferred."[41] In summing up the study, psychologist Dorothy Singer comments as follows: "All the constructive characteristics seem to be correlated with imaginary playmates in our children. . . . So although the emphasis used to be on pathology, we see these imaginary companions as a sign of health."[42]

Brussel is correct in noting that children, like psychotics, have imaginary companions. He appears to be wrong in imputing pathological characteristics to such children. Our children's distrust of imaginary processes has again distorted the positive significance of imaginary social relationships. Speculating on the positive aspects of these relationships, Julian Jaynes has even gone so far as to argue that in "a proper society" children might be permitted to keep their imaginary friends, who "could become full-fledged gods, guiding persons into adulthood."[43] In psychiatric writing, psychotics may be compared to children, but it is explicitly assumed that they are radically different from normal adults. "Normals" are assumed to be fully in touch with "reality," since they are not caught up in pseudo relationships with a delusional community of imaginary beings. As we saw earlier, this assumption is erroneous. People in our society do not give up imaginary companions at all. As they get older, they merely change their gods and their modes of friendship. Through media relations, dreams, stream-of-consciousness processes, and fantasy, normal American adults extensively engage in imaginary social interactions. Brussel is correct in noting some similarities among the imaginary relations of children, psychotics, and "primitives." He is wrong in assuming that imaginary relations distinguish such people from normal American adults.

This is not to say that there are no significant differences between normals and psychotics. Rather, the differences which probably do exist are more complex and less clear-cut than is often assumed—partly because formulations about psychotic imaginary relationships are not sufficiently informed by an accurate appraisal of the power and elaborateness of normal pseudo communities. It may be argued that what distinguishes psychotic imaginary relationships from those of normals is that psychotics "hallucinate" while normals "fantasize." However, this distinction is far from clear-cut. Some of my normal informants not only experience vivid visualizations of media figures in "fantasy" but also sometimes take these experiences to be real communications. Normal people also readily experience powerful waking hallucinations while influenced by consciousness-altering drugs such as LSD. Here again people often experience vivid "meetings" with imaginary beings. One study of 206 subjects who had taken LSD reported that 58 percent saw images of figures such as Christ, Buddha, and William Blake.[44]

The hallucinations of drug use are paralleled by hallucinations associated with the fevers of infectious illness. Such conditions not only produce simple hallucinations such as seeing dots or fog; they often lead to imaginary social relationships. One informant, hospitalized and delirious after a complex arm fracture, experienced the following encounters:

While lying in my hospital bed, I saw people peering around the corner in the window at me. I could never get a good look at them until a man in an overcoat tried to get in, rapping on the window. I called a nurse, who explained we were on the eighth floor.

A fellow across the hall had hobbled over to chat with me. He was recuperating from a car wreck but could get up and around. I liked him a lot, but noticed that a group of people visiting him were laughing and talking about me. Were they part of the plot (it was becoming a plot now) that I was unearthing operating in this hospital?

A Hasidic Jew, his long black beard hanging down over his black coat, stood to the right of my bed. Every now and then he would push my left arm and the slightest movement of that arm in traction would cause me intense pain. "Stop it!" I cried, but he would just smile and do it again. . . .

Not all my spectral visitors were malevolent. In particular, I remember a Russian count and countess, in elegant garb such as they would wear to a court ball in the eighteenth or nineteenth century, dancing around my bed. They ignored me, but their presence was a relief and a source of comfort.

It should also be noted that many ordinary Americans under quite ordinary conditions occasionally experience quasi-mystical visionary states of consciousness. Some of these involve the felt presence of mysterious beings. As sociologist Andrew Greeley notes, most social scientists have either ignored such experiences or dismissed them as "abnormal." Greeley argues that such experiences are both healthy and common. A study by Greeley and one of his associates suggests that such experiences may occur regularly in as much as a fifth of the American population.[45]

Schizophrenics, to be sure, often seem to have negative and destructive hallucinatory relationships involving hostility, anxiety, depression, and an inability to function acceptably in ordinary social roles. However, in comparing normal and schizophrenic imaginary systems, we are typically comparing free "normals" and institutionalized "schizophrenics." This difference in actual social situations is significant. It may be that the seemingly distinctive marks of psychosis—including psychological distress and inability to function appropriately—are not so much the product of the schizophrenic's hallucinatory systems as they are of the negative treatment the person has received from society—both before and after hospitalization. Certainly the experience of labeling and institutionalization is an extremely traumatic and damaging psychological experience.

This suggests that a more adequate understanding of hallucinatory and delusionary social systems will call for a number of revised ethnographic procedures. First, we need to know a great deal more about the "subjective cultures" of normals, including the quasi-hallucinatory social interactions experienced by ordinary socially successful adults.[46] We will also need to study more carefully the inner worlds of schizophrenics. We need to know more about the delusionary systems of hospitalized schizophrenics, but even more we need to investigate the imaginary systems and actual social situations of nonhospitalized schizophrenics or schizophreniclike individuals. The study of such cases might contribute greatly to our understanding of the inner worlds of hallucinatory systems and to our understanding of the social and cultural dimensions of such systems.

Let us consider one example, a case study by June Macklin based on anthropological field work in Connecticut. Rita M., the sixth of her parents' nine children, was born in Vermont in 1909. She grew up in a small town in Connecticut, where her father worked as a railroad foreman, and the outward events of her early years were not unusual. She attended school through the eighth grade, worked in a variety of sales clerk jobs, and married at age nineteen. However, even as a child Mrs. M. was different from her siblings. "I was kind of a dreamer, I lived in a world of my own. I don't mean I was odd. I had friends, but books fascinated me. My sister, the one next to me, was more of a tomboy and I was more of the quiet type."[47] She was not just a quiet type. At about age five she had a frightening vision of a child kneeling near her bed. As she grew older she saw strange beings wandering about the house. "They looked real. They had clothes, and they looked like flesh. There was nothing ghostlike or vaporish about them."[48] But

219

the rest of her family could not see them. Her mother became anxious that Rita was "a little off." Her brothers took the same view and used to torment her, saying, "You're crazy. You belong in the bug house!" Given such social reactions, Rita learned to keep quiet about these special perceptions. As she grew older, however, she continued to have visionary experiences and "floating away spells."

I would actually have the sensation of floating. I know now that it's called cataleptic clairvoyance or astrotraveling. It could happen anywhere. I could have been washing dishes, and I'd all of a sudden be looking at different cities or different country scenes. One time I remember looking down, seeing a big building, and I know now that what I saw was Westminster Abbey, although I didn't know it then.[49]

As a thirteen-year-old, Mrs. M. wanted to go to college and to become a teacher or a nurse, but her parents opposed her. At age nineteen she married a man of Italian-American background, concealing from him as well her visions and floating away spells. After the birth of her first child she began to experience considerable physical and mental distress associated with an increase in her hallucinatory experience: "From the time he was about three months old was when psychic things began to happen more and more to the point where I wasn't feeling well. I went to doctor after doctor. I had terrible stomach trouble. . . . I realize that if psychiatry was as prevalent then as it is today, they would have sent me to a psychiatrist first thing."[50] On one occasion she saw a vision of her great-grandmother, and on another she saw a man in the garb of a monk next to her baby's crib. Her anxiety increased to the point of terror, she felt like she was being watched constantly, she was frightened to go into her son's dark room at night, and she was scared of being left alone. Then she had an even more dramatic encounter with the mysterious monk figure. Her sister was sick and she had gone to her house to help.

I had fed and bathed her four children and my own son, and sank exhausted onto the closed toilet seat in the bathroom, the children's soiled clothing in my hands. Suddenly a figure was in front of me, dressed in a monk's habit, and the face cowled so that one could not see it. This figure stood a table length's away from me. I was petrified. The light was on in that room, so it was illuminated. I said, "Oh my God don't show me your face." I thought that if I saw a face, I'd faint dead away. In the meantime, all the kids had gone to sleep. The figure flashed out. Right where the figure had come, these eyes came and stood about a foot and a half from me. The eyes were brown. They had the most kindly look I've ever seen in anybody's eyes. They stood in front of me and just stared right into mine. I couldn't take my eyes away if you paid me a million dollars.

I was so scared that I couldn't move anyway. All of a sudden, after staring at me for a few seconds, they flashed off. They came again in the corner of the room up over the sink, looked at me, and all of a sudden they were gone. Then over the sink in little blue chip diamonds, it started to form this thing. It spelled out my initials, R.A. (A.'s my maiden name). I saw them etch it. By the time that was finished, I had gotten hold of myself. I went out of the house flying and onto the porch. I got myself in the corner with my knees up against my chest. I'm in the corner of the house and I'm just rigid, I'm so scared. It's a good thing that the kids didn't wake up. . . . They could have screamed bloody murder; I wouldn't have gone back into the house.

After I had been out there about a half hour—holding myself rigid, visualizing it over and over again, scared to death—my husband stepped onto the porch. He looked over and said, "What are you doing there?" That's all he had to say. Suddenly I was laughing, crying, shaking, I went hysterical. He didn't know what the devil had happened. He ran in the house, wet a towel and mopped my face with it. He got me up. I just cried and cried, and shook, and laughed. I just didn't know what I was doing. Finally, after fifteen to twenty minutes, he got me calmed down.[51]

At this point in her life, Mrs. M. was clearly a person in very poor psychological condition. She was not only anxious and nervous about her special perceptions; she was terrified. Partly her fear was based on the strangeness of the visionary experience itself, but partly it had to do with her interpretation of what these visions meant. Her husband thought she was going crazy and Mrs. M. shared this view; she felt she was "losing her mind," she "feared for her sanity."[52]

From a psychiatric perspective, this interpretation seems correct. If she had presented the above symptoms to a psychiatrist on the ward I studied, she would undoubtedly have been diagnosed as a "paranoid schizophrenic" and committed to a state mental hospital. She had all the "classic symptoms." Her visions, of course, would be seen as extreme "hallucinations." She was extremely anxious and was losing emotional control. She was potentially dangerous to herself and others. What if her child was choking in his crib but the monk was there too? What if the monk appeared beside her while she was driving a car in traffic? She seemed to be well into the throes of a severe psychotic episode. Mrs. M. recognized this herself. On her visits to the doctors, she avoided mention of her psychic experiences because she knew "they would put me down in the state (mental) hospital." [53]

Instead her life took a very different course. Although she received no psychological therapy, a few years later she was characterized as a "self-actualized" woman of "superior competence," an "energetic," "intelligent," "articulate," "optimistic," "self-confident," "warm, nurturing woman," with a good sense of humor. [54] She was characterized, that is, in terms suggesting the very picture of positive mental health. What had happened?

Worried about her daughter and seeking an explanation for her problems, Rita M.'s mother took her to a local card reader and spirit medium. This medium offered an interpretation at odds with the pathology-oriented explanation she and her family had previously suspected. The reader said that Mrs. M. was not sick but that she was "going under control," that is, making contact with a guide from the spirit world. The reader said she was a potential spirit medium. Told about the monk's visit, the reader was not surprised: "She knew about that spirit's visit, and told me that I shouldn't have been so frightened, that it was only my 'guide,' and that someday he would put me under control. I told her I didn't want to see anything like that, but she responded that what I wanted didn't matter: it is what "they" [the spirits] wanted that counted." [55] Reluctantly at first, and later with enthusiasm, Mrs. M. began to study spiritualist books and to attend meetings of the National Spiritualist Association of Churches. There she encountered other mediums who recognized her as a potential medium and urged her to develop her spiritualist talents. Pursuing a course of spiritualist study, she gradually learned to deal with her special perceptions as "gifts," and she achieved the ability to go into a trance at will. In this "unconscious state" she "communicates with beings in Summerland" (the spirit world). Ordinarily her guide puts her in contact with the spirits of particular deceased persons, who then take possession of her and speak their own words through her mouth.

Now, at age sixty-five, she is a highly successful trance medium. She is an ordained spiritualist minister, instructs a group of apprentices, and conducts a highly successful and lucrative business "reading" for clients. By entering trance states, she provides hidden information from the spirit world. Among others, she helps clients who are suffering from "mental problems." Aside from the time spent on her annual six-week vacation in Florida, she works every week. She has four appointments a morning, five days a week, and, without advertising, is booked up two months in advance. For years she has had no symptoms of anxiety. On the contrary, she is a happy and successful woman.[56]

This case raises a number of important points. First, it provides vivid illustration of the relativity of imagination and reality that exists within American society. Even in a small Connecticut town, it is possible to move from a social circle that views "seeing things" as psychotic hallucinations to a spiritualist group in which the same phenomena are viewed as a sign of special talent. Even more striking is the effect that social transit between these groups—and their schemes of interpretation—had on the psychological and social functioning of Mrs. M. In her younger days, her special perceptions were seen by herself and by others as a distressing sign of mental illness. Reinterpreted by the spiritualist culture, the same characteristics—her imaginary social interactions—emerged not as attributes of illness but as special gifts. This reinterpretation allowed a radical and far-reaching shift in self-conception, and she now sees herself as an unusually gifted and talented person. This shift also led to a radical change in social competency and social functioning. Because of her gifts, she is now admired and respected by others and placed in a rewarding social role that allows for American dream style success—professional expertise, collegial respect, admiring and grateful clients, and financial reward. Her case provides direct confirmation of the view that the negative attributes of persons we view as mentally ill can be a product of their social treatment, not of their hallucinatory experience. The very basis of Mrs. M.'s success is her hallucinatory social relationships with spirit beings.

Among the galaxy of spirit associates who regularly speak through Mrs. M. are her guide, the all-knowing and wise monk; a Baptist minister, Dr. Denton; a little girl named Daisy; and Nadaena, an ancient Egyptian ruler's daughter. Macklin suggests that Mrs. M. is herein solving her Oedipus-Electra complex. Without resorting to such psychoanalytic interpretation, it is nonetheless easy to agree that these spirit relationships are satisfying—they provide not only social respect and financial success but also strong personal satisfaction. The monk and Dr. Denton can be seen as providing Mrs. M. with a kind of vicarious fulfillment of her frustrated desire for academic credentials and a professional career, while the willful Nadaena allows her to express the rebellious side of her personality. Macklin gives this succinct summation:

Supported by a band of diverse spirit guides orchestrated by an all-caring, all-knowing, and constantly attentive monk control, she is able to become whatever she wishes by complementary projection: an all-powerful and wise male; a well-educated male doctor whose credentials are impeccable; a mischievous child, center of attention which she herself never had; a high-born self-indulgent and powerful Egyptian woman; and so forth. By supplementary projection, she can also foist onto the spirits the unacceptable attributes she finds in herself: the engaging child spirit also is irresponsible; the Egyptian was not only selfish, she also wilfully destroyed those who crossed her.[57]

Socially, such beings allow spiritual mediums to achieve roles that have been denied them or to repair flawed roles and relationships. For some mediums, this even extends to romantic love relationships. While Mrs. M. denies that the monk serves this role for her, some mediums carry out love relationships with their guides and may even have sexual relationships with them.[58] It is also possible for the medium to restructure social relationships with actual others once they have died. The powerful satisfaction to be had here is vividly illustrated by the report of another medium, a sixty-year-old man who had always experienced difficulties with his strict father.

We always called my father the Boss, never Father or Dad. Well, after he died he came back as he was in life, just like a bull in a china shop, blustering and giving orders. I told him "You think you're still alive: well you're not! You're not the boss any longer. I'm the boss, now. And don't you come back until you can behave yourself, and conduct yourself civilly." When he did return he came back on his knees—*on his knees*—humble and asking forgiveness.[59]

These spirit relationships also have interesting connections to cultural values. Some authors have seen the schizophrenic's pseudo community as a negation of cultural values, but in Mrs. M.'s situation, the hallucinatory relationships *support* basic cultural values. June Macklin explicitly develops the social aspect of this connection: "Furthermore, the spirit teachers always counsel in terms of the values of a stable society and plump for the re-establishment of traditional family and marital relationships."[60] The importance of work, achievement, and success are strongly emphasized. "The spirits appear to be inner-directed nineteenth century individualists and counsel accordingly."[61] The hallucinatory system of social relationships thus operates to reinforce and support the traditional values of middle-class American society.

The case of Mrs. M. shows that a person with a "schizophrenic" set of hallucinatory relationships can function successfully within the context of American society. It also suggests that at least some of our seemingly bizarre, incompetent, institutionalized schizophrenics might have achieved mental health and social competency had they been fortunate enough to experience a more favorable social and cultural context within which to make use of their special hallucinatory or visionary talents. Likewise, it is easy to imagine what Mrs. M. would have become had she been institutionalized in the state mental hospital at age nineteen.

Her case raises another interesting question as well. What is the proper diagnosis for Mrs. M. now? On the one hand, she has most of the attributes of positive mental health; on the other, she has primary attributes of psychosis. Macklin seems unsure about the proper diagnosis and, apparently as a compromise, settles for "neurotic." This seems unjustified. Mrs. M. lacks the definitive attribute of neurosis, subjective anxiety; her only psychiatric symptoms, hallucinations and dissociation, indicate psychosis, not neurosis.

One October day, on the psychiatric ward I studied in Philadelphia, I happened to observe a somewhat similar case. Mrs. J. was a heavyset, forty-year-old black woman from New York who spoke English with a Caribbean accent. She had been picked up by the police at Philadelphia International Airport for acting "strangely," for breaking the rules of comportment in American airports. She had been haranguing other travelers about "the end of the world," she was carrying a paper bag full of money, and she was nude underneath her dress. The mental status exam proceeded as follows:

Psychiatrist: Who are you?

Mrs. J.: (no response)

Psychiatrist: You were confused yesterday. Maybe you can give us a better story today. Open your eyes! Who are you?

Mrs. J.: I am the prophetess of destruction. I am Jeremiah, I am a Jewish angel.

Psychiatrist: What were you doing at the airport?

Mrs. J.: I have been sent here to warn people to repent. The end of the world is coming and everything is going to be destroyed. God only uses me as an instrument. I am like a carcass, I have no flesh.

Psychiatrist: Where did you get the money?

Mrs. J.: The Lord supplied me. I work in a nursing home. It's not me here now. God sends it through me. You are hearing it, I am talking it, He is speaking it. I only open my mouth, as a telephone. (Mrs. J.'s tone of voice changes; she continues in a deeper voice) This is God speaking. Love, smile, cry.

Psychiatrist: (interrupting) You are *God* speaking?

Mrs. J.: Don't plan no more, it's all over. There will be no more mercy. . . .

Psychiatrist: (interrupting) Describe God!

Mrs. J.: God resembles Satan but He is not Satan. . . . I came here as the mother of Jesus, I don't have a mother and father now. . . . My husband is in Heaven.

Psychiatrist: We know he is in Jamaica.

Mrs. J.: The Rapture. . . . (she drifts into a long, rambling, seemingly garbled religious harangue)

Mrs. J., like Mrs. M., was a possession trance medium. She belonged to a Protestant sect based in both the eastern United States and Jamaica, and she was engaged in missionary work. Asked about who she was, she had responded by listing the spirits who possessed her and by demonstrating her role through entering a trance state and having God speak through her. Unfortunately, such behavior is not considered "appropriate" in the mental status examination. The psychiatrists viewed Mrs. J. not in terms of her cultural background but in terms of their conceptualizations of individual pathology. She was characterized as "having just about all the dynamics you can think of: schizophrenic withdrawal, depersonalization, dissociation, blocking, evasiveness, avoidance of reality, guilt, religiosity, autistic thinking, inappropriate affect, and loose associations." The diagnosis was "paranoid schizophrenic," the prognosis was considered poor, and the recommendation was for institutionalization.

It is possible that the psychiatrists were right. It may be that Mrs. J. was indeed a seriously disturbed person psychologically. There were indications—from phone conversations to New York—that some of her fellow church members regarded her as unstable. It is also possible that Mrs. J.'s apparent psychological distress was due less to underlying mental problems than to her current social circumstances—to culture shock, to the police action, to her involuntary incarceration on a locked mental ward, to forced drug medication, and to the threat of permanent institutionalization. If this is so, then the diagnosis was both misguided and destructive.

Whatever the case with Mrs. J., such a diagnosis would clearly be inadmissible in the case of Mrs. M. Knowing her nonhospital context, we know that here is no evidence of symptoms that could provide reasonable legal justification for involuntary institutionalization. Mrs. M. does not need help. If she is "schizophrenic," she is a highly successful, happy, socially well-adjusted schizophrenic.

One important difference between Mrs. M. and L. Percy King is that Mrs. M.'s hallucinatory system is integrated into the cultural knowledge and social order of the spiritualist subgroup. Mrs. M.

began her hallucinatory relations with the monk on her own, but she later made adjustments in this relationship as she converted to the spiritualist subculture. By contrast, L. Percy King has developed his relations with the pursuers entirely on his own. Theoretically, at least, these beliefs could be not only understood but accepted by others, and King has energetically tried to persuade others of the validity of his "discoveries." However, there is no evidence that anyone else accepts his reality.

This is the usual situation of the paranoid schizophrenic. This too is his tragedy. Since the pseudo community is a solitary system, it does not provide the basis for cooperative and satisfying actual social relations with real others. Norman Cameron suggests that such paranoid systems cannot be shared. "His attitudes and interpretations are not and cannot be shared by other individuals within the social field, since these others do not and cannot share his delusional reconstruction."[62] But this is not always true. There are well-documented cases in which a paranoid schizophrenic's system has been partially or totally accepted by others. Cameron himself presents such an example. He illustrates his discussion of the paranoid pseudo community by reference to the case of a businessman who falsely believed that murderous gangsters were after him. As Cameron's account shows, this man succeeded in temporarily converting a real relative into an ally.

From his room the patient telephoned a relative and told him the whole story. The relative, who was well aware of the patient's intelligence and business acumen, accepted everything and agreed that the patient must somehow escape the murderers. The two arranged to leave the next morning secretly by car and take a long trip.[63]

In this case the conversion was only fleeting—the businessman actually fled alone—but there are other cases in which a more lasting conversion develops. This has even occurred in therapy, in the context of a social relationship explicitly designed to destroy the hallucinatory system of meaning. Psychiatrist Robert Lindner's description of his treatment of the schizophrenic Kirk Allen illustrates the powerful appeal a hallucinatory system of social relationships can have not only for its creator but for another person as well.

228

Lindner's account begins in the late 1940s, when he is called by the doctor of a government installation in the Southwest where work is being done on a secret project. The doctor is concerned about one of the physicists whose work has dropped off and who, in explanation, claims to have been involved in mysterious outer space journeys. Before agreeing to take the case, Lindner asks the project doctor about the patient's condition. Is he dangerous, will he need hospitalization? The answer is no.

"I really can't explain how it works exactly," the doctor continued, "but I have the impression his psychosis—I suppose that's what it is—doesn't interfere with his ability to take care of himself or get around in a normal fashion. At least not at this point. I'd say from what he's told me that he has a certain control over it—can get in and out of it when he wants to, I mean. And he's really one of the mildest, nicest chaps ever." [64]

Intrigued, Lindner agrees to take the case. Kirk Allen comes to Baltimore, takes up residence in the city, begins to participate in its social life, and visits Lindner's office an hour a day for psychiatric therapy. Lindner finds that Allen does claim to take journeys to outer space but that he is also absolutely convinced of his own sanity. To begin the treatment, Lindner decides to explore Allen's unusual background.

His American parents were living on Hawaii when Allen was born, and they hired a young Polynesian woman just down from the hills to serve as his nurse. Neglected by his father and mother, Allen was cared for largely by this nurse, whom he loved dearly and from whom he learned his first language, a local Hawaiian dialect. The nurse died when he was six. By then he and his family were living on an outer Pacific island, where his father was district commissioner. Allen had no contact with white children and was thrown instead into the activities of the native children of this traditional Pacific island. Continued neglect by his parents and unpleasant encounters with a series of American governesses—one of whom seduced and sexually abused him at age ten—continued his unusual enculturation.

Noting the parental neglect, the trauma of his nurse's death, and the sexual abuse, Lindner offers a quasi-psychoanalytic interpretation of how this background may have led to the development

229

of his "psychosis," but cultural interpretation is also possible. Brought up by a Hawaiian nurse, Allen initially learned Polynesian ideas about the distinction between imagination and reality. This influence continued through Allen's association with the Pacific island children—as Lindner observes, "In his soul he was an islander." But at the same time Allen was taught American reality by his parents, his governesses, and his books. This contradictory enculturation may have contributed to the formulation of both his hallucinatory world and his ability to alternate between different systems of reality.

In any case, the origin of his delusionary system was a standard media relationship. Lonely on his island, Kirk Allen developed an intense admiration relationship with the all-conquering hero of an adventurous series of American science fiction novels. He was attracted to this heroic space explorer partly because he happened to share the name Kirk Allen.

As I read about the adventures of Kirk Allen in these books the conviction began to grow on me that the stories were not only true to the very last detail but that they were about me. In some weird and inexplicable way I knew that what I was reading was my biography. Nothing in these books was unfamiliar to me. I recognized everything—the scenes, the people. . . . My everyday life began to recede at this point. In fact, it became fiction—and, as it did, the books became my reality. To daily affairs, to the task of staying alive, eating, studying, moving about on the island, I gave little attention—for this was dream. Real life—my real life—was in the books. There I lived; there I had my being. . . . It was, of course, a curious position to be in—an adolescent boy remembering the adventures of himself as a grown man. But I got around this difficulty by convincing myself that the books had been composed in the future and had been sent back by some means into the present for my instruction. . . . At any time of the day or night, with hardly any effort, I could select an incident or an adventure and, while appearing to be doing what was expected of me at that moment, I would actually be living a completely different life by simultaneous process of recall of the past and experience in the present.[65]

Meanwhile, on this planet, the earthly Kirk Allen continued his education through college and graduate school—where he obtained his Ph.D. in physics—and obtained his job on the government project. There he developed yet another aspect of his system, the ability to teleport himself into the space world. Unable to "remember" the details of some important photographic maps that he knew to be located in a file in his outer space palace, Kirk became intensely frustrated.

I wracked my brains trying to recall the landscape I had flown over, and the pictures I had glanced at casually before putting them away. No use. I was furious. . . . And then I thought: "If only . . . if only I were there, right now, I would go directly to those files and get those pictures!"

No sooner had I given voice to this thought than my whole being seemed to respond with a resounding "Why not?"—and in that same moment I was there!

How can I explain this to you? One moment I was just a scientist on X Reservation bending over a drawing board. . . . the next moment I was Kirk Allen, Lord of a planet in an interplanetary empire in a distant universe, garbed in the robes of his exalted office, rising from the carved desk he had been sitting at, walking toward a secret room in his palace. . . .

It was over in a matter of minutes, and I was again at the drawing board—the self you see here. But I knew the experience was real; and to prove it I now had a vivid recollection of the photographs. . . .

You can imagine how this experience affected me. I was stunned by it, shaken to the core, but excited as I had never been. In some way I could not comprehend, by merely desiring it to be so, I had crossed the immensities of Space, broken out of Time, and merged with—literally become—that distant and future self whose like I had until now been remembering. . . . From that night on I have spent more and more time being the Kirk Allen of the future. At any time, no matter where I am or what I am doing, I can will to be him, and at once I am. As him, as my future self, I live his life; and when I return to this present self, I bring back the memories I have of that future and so am able to correct the records I am keeping. . . . But what got me in trouble, I think, and led to my being sent here, is the fact that I've been spending more and more of my time as the other Kirk Allen. . . . I don't think I can be blamed for this—his is such an exciting life compared with mine; but of course I have a job to do here.[66]

In the early phase of therapy, Kirk Allen's personal system of knowledge includes the following postulates. First, there are two separate worlds, the world of ordinary American society and another world out in space that is in the future but coexists with the present on another temporal plane. Second, Kirk believes that he has the power to travel back and forth between these two worlds by means of a mysterious mechanism he does not fully understand but that he thinks may involve a "telepathic state" or "teleportation." Whatever the mechanism, Kirk believes that he "really" experiences visits to the outer space planet. This other planet is not empty. It is full of other beings—it is a social world, and that constitutes much of its appeal. When he goes there, he assumes a heroic self and plays out dramatic interactions in the roles of Lord of the Planet, Space Pilot, Warrior, and Notorious Lover of Beautiful Women. This is his experience, and this for him is reality.

Robert Lindner believes otherwise. He is convinced of two things—first of Kirk's "utter madness" and second of the "life-sustaining necessity of his psychosis." He recognizes that it is a highly meaningful and gratifying system. However, as his report indicates, he never considers leaving this system intact. Theoretically, at least, it would have been possible to assume that Allen's temporary job difficulties might be adjusted—thus returning him to full-time work—without attacking his meaning system. After all, Allen had lived with it successfully for years, was even now able to function quite well, to go in and out of his system at will, and was recognized as "one of the mildest, nicest chaps ever." But such nonintervention is not the role of a psychiatrist in our society. Instead Lindner sets out with cool calculation and deliberate deceit to destroy Kirk Allen's other world—to "assault his psychosis" and to "wean him of his madness."[67]

Frustrated by the ineffectiveness of his initial attempts at "therapy" and discouraged by Kirk Allen's continued matter-of-fact insistence on the reality of his other world., Lindner considers and rejects the more drastic "therapeutic" methods of shock treatment and lobotomy. He settles instead on the unusual technique of "participation therapy." In essence this means that he pretends to go along with the validity of Kirk's system as a maneuver for destroying it. Pretending sympathy and belief, he asks for Kirk's written records, maps, and charts. He pores over this material and enculturates himself into Allen's system. He also sends Kirk off on special journeys to the other world in order to work out gaps and contradictions in the record.

In the course of his feigned involvement, an interesting transformation takes place—in Lindner. He becomes attracted to the system he had intended to destroy. As he becomes increasingly "obsessed" with Kirk's world, his concern with real matters fades. He loses interest in his other patients and his work begins to fall off. Poring over the manuscripts by night and thinking about them by day, Lindner begins to lose contact with ordinary American reality.[68] Lindner attributes his fascination with Allen's world to several different factors. He is bored with his current social situation and depressed by his sense that he is growing old. He has had a lifelong "addiction" to science fiction and an active fantasy life. But the primary appeal of Kirk's system is that it provides a vehicle through which he can realize certain personally satisfying social relationships. Through identification and fantasy, Lindner begins to participate vicariously in Allen's social world.

With but a small step of an already lively imagination, I could escape from the prison of time: I could be geologist, explorer, astronomer, historian, physicist, adventurer and all those other enviable beings whose roles I had, at one time or another, played in my own pallid fantasies and whose knowledge I have always wanted to possess. This was a potent allure. . . . The materials of Kirk's psychosis and the Achilles heel of my personality met and meshed like the gears of a clock.[69]

Lindner claims that he never fully entered Allen's world—that he always realized that the "trips" were impossible. He "overlooked" this, however, and in doing so took part in Allen's reality. His consciousness was invaded to the point of "obsession," as he felt the magnetic pull of Allen's enticing world. During this period, therapy ceased. Kirk arrived each day for his hour of therapy, but his interactions with Lindner were no longer structured by the roles of patient to psychiatrist, they were structured by their shared, mutual involvement in Allen's outer space world.

Eventually, as Lindner writes, "The folly we shared collapsed." Allen confesses that he has been "lying" to Lindner, that he had seen through the "trips" weeks ago. When asked why he continued to pretend, Allen replies, "Because I felt I had to . . . because I felt you *wanted me to*!" [70]

Lindner admits that his extraordinary experience helped to shake him out of the smug sense that schizophrenic realities are only for others. But the importance of this case for our purposes is that it shows how a schizophrenic style imaginary social world can exert such a powerful appeal that it may draw others into its orbit. Here we see how a shared hallucinatory social world can structure actual social relationships. While the concept is controversial, the possibility of this process is recognized in the technical vocabulary of psychiatry as "folie-à-deux," a madness shared by two people. (If madness is shared by three it becomes "folie-à-trois," and so forth.) This appears to be the situation that began to develop during Milton Rokeach's study *The Three Christs of Ypsilanti*.

Rokeach may have been inspired by Lindner, since he cites the Kirk Allen case in his introduction, but he takes a somewhat different approach to the problem. He raises the possibility that a confrontation between two deluded persons might lead to a cure, since, he theorizes, two people cannot share the same delusion. In effect, Rokeach does not believe in folie-à-deux. He thinks Lindner's and Allen's folly collapsed precisely because the delusion became socially shared. He also cites another case described by Lindner.

This fantastic situation can also be represented by imagining an encounter between two victims of, let us say, the Napoleonic delusion. The conviction of each that he is the real Napoleon must be called into question by the presence of the other. . . . Some years ago I observed exactly this while on the staff of a psychiatric sanitarium in Maryland. At that time we had a middle-aged paranoid woman who clung to the delusion that she was Mary, Mother of God. It happened that we admitted another patient with the same delusion some months after the first had been received. . . . On the lawn one day, happily in the presence of another staff member and myself, the two deluded women met and began to exchange confidences. Before long each revealed to the other her "secret" identity. What followed was most instructive. The first, our "oldest" patient, received the information with visible perturbation and an immediate reaction of startle. "Why you can't be, my dear," she said, "you must be crazy. I am the Mother of God." The new patient regarded her companion sorrowfully and, in a voice resonant with pity, said, "I'm afraid it's you who are mixed up. I am Mary." There followed a brief but polite argument which I was restrained from interfering with by my older and more experienced colleague. . . . Finally, the "older" patient beckoned to the doctor standing with me.

"Dr. S.," she asked, "what was the name of our Blessed Mary's Mother?"

"I think it was Anne," he replied.

At once, this patient turned to the other, her face glowing and her eyes shining. "If you're Mary," she declared,"I must be Anne your mother." And the two women embraced.

As a postscript to this story, it should be recorded that the woman who surrendered her Mother of God delusion thereafter responded rapidly to treatment and was soon discharged.[71]

Actually, of course, this case, like that of Lindner and Allen, demonstrates that madness can be shared. When the two women operate as "Mary" and "Anne," their social interactions are structured by a shared schizophrenic reality—they are engaged in a "folie-à-deux." What Rokeach appears to be arguing is that the sharing of a schizophrenic reality dooms the structure to rapid destruction, that one or more of the former participants will be rapidly "cured." To test this hypothesis, Rokeach plans an experiment. Through a survey of the Michigan state mental facilities, he locates three paranoid schizophrenics, each of whom claims to be Jesus Christ.

The three Christs were originally Leon, Clyde, and Joseph. Each had once made a minor social nuisance of himself. Leon threatened his mother and broke up her religious icons, Joseph antagonized his relatives, and Clyde was disorderly and destructive after having been jailed for drunkenness. These offenses would not have merited the punishment they received—life incarceration—had the three not also displayed evidence of hallucinations and delusions. Each claimed contacts with a variety of imaginary beings. Clyde received communications from his deceased first wife and frequently hallucinated contacts with a friend named Gloria. Joseph said his uncle was the king of England, and Leon spoke often of his "wife," the mysterious Madame Yeti. Furthermore, each claimed to be Jesus Christ.

Hoping to break down these schizophrenic systems, Rokeach has the three Christs locked up together in the same ward of Ypsilanti State Mental Hospital. He seeks to drive them sane by confronting each of them with two other persons who claim the same identity. He also seeks to manipulate their pseudo communities by sending them real letters from their imaginary companions.[72]

Despite Rokeach's manipulations, none of the three is cured. On the contrary, each holds fast to his own schizophrenic reality. As Rokeach notes, one of the major implications of his study is that paranoid schizophrenic systems are much more resistant to outside manipulation than many had supposed—presumably, in part, because of the gratifications these imaginary systems hold for their creators. Even more interesting is what happens among the three. Instead of abandoning their delusions or continuing to argue with their competitors, the three become friendly and engage in cooperative social interaction. In the course of their conversations they also work out certain compromises that begin to bring their belief systems into line with each other. The development is analogous to what happened when the two Marys agreed to play complementary roles. Each Christ makes certain concessions to the others' beliefs or invents solutions that resolve contradictions. Clyde, for example, claims that in his role as God he made not one but forty different Christs. The direction of these adjustments is not toward "cure"—that is, acceptance of standard American reality—but toward folie-à-trois.

This raises an important question. What is the difference between a shared delusionary system and a shared culture? Is it numbers? If only three persons survived a war, their belief system would still constitute a culture. Is it possession of truth? The cross-cultural evidence suggests otherwise. People who believe other than we do are still granted possession of culture. All cultures appear to be mixtures of truth and delusion.

But, it may be argued, the basic difference is that the three Christs are "schizophrenics." This does not suffice. Judgments about madness and sanity are social judgments, about which disagreement is not only possible but frequent. Ultimately, the resolution of any disagreement depends on who has the power to enforce a given definition of reality.[73]

By the end of Rokeach's study, the three Christs did not share a single belief system. But that is the direction in which they were moving. If they had reached further accommodation, the three

Christs could be said to have developed a cultural system. There is, in fact, considerable evidence that hallucinatory and delusionary worlds can sometimes provide the basis for actual sociocultural systems. This connection leads us to another basic connection between imaginary worlds and actual social relationships.

Cultures, we know, are never stable—both the nature of "reality" and the structure of the social order are always moving. Commonly, change proceeds slowly and gradually through mechanisms such as cultural drift. Yet sometimes there is rapid change—reality is radically redefined, and an old social order is torn asunder and replaced by one that is drastically different in its organization and roles. One of the mechanisms through which rapid change takes place is the process Anthony F. C. Wallace has referred to as a "revitalization movement." A revitalization movement involves radical cultural reform based on "a conscious and deliberate effort by the members of a society to construct a more satisfying culture."[74] Sometimes revitalization movements are revivalistic; they attempt to restore some image of a better past. More often they are future-oriented or utopian; they attempt to establish a new social order to solve what are perceived to be the evils of the present. Such movements often seem to begin when the society has reached a point of disruption such that meaninglessness and despair are rampant, traditional values cannot be realized, and the old identities are no longer satisfying.

For Wallace the prototype of revitalization is the Handsome Lake movement among the Seneca Indians. By the mid-eighteenth century, political developments in colonial America had wreaked disastrous consequences on the Iroquois in general and the Senecas in particular. The formerly powerful tribe was confined in tiny, slumlike reservations. They were economically impoverished, subject to severe conflicts, and plagued by widespread drunkenness. The former ideal identities of Hunter, Political Statesman, and Warrior could no longer be realized.

Handsome Lake, a fifty-four-year-old former warrior, was now a sick bedridden alcoholic who was despondent over his personal losses and the fallen state of the Iroquois. He was evidently in a seriously depressed and disturbed psychological state. But suddenly everything changed.

In June 1799, Handsome Lake experienced the first of a series of visions that were to transform not only his own life but the lives of the Seneca people and, indeed, of the Iroquois generally. During a deathlike trance he dreamt that 3 angels came down from heaven to talk to him. After explaining that his illness was owing to the sin of drinking liquor, and that the trouble with the Seneca as a nation was that too many of them drank too much and practiced witchcraft, the angels assured him that if he gave up drink and behaved well he would not die that summer. Handsome Lake came out of the trance while his relatives were preparing him for burial. He told them what he had seen (by fortunate chance, a Quaker missionary happened to be living close by and recorded a translation of his words) and, at Handsome Lake's direction, Cornplanter assembled the people and reported the vision. Handsome Lake felt better and after a few more visions, was able to leave his bed and take up the mission to which he felt he had been appointed. He had many subsequent visions, preached vigorously to the Seneca and the other Iroquois tribes on their several reservations, and was appointed the spiritual and moral censor of the Seneca nation.[75]

In his later visions, the three angels, who came in traditional Indian garb, explained the problems of current Seneca society and specified programs of social reform to solve the tribe's current problems. They said that a new social system should be established, that emphasis should be placed on the nuclear family instead of the old clans, and that the men should take up farming, formerly the work of the women. The angels also took Handsome Lake on a tour of heaven and hell and showed him how the wicked and disobedient would be tortured.[76] This new "way" was preached by Handsome Lake and his early converts, and their code was eventually accepted by the tribe as a whole. The consequences were dramatic. The Seneca reservation was transformed from a frontier slum into a vigorous and enterprising society.

On the basis of the Handsome Lake movement and some 100 other cases, Wallace defines the stages of revitalization as follows. First, there is a period of "cultural distortion" in which the old social system breaks down—the old customs prove ineffective and there is increased individual stress. Next comes the period of "revitalization," in which a new code is introduced, specifying the evils of the present, the goal culture to be achieved, and the transfer culture by which it is to be reached. The period of revitalization includes a number of steps including communication of the code, organization, and adaption. Sometimes the code proves destructive. The *terre sans mal* movements of South America inspired large numbers of Indians to leave their homes in search of the promised "land without evil." Instead they often found only destruction and death. However, if the movement is workable, and if it overcomes opposition, it often leads to a more satisfying social order significantly different from the one that preceded it.

At the center of the process is the prophet-leader's innovation of an image of the ideal social order. This "mazeway resynthesis" consists of a "break" in which the individual suddenly shifts his sense of reality. Usually this occurs under the impetus of a hallucinatory vision. Wallace regards the hallucinatory experience as common to revitalization movements in general and standard in religiously oriented revitalization movements.

With a few exceptions, every religious revitalization movement with which I am acquainted has been originally conceived in one or several hallucinatory visions by a single individual. A supernatural being appears to the prophet-to-be, explains his own and his society's troubles as being entirely or partly a result of the violation of certain rules, and promises individual and social revitalization if the injunctions are followed and the rituals practiced, but personal and social catastrophe if they are not.[77]

The essence of the vision is a social interaction with an imaginary being who communicates the design of the new social order to the prophet. Imaginary social interaction provides the very basis for revitalization movements. As Wallace observes, this hallucinatory experience and personal reality change is not "pathological." On the contrary, it is therapeutic for the individual prophet and— when successful—beneficial to society. In Wallace's formulation, revitalization movements include well-known reform movements such as the Cargo cults, the Ghost Dance religion, the Sudanese Mahdi movement, the Taiping Rebellion, the origin of Christianity, the Mormon movement, and John Wesley's early Methodism.

An intriguing addition to Wallace's approach has been formulated by the anthropologist-psychiatrist Edward Foulks. Following the World Health Organization's definition, Foulks defines schizophrenia as "a condition of human psychologic functioning characterized by hallucinations, with the person hearing his own thoughts spoken aloud and voices talking to each other."[78] Citing the substantial but still controversial evidence, he argues that a proclivity to responding to stress in this way is under genetic control and occurs in approximately five out of every 1,000 people in all societies. He argues that its prevalence may be based on some selective evolutionary advantage and discusses the similarities between the revitalization leader's vision and the schizophrenic's hallucination. He concludes that they are one and the same. The revitalization prophet-leader is a schizophrenic whose hallucinatory vision answers the needs of others and is accepted as valid.

The prevalence of schizophrenia is to be accounted for by its usefulness during periods of cultural distortion.

The experiences of the schizophrenic may have provided a mechanism for rapid cultural resynthesis through revitalization during periods of social disintegration. . . . Schizophrenia is a condition which occurs at a relatively constant prevalence rate around the world and most probably is inherited polygenically. These observations lead us to consider that schizophrenia may be found in all human populations because it has had a selective advantage in triggering social change.[79]

If Foulks is right, then the cultures of many social groups are the products of schizophrenic hallucinations; they are, in effect, shared schizophrenic realities.

In fact, it is unnecessary to label revitalization prophets as schizophrenics. That would appear to be the Western psychiatric bias again. "Schizophrenic" is perhaps best kept, in its traditional American sense, as a pejorative label for deviants whose visions we do not like.

But what *is* clear from the extensive ethnographic evidence is that the hallucinatory social interactions of the prophet-leaders of revitalization movements have often provided the blueprints for new sociocultural systems. Far from being peripheral, bizarre, or pathological, "hallucinatory" social interactions have often defined the social and cultural "realities" by which humans live their lives.

Chapter 7

Conclusion: The Cultural Significance of Imaginary Social Worlds

We do not live only in the objective world of external objects and activities. On the contrary, much of our experience is inner experience. Each day we pass through multiple realities—we phase in and out, back and forth, between the actual world and imaginary realms. We awake in the morning after spending six or seven hours entangled in the phantasmagorical world of dreams. During our early morning routines, we regularly drift off into the stream of consciousness. As we dress, our attention wanders, we experience moments from the past, imaginatively engage in scenes of the day ahead, and silently converse to ourselves about these non-present worlds. At breakfast we may sleepily talk with our families but then, picking up the morning newspaper, we are off again, caught up in the political machinations of Washington and the doings of the sports worlds and comic strip characters. Driving to work, we are only partly aware of the familiar route. Much of the time we are "away," lost in anticipations of the hours or years ahead or in fantasies about how things might otherwise be . . . and so on throughout the day, hour after hour, day after day.

This complex dimension of experience, so little attended to in social science, is of considerable interest for culture studies. In this ethnographic study, I have explored the social aspect of these inner experiences. I have shown that in passing much of our lives in imaginary worlds, we are engaging not in private but in *social* experiences. Cultural studies of social organization have neglected a fundamental aspect of our subjective experience— our pervasive involvement in imaginary social relationships. In dreams we enter imaginary worlds in which we are almost never alone. We take on varied identities, assume roles, and play out social interaction with dream beings. Similarly, when we attend to virtually any form of the media, we leave our objective social situation but are transported into artificial or vicarious social situations. Through processes like identification, we play out pseudosocial roles with images of media figures. In the stream of consciousness as well—in memories, anticipations, and fantasies—we typically become entangled in pseudosocial interactions with imaginary replicas of our actual friends and acquaintances. Our imaginary worlds are dominated by social interaction. Our lives are pervaded by imaginary social relationships.

Imaginary social relationships are subjectively compelling. Experiences in fantasies, memories, dreams, and media involvements are often more engrossing than actual social encounters. These experiences are not only engaging, they are elaborately patterned. Through the use of ethnographic methods—through approaching these realms as alternate social worlds—I have uncovered some of their distinctive characteristics. I have described the kinds of settings involved, the identities and roles assumed by the self and others, and the patterns of interaction that occur. I have shown that these imaginary experiences are not structured just by individual personality factors, but that in a variety of different ways, they are culturally structured as well. In some cases the imaginary system mirrors the actual social structure. In others the reflection is distorted, as when there are exaggerations of cultural values or violations of cultural norms. Whatever the connection, the imaginary world is extensively influenced by culture. In our imaginary social relationships, as in our actual social behavior, our lives are dominated by cultural forces.

The imaginary worlds we have considered are interconnected by the imaginary social relationships within them.[1] Recalled during waking consciousness, dream figures may become significant in memories and self conversations; the fictional figures of the media are themselves the product of an author's personal fantasies. Such connections indicate that the study of any one of the imaginary worlds we have considered—media involvements, dreams, stream-of-consciousness processes—can often be advanced by considering how the social relationships in one realm connect to those of another. For example, a perennial issue in media studies is the question of the effects that mass communications have on audience members, the extent to which media consumption serves as a "socialization" mechanism. Traditionally, media researchers have sought the direct behavioral effects of media exposure, but is has increasingly been recognized that we need first to consider media effects on knowledge and consciousness. The "social relationships" approach adopted here opens up another perspective on this problem. Media consumption, itself a form of pseudosocial interaction, introduces the individual to a swarming throng of media figures. These figures do not simply remain on the screen or the printed page. On the contrary, they invade the individual's personal imaginary systems. When an individual enters the worlds of dreams or fantasies, he often becomes emotionally involved, through admiration, love, or hatred, with media figures and plays out intense pseudosocial interactions with them. An adequate assessment of "media effects" demands consideration of the roles media figures play in personal imaginary systems. In short, the understanding of any one imaginary world requires ethnographic attention to its social interconnections with other imaginary systems.

Imaginary social worlds are also significant because of the important effects they have on actual behavior. As we have seen in a variety of different ways, imaginary social relationships have complex and pervasive effects on actual social relationships. In our society, imaginary relationships with media figures influence the conduct of actual interactions because people often use these figures as mentors and role models. Dreams affect actual social relationships because dreams about people we know color our emotional orientations to them and because our waking interpretations of dreams affect our decision making. Through stream-of-consciousness processes, much of our actual social conduct is scripted out beforehand during anticipations. Such imaginary processes often have important reality-defining and social control functions. Fantasies too are socially significant. By providing vivid pseudosocial experiences of value realization, they may acquire considerable motivating force. In mental illness as well, when the individual takes a pseudo community of imaginary others as real, the actual social consequences may be significant—sometimes dangerously so. But the imaginary social experiences of so-called schizophrenics may sometimes have positive social effects as well. The schizophrenic's "hallucinatory" experiences have sometimes provided the visionary bases for cultural revitalization movements. In such cases the actual social order becomes a product of imaginary social relationships.

This ethnographic exploration of imaginary worlds shows, then, that attention to imaginary social experiences is of considerable importance for the study of culture. Our understanding of many basic aspects of culture can be enhanced through systematic attention to imaginary experiences. Studies of values, for example, can clearly benefit from a careful examination of the ways in which people play out conceptions of the desirable in fantasies, dreams, and anticipations. Certainly, given the patterns considered here, any study of American social organization that ignores imaginary social relationships must be regarded as incomplete.

Such findings are important for the development of both ethnography and culture theory. But what of the "applied" implications of this study? What does the prevalence of imaginary social experiences tell us about the state of contemporary American society? This was a question newspaper interviewers wanted to discuss during my own brief experience in the role of media consultant.

Five days after John Hinckley shot President Reagan, I drove to a nearby drugstore to buy a newspaper. I had already seen the *Washington Post*. Reagan was all right, Brady was a little better, and there was nothing new on Hinckley's imaginary love relationship with Jodie Foster. But I wanted to check the *Washington Star* to see if my article had appeared. An acquaintance who knew of my research had persuaded me to do an interview with a reporter she knew on the *Star*. He and a photographer had come to my office the day before, and they had said that the article might appear today.

I walked into the drugstore and picked up a paper from the stack. Scanning the front page, I saw the small picture of Jodie Foster and the "Today's News" contents caption: "A University of Maryland anthropologist believes that fantasy relationships—even the one which may have motivated the man accused of trying to kill President Reagan—are anything but abnormal."[2] I sat down at the lunch counter and ordered a cup of coffee from the waitress, a pleasant-looking blonde teenager. I opened the paper to section C, and there, spread across the page, was the picture: Eddie Waitkus, Jodie Foster, and me. As the waitress set down my coffee, she offered a media joke.

"This is our rich new coffee," she said. "We put it in a crummy restaurant to see if you liked it."

I read the article carefully, sipping my coffee. I felt relieved that the reporter had my major points right—that the fantasy relationship Hinckley had with Foster is not in itself unusual, that such relationships are now prevalent in our society, that there is a certain logic to why people would choose these imaginary figures over real acquaintances. I felt a mild glow at seeing my words in print. I asked the waitress for another cup of coffee. Taking my order, she was pleasant but distant. I was just another customer, nobody. I decided to perform an ethnographic experiment on her.

"Did you see the paper today?" I asked her, casually indicating the picture. She glanced down at the picture and up at me. Then she did a quick double take and her face broke into an expression of wonder. She skimmed the article lead quickly.

"Wow!" she said, giving me a big smile. "That's really neat! Can I tell the others that you're a star?"

"Jane!" she hissed to the other waitress. "Jane, come here!"

"I can't," said Jane, busy at the cash register.

My waitress picked up the paper and took it over to Jane. They huddled together whispering, giggling, and looking back at me. My waitress came back with the paper. She put it down before me and looked at me again.

"Can I have your autograph?" she asked. "I want to take it home and show my family."

"You're kidding," I said.

"No, really."

And I saw that she was not. She placed a battered "Star Wars" pocket notebook down before me. Other customers were now calling for service.

"I'll pick this up later," she whispered, and off she went to attend them.

I finished my coffee, marveling at the change in her attitude.

"Do you really want me to write something?" I asked when she came back.

"Yes. Please. And will you do one for Jane? She wants one too."

"What's your name?" I asked.

She pointed to her blue plastic name tag. "Sally" was inscribed there.

"You can write 'To the most wonderful person in the world,'" she suggested. I scrawled, "To Sally—the most wonderful person in the world," and autographed it.

"You're a celebrity!" she said again, almost adoringly.

"For a few minutes," I said with appropriate Gary Cooper modesty.

"Awww."

One theory of mass communication holds that in our society the media performs a "status conferral" function.[3] It gives recognition and legitimacy not only to public issues, organizations, and ideas, but also to persons. Americans tend to view people who gain media recognition—by whatever means—as superior beings; we give such people immediate, inflated status. John Hinckley knew this well. By performing a "historic deed," he would transform himself from a nobody into a media figure—and thereby elevate himself to the level of Jodie Foster and the stars. In a minor way, I had experienced a similar elevation during my experiment in the drugstore. While Sally's response was the most extreme, the phenomenon continued for several days afterwards. Many of my friends, colleagues, and students were unduly impressed. In giving an interview, I had not really done anything extraordinary—I was the same person as before—but their image of me had radically, if temporarily, shifted.

Through this elevation, I was also cast temporarily in the role of "media consultant." After the *Washington Star* article appeared, I was invited to appear on radio and television talk shows, and several other reporters called with questions. They wanted to know about Hinckley's relationship with Foster, about fantasy relationships in general—and about what it all meant. Did the prevalence of fantasy mean that psychosis was running rampant? Was our society beginning to decline? Were we on the edge of an epidemic of celebrity shootings?

Given our current knowledge, many of the questions I was asked are unanswerable. But a general issue behind the questions is worth some brief speculation. What does the prevalence of fantasy relationships suggest about our society?

To assess properly the implications of imaginary relationships in American society would require placing American imaginary processes in systematic cross-cultural perspective. Since we still know relatively little about American imaginary relationships and even less about those of other societies, this is difficult. Nevertheless, it does seem that our imaginary relationships have certain elements that are widely shared by other cultures and other elements that are distinctive.

Intense imaginary experiences—fantasies, dreams, anticipations—seem to be characteristic in all societies. This is suggested by the available literature as well as by the material on Fáánakkar and Pakistan that I have discussed above. However, imaginary experiences are organized differently in different societies, and while more comparative studies would be needed to fully document this, it appears that certain forms of imaginary interaction have become particularly important in our society. Certainly, technologically developing countries like ours are distinctive in that the population has become intimately involved with a swarm of media figures through a powerful mass communications system. It is only in the past seventy-five years that the electronic media have begun to feed such figures into our personal imaginary systems in the ways examined above. These figures exert important influences on other imaginary systems and on actual social conduct.

Some of these influences are negative. To a significant extent our indulgence in imaginary relationships seems to reflect problems in the wider social system, including the disruption of traditional social relationships and the erosion of value systems. For many of my informants, intense engagement in imaginary relationships reflects a spuriousness in their actual social experience. At the same time, the negative features of many media-structured imaginary relationships—with their glamorization of violence, selfishness, predatory sexuality, and materialism—often have negative consequences when the individual returns from media consumption or media-derived fantasy to the realm of actual social behavior. One symptom of this is the widely acknowledged fact that media relationships contribute to the performance of antisocial conduct, including violence. Given expected new developments in media technology, the intensity and negative influence of media relationships is likely to increase.[4] This may contribute to an increase in antisocial conduct generally—including an increase in attacks on media celebrities. John Hinckley was inspired not only by *Taxi Driver* and his own personal fantasy relationship but also by the media presentation of Mark Chapman.[5] Hinckley himself has served as a role model for more recent celebrity attackers.[6]

One aspect of this problem is clearly the status conferred upon celebrity attackers by the media. Along with complex personal motives behind such attacks (including feelings of love, admiration, envy, anger, and resentment) is often found a desire for celebrity status. Ruth Steinhagen was explicit on this point. "I wanted publicity and attention for once."[7] And John Hinckley reportedly feels that his attack on Reagan has "accomplished its intended purpose" by linking him "forever in history" with actress Jodie Foster.[8] After all, his face has been on the cover of *Newsweek* and his quotes have been featured in the press. It will be interesting to see if we can learn not to reward such attackers with the media attention they desire.

However, it would be erroneous to conclude that imaginary relationships—including those with media figures—are generally pathological because a few of them end in violence. This would be like saying that an actual social relationship such as marriage is pathological because a few marriages end in violence. Intense imaginary relationships with media figures have become a prevalent, statistically normal feature of contemporary American social organization. Even if such relationships often reflect problems in the wider society, very few of these relationships are dangerously antisocial. On the contrary, such relationships often lead to socially approved forms of thought and behavior very much in line with current American value orientations, norms, and definitions of reality. This does not mean that we should not be concerned, but the issues are complex. The media constitute but one factor influencing imaginary and actual forms of behavior. Changes in the wider culture will also have their effects. Furthermore, the assessment of whether a given media-derived relationship is positive or negative is often a relative judgment subject to considerable disagreement among the multicultural segments of contemporary society. For example, evaluations of a recent television attempt to promote "prosocial" behavior in children by changing their sex role beliefs depend on particular value orientation on this issue.[9] However, as media influence becomes stronger and as our understanding of its effects on social behavior becomes clearer, the issue of what power groups control the media, with what goals and what effects, will become even more significant. It is clear that future forms of the media will have an important effect on our imaginary social experience. This means they will affect our psychic life, consciousness, and systems of meaning, and thereby the structure of actual American social relationships.

During my days as "media consultant," I also received requests for personal assistance from people who wanted advice on dealing with imaginary social relationships. I was asked about the meaning of recurrent fantasies and invited to interpret disturbing dreams. A woman from Baltimore wrote me a letter about her husband's fixation on a popular female singer. He was spending so much time in this relationship, listening to her records and staring at her photographs, that she was thinking of leaving him. She wondered if there was any hope; would her husband ever get over this problem? Another woman called me about her involvement with a TV newscaster. She had never met him, but she had been in love with him for years. She was "not violent," but she was worried about the parallels between her own fantasy relationship and that of Hinckley and Foster. "I guess I should find someone else," she said. "But other men are not up to par, not up to his level. Could you tell me, do you know how a person can get *out* of such an infatuation?" Being an ethnographer, not a psychiatrist, and not believing in long-distance therapy, I could not really help—other than to offer some reassurance. But the irony was intense. In an earlier article I had criticized the fact that many people in our society will seek the advice of an unmet media figure in trying to deal with personal problems. And now I was cast in the role of a "Dear Abby" myself.

Such cases raise another issue which can be partially illuminated by the kind of cultural analysis employed in this book. For the people involved in them, what are the personal implications of the imaginary relationships we have examined? Clearly, some individuals suffer subjective distress because they are involved in imaginary relationships that they themselves feel are somehow wrong or unhealthy. Sometimes this anxiety is both unjustified and culturally constituted. People can become overly concerned about their own imaginary experience when they do not realize that it is culturally standard. This may have been the case with the caller who was worried about the supposed similarities between her own fantasy relationship and that of Hinckley. It was certainly true of an eighteen-year-old informant who was disturbed by her own vivid fantasies until she realized that other people have similar experiences. Her anxiety was largely a product of cultural rules against talking about such experiences. Occasionally something more serious is involved. While this is rare, a few people are justifiably concerned that, as one informant put it, "I have gone too far in this relationship." As the cases of Ruth Steinhagen, Mark Chapman, and John Hinckley show, attempts to resolve such a situation can sometimes be dangerous.

What is obviously needed is therapeutic attention to the problem of identifying and treating cases in which imaginary relationships have become pathological. However, many therapists are poorly equipped to diagnose and treat problems with imaginary relationships because they lack sufficient appreciation of the extent to which powerful fantasy relationships are common among normal Americans. An adequate therapeutic understanding of imaginary relationships will require further attention to normal as well as pathological imaginary social experiences.[10]

But if we consider the ways in which "normal" Americans operate with imaginary social systems, should we see this statistically normal pattern as positive? My own ethnographic investigations of imaginary systems suggest that the average American, while neither subjectively disturbed nor dangerous, is not using imaginary experiences in a particularly beneficial manner. There are various reasons for this, chief among them the fact that most Americans are only dimly aware of the contents and scope of their daily imaginary experience. They are unaware of the patterns involved and they have a poor understanding of the effects that such experiences may have on their actual life. This is partly a cultural phenomenon. Implicitly, at least, our society mistakenly teaches us to attach little importance to imaginary relationships. But it is also quite possible for people to make their imaginary processes the subject of personal observation and thereby to increase greatly their awareness of their own imaginary life. The texts quoted throughout this book show that people can become highly aware of their own imaginary systems. At first, most informants are amazed at the extent of their imaginary experience; when the amount of their participation in all forms of the media is added up, people are typically surprised and often appalled. They are usually even more surprised at the number of hours they are "away" in fantasies, memories, self-talk, and anticipation. Monitoring their own imaginary experiences is disturbing to some people, but most find this process both interesting and "therapeutic." An examination of the imaginary relationships in one's fantasies, dreams, anticipations, and media involvements is a potentially rich source for increasing self-understanding. In part, one is learning here about the shape of one's own personality, but the process also reveals social and cultural influences. By paying attention to imaginary systems, the individual can increase significantly awareness of cultural conditioning. If a person is happy with what he or she finds here, no action is necessary, but in some cases it may be appropriate to try and alter passive, uncontrolled use of imaginary experience. People have the power to become aware of their own imaginary worlds, they also have the ability to modify these experiences.

Our culture often makes a distinction between people who deal with problems actively by trying to affect the external environment (the so-called problem solving approach) and those who deal with them through "intrapsychic" or "emotion-focused" methods—that is, by trying to accomplish shifts in their own states of mind. Our culture has tended to assume that healthy people use problem-focused modes and that sick people use emotion-focused methods.[11] But, as the cognitive therapists have shown, everyone uses both techniques. As they have also shown, people can increase the effectiveness of intrapsychic methods by the cultivation of deliberate internal strategies.[12] For many Americans the stream of consciousness includes an extensive amount of critical self-talk, as when a person tells himself, "This situation is too difficult, I can't cope with it." Often it is possible deliberately to modify the structure of such negative inner conversations. It seems likely that similar modifications might be accomplished in other aspects of the stream of consciousness and in imaginary systems generally.

Such processes have long been used in various Eastern modes of therapy. Among the Sufis with whom I worked in Pakistan, as with many other Eastern cultures, emphasis is placed on techniques for observing and modifying negative inner imagery.[13] In the Sufi system, the cultural obstacles to internal work are clearly recognized, since it is explicitly believed that many negative images derive from the false values of worldly society. Conversely, emphasis is also placed on the deliberate use of positive imagery. In the West, "guided imagery" offers a similar indication of how imaginary systems might be used more creatively.[14] In our society, progress here would often require taking more personal control over media consumption. Learning to use the media is something like learning to use a powerful drug; controlled doses and careful monitoring of effects on inner experience are worth the effort. On the positive side, some psychologists suggest that benefits can be obtained from cultivating imaginary dialogues with unmet but admired figures.[15] A similar approach is also applicable to dreams. As we saw in Chapter 3, people in some societies have learned to restructure the negative social situations of their dreams and to turn these dream relationships in positive directions—with reportedly major effects on waking mental health and social relations. There have been attempts to apply similar techniques to American dream therapy.

Given our limited understanding of these complex and powerful processes, imaginary relationships are likely to remain well beyond our complete control. However, the methods just described offer some hope that we may eventually learn to make better use of our pervasive involvement in imaginary social worlds.

Notes

Prologue

1. Most of the information summarized here comes from the official psychiatric "Report to Felony Court" as reproduced in Charles Einstein, ed., *The Fireside Book of Baseball* (New York: Simon and Schuster, 1956), 118–22. Cf. Rich Ashburn, "Waitkus Tragedy Recalled," *Philadelphia Evening Bulletin*, 22 April 1975.
2. "Report to Felony Court," 121.
3. Allan J. Mayer et al., "Death of a Beatle," *Newsweek*, 22 December 1980, 31–36.
4. Art Harris, "Memories of Chapman," *Washington Post*, 12 December 1980.
5. Ibid.
6. Mayer et al., "Death of a Beatle," 32.
7. John Langone, "The Lennon Syndrome," *Discover*, February 1981, 75; "Death of a Beatle," 33; "Up Front," *People*, 20 April 1981, 38.
8. Langone, "The Lennon Syndrome," 75; Mayer et al., "Death of a Beatle," 33.
9. Althelia Knight and Neil Henry, "Love Letter Holds Clue to Motive in Shooting," *Washington Post*, 1 April 1981.
10. Laura Kiernan, "Clashing Portraits of Hinckley Offered," *Washington Post*, 5 May 1982; Laura Kiernan, "Hinckley's 'Suicide Impulse' Claim Draws Sharp Attack from Prosecutor," *Washington Post*, 18 May 1982.
11. Neil Henry and Chip Brown, "An Aimless Road to a Place in History," *Washington Post*, 5 April 1982.
12. Neil Henry, "Courtroom Erupts with the Verdict," *Washington Post*, 22 June 1982.
13. "Text of Letter to Foster," *Washington Post*, 21 May 1981.

14. Harris, "Memories of Chapman."
15. "Report to Felony Court," 119.

Chapter 1

1. Roger M. Keesing, "Theories of Culture," in Bernard J. Siegel, Alan R. Beals, and Steven Tyler, eds., *Annual Review of Anthropology* 3 (1974), 73–96.
2. Ward H. Goodenough, *Cultural Anthropology and Linguistics*, Georgetown University Monograph Series on Language and Linguistics, no. i (Washington, D.C., 1957), 167.
3. For more on this approach, see Janet W. Dougherty and James Fernandez, eds., "Symbolism and Cognition," special issue of *American Ethnologist* 8 (1981), 413–660; and J. Mechling, "In Search of an American Ethnophysics," in L. Luedtke, ed., *The Study of American Culture* (Deland, Florida: Everett Edwards, 1977).
4. John L. Caughey, *Fáánakkar: Cultural Values in a Micronesian Society*, University of Pennsylvania Publications in Anthropology, no. 2, (Philadelphia, 1977).
5. Peter Berger, "The Problem of Multiple Realities: Alfred Schutz and Robert Musil," in Thomas Luckmann, ed., *Phenomenology and Sociology* (New York: Penguin, 1978), 347.
6. Cf. Anthony F. C. Wallace, *Culture and Personality* (New York: Random House, 1970), 165–206.
7. James P. Spradley and David M. McCurdy, *Anthropology: The Cultural Perspective* (New York: John Wiley, 1975), 111.
8. Cf. John Caughey, "Personal Identity and Social Organization," *Ethos* 8 (1980), 173–203; and Ward H. Goodenough, "Rethinking 'Status' and 'Role' Toward General Model of the Cultural Organization of Social Relationships," in Michael Banton, ed., *The Relevance of Models for Social Anthropology* (London: Tavistock, 1965).
9. This account is based on fieldwork carried out in Pakistan in 1976–77. Cf. John L. Caughey and J. Michael Mahar, "Ritual Remedies at a Sufi Shrine," paper presented to the seventy-sixth annual meeting of the American Anthropological Association (Houston, 1977).
10. Spradley and McCurdy, *Anthropology*, 112.
11. A. I. Hallowell, "The Self and Its Behavioral Environment," in his *Culture and Experience* (Philadelphia: University of Pennsylvania Press, 1955), 92.
12. A. I. Hallowell, "Ojibwa Ontology, Behavior and World View," in S.

Diamond, ed., *Culture in History* (New York: Columbia University Press, 1960), 22–23.

13. Caughey, *Fáánakkar*, 21.
14. Yi-Fu Tuan, *Landscapes of Fear* (New York: Pantheon, 1978), 5–6.
15. Melford Spiro, "Ghosts, Ifaluk, and Teleological Functionalism," *American Anthropologist* 54 (1952), 497–503.
16. Joe Kamiya, "Operant Control of the EEG Alpha Rhythm and some of Its Reported Effects on Consciousness," in Charles Tart, ed., *Altered States of Consciousness*, (New York: John Wiley, 1969), 508.
17. Ibid. Ironically, EEG dream detection methods have required correction by introspective methods. See Jerome Singer, *The Inner World of Daydreaming (New York: Harper and Row, 1975), 47–49.*
18. Singer, *The Inner World of Daydreaming.* Cf. J. Radford, "Reflections on Introspection," *American Psychologist* 29 (1974), 245–50.
19. Jacques Maquet, *Introduction to Aesthetic Anthropology* (Reading, Mass.: Addison-Wesley, 1971), 2.
20. Anthony F. C. Wallace, "Driving to Work," in James P. Spradley, ed., *Culture and Cognition* (San Francisco: Chandler, 1972), 311.
21. Ibid. Cf. Victor Turner and Edith Turner, *Image and Pilgrimage in Christian Culture: Anthropological Perspectives* (New York: Columbia University Press, 1978), xv: "When the deeper levels of the self, deeply tinctured by culture, are reflexively engaged, the knowledge brought back from the encounter between self as subject and self as object may be just as valid as knowledge acquired by 'neutral' observation of others."
22. Wallace, "Driving to Work," 312.
23. David M. Hayano, "Autoethnography: Paradigms, Problems, and Prospects," *Human Organization* 38 (1979), 103.
24. For further discussion of introspection and ethnography, see my "Ethnography, Introspection, and Reflexive Culture Studies," *Prospects* 7 (1982).
25. A university class provides one version of the "focused group" method that seems particularly suited to research in this area. Since it takes some time to get informants attuned to this area of experience, a class provides one efficient way of accomplishing this with a group of people. Students were asked to independently monitor a given aspect of imaginary experience (e.g., the stream of consciousness) and then to write a report describing the results. This material was then discussed in class. Such discussion often produced interesting indications of patterns in imaginary experience. It can be objected, of

course, that the use of a class—or any focused group—might lead to biased results, that people may provide material the ethnographer wishes to hear. But, as is well known, this is a problem that must be guarded against in any type of informant interviewing. Subsequent interviews with individual class members, independent interviews with other informants, surveys of published autobiographical accounts, reviews of other research on imaginary processes, and self-ethnographic monitoring all provide useful checks on the results obtained in focused groups.

26. Some of the illustrative texts quoted below come from interviews. Other texts were initially written for class exercises involving self-reports on imaginary processes. When a given class report interested me, I usually interviewed the informant further. Some students and other informants also kept journals on their imaginary experiences; I did the same. Thus the quoted material presented in the chapters that follow consists of verbatim quotes from interviews or verbatim extracts from class exercises or journals.

For discussions of the differences between ethnography and other social science approaches, see Michael Agar, *The Professional Stranger: An Informal Introduction to Ethnography* (New York: Academic Press, 1980) and John L. Caughey, "The Ethnography of Everyday Life: Theories and Methods for American Studies," *American Quarterly/Bibliography Issue* 34 (1982).

27. Peter Berger and Thomas Luckmann, *The Social Construction of Reality* (New York: Anchor, 1966), 23.

28. Alfred Schutz, "On Multiple Realities," in Maurice Natanson, ed., *The Collected Papers of Alfred Schutz* (The Hague: Martinus Nijoff, 1962), 232.

29. Peter Berger, "The Problem of Multiple Realities," 232.

30. Peter Berger and Thomas Luckmann, *The Social Construction of Reality*, 112–115.

Chapter 2

1. Cf. Ward H. Goodenough, *Cultural Anthropology and Linguistics*, Georgetown University Monograph Series on Language and Linguistics, no. i (Washington, D.C., 1957), 167.

2. John L. Caughey, *Fáánakkar: Cultural Values in a Micronesian Society*, University of Pennsylvania Publications in Anthropology, no. 2 (Philadelphia, 1977), 17–23.

3. Cf. John L. Caughey, "Identity Struggles in the Mental Status Examina-

tion," paper presented at the seventy-seventh annual meeting of the American Anthropologcial Association (Los Angeles, 1978).

4. The large set of beings I refer to here as "media figures" could be subdivided by many different criteria. In certain ways historical figures and live celebrities *are* different from fictional characters. For my purposes, however, they may all be usefully classified together. All three groups represent unmet figures beyond the circle of our actual social acquaintances. Historical persons like living authors or politicians are "media figures" because we know about them largely through biographies, essays, autobiographies, and documentaries. Even if an actual social acquaintance should tell us something about a media figure, he is likely to have obtained this information through the media.

5. Gary Pomerantz, "On the Road With the Dukes," *Washington Post*, 7 July 1981.

6. One study of blue collar workers showed that a large majority (85 percent) regularly read newspaper comic strips and that most of them habitually discussed them with each other. See Leo Bogart, "Adult Talk About Newspaper Comics," *American Journal of Sociology* 61 (1955), 26–30. Cf. Irving L. Allen, "Talking About Media Experiences," *Journal of Popular Culture* 16 (1982), 106–15, and Garth Jowett and James Linton, *Movies as Mass Communication*, (Beverly Hills: Sage, 1980), 83, on media as social integrators; James Lull, "The Social Uses of Television," *Human Communication Research* 6 (1980), 197–209, on the social uses of television in family interactions; and John M. Roberts, Chien Chiao, and Triloki N. Pandey, "Meaningful God Sets From a Chinese Personal Pantheon and a Hindu Personal Pantheon," *Ethnology* 14 (1975), 121–48, on "significant figure sets."

7. Peter Berger and Thomas Luckmann, *The Social Construction of Reality* (New York: Anchor, 1966), 25. Cf. Peter H. Wood, "Television as Dream," in Horace Newcomb, ed., *Television: The Critical View* (New York: Oxford, 1979), 517–35.

8. John L. Caughey, "Artificial Social Relations in Modern America," *American Quarterly* 39 (1978), 73. Cf. Donald F. Roberts and Christine M. Bachen, "Mass Communication Effects," in Mark Rosenzweig and Lyman Porter, eds., *Annual Review of Psychology* (Palo Alto, 1981), 310–17. For other reviews of the mass media, see Michael R. Real, "Media Theory: Contributions to an Understanding of American Mass Communications," in *American Quarterly* 32 (1980), 238–58; and Lawrence E. Mintz, "Recent Trends in the Study of Popular Cul-

ture," in Robert Walker, ed., *American Studies* (Westport, Conn.: Greenwood, 1983).

9. Arthur Knight, *The Liveliest Art* (New York: Mentor, 1957), 8.

10. Cf. Orinn Klapp, *Heroes, Villains and Fools* (Englewood Cliffs: Prentice-Hall, 1962).

11. Cf. Marie Winn, *The Plug-In Drug* (New York: Bantam, 1977).

12. D. Horton and R. Richard Wohl, "Mass Communications and Para-Social Interaction," *Psychiatry* 19 (1956), 215–28. For an elaboration on this classic essay, see Jan-Erik Nordlund, "Media Interaction," *Communication Research* 5 (1978) 150–75.

13. Ibid., 217. On newscasting as parasocial interaction, see Mark Levy, "Watching TV News as Para-Social Interaction," *Journal of Broadcasting* 23 (1979), 69–80.

14. Alan Blum, "Lower Class Negro Television Spectators: The Concept of Pseudo Jovial Skepticism," in Arthur Shostak and William Gomberg, eds., *Blue Collar World* (Englewood Cliffs: Prentice-Hall, 1964), 432.

15. Horton and Wohl, "Mass Communications and Para-Social Interaction," 228.

16. On media identification, see Jowett and Linton, *Movies as Mass Communication*, 91–92.

17. Frederick Exley, *A Fan's Notes* (New York: Ballantine, 1968), 2.

18. *Webster's Third New International Dictionary* (1966).

19. Linda Witt interview with Lawrence Freedman, "Up Front," *People* 15 April 1981.

20. Jerry Hopkins, "The Fans," in Harry Hubel, ed., *Things in the Driver's Seat: Readings in Popular Culture* (Chicago: Rand McNally, 1972), 166.

21. "Dear Abby," *Philadelphia Evening Bulletin*, 1 April 1974.

22. "T.V. Time," *Philadelphia Evening Bulletin*, 17 November 1973.

23. John L. Caughey, "Media Mentors: Adults' Fantasy Transactions with Celebrities," *Psychology Today* 12 (1978), 47.

24. Elihu Katz and Paul Lazarsfeld, *Personal Influence* (Glencoe: Free Press, 1955).

25. These data are patterned along a number of different social dimensions. For example, admired figures tend to be both older than the fan and of the same sex. If the admired figure is of the opposite sex, the fan is more likely to be female.

26. Seymour Fesbach, "The Role of Fantasy in the Response to Television," *Journal of Social Issues* 32 (1976), 71–85, makes a strong case for the importance of fantasy in analysing mass communications effects. However, he takes the argument in a very different direction

from that developed here. He argues that it is important to distinguish "fantasy" programs (such as fictional movies) from realistic programs (such as news broadcasts) in assessing media effects. My concern here is with the fantasies induced by media consumption. While I agree that it is sometimes important to assess the viewers' definition of the reality of media productions, I regard all media consumption as similar to fantasizing. For a supporting argument, see Thomas R. Lindlof, "Fantasy Activity and the Television Event: Considerations for an Information Processing Construct of Involvement," *Communication Year Book* 4 (1980), 277–91. As is usual with such work, neither of these researchers is concerned with the pseudosocial relationships that dominate such processes.

27. The extreme case here is plastic surgery designed to make the fan resemble his or her idol. According to the president of the American Nasal and Facial Surgery Institute, "Many people have been requesting surgery to make them look like celebrities." Among the most requested features are Brooke Shields's lower lip, Bo Derek's ears, and John Travolta's cheekbones. "People," *Washington Post*, 25 August 1981.

28. Caryl Rivers, "I Fell in Love With Montgomery Clift," *New York Times*, 2 August 1973. Cf. her *Aphrodite at Mid-Century* (New York: Doubleday, 1973).

29. Ibid.

30. Ted Rodgers, "Groetsch Isn't Hazy About Tennis Goals," *Philadelphia Evening Bulletin*, 26 April 1978.

31. For a recent review of the research, see Roberts and Bachen, "Mass Communication Effects," 340–42.

32. Cf. Donald Roberts, "The Nature of Communications Effects," in Wilber Schramm and Donald Roberts, eds., *The Processes and Effects of Mass Communications* (Urbana: University of Illinois, 1971), 363.

33. Otto Larsen, quoted by Melvyn DeFleur, *Theories of Mass Communications* (New York: McKay, 1970), 136.

34. From *TV Guide*, as quoted by Action for Children's Television in an untitled, undated pamphlet distributed by ACT, 46 Austin St., Newtonville, Mass. 02160.

35. Similar gatherings include Star Trek, Beatles, and science fiction conventions. Again there are parallels with religious groups.

36. Caughey, "Artificial Social Relations," 66. Cf. Timothy Meyer et al., "Non-Traditional Mass Communication Methods: An Overview of Observational Case Studies of Media Use in Natural Social Settings," *Communication Yearbook* 4 (1980), 261–75.

37. Phillip Slater, *The Pursuit of Loneliness*, second ed. (Boston: Beacon Press, 1976), 26.

38. For a recent critical view, see Jerry Mander, *Four Arguments for the Elimination of Television* (New York: Morrow, 1978).

39. On "prosocial effects," see Roberts and Bachen, "Mass Communication Effects," 342–44.

40. Paul Wilkes, "Robert Coles: Doctor of Crisis," *New York Times Magazine*, 26 March 1978.

41. Miguel de Cervantes, *Don Quixote*, trans. Samuel Putnam (New York: Modern Library, 1949), 32.

42. Cf. Alfred Schutz, "Don Quixote and the Problem of Reality," in *Alfred Schutz: Collected Papers II*, ed. Arvid Brodersen (The Hague: Martinus Nijhoff, 1964).

43. Richard Nyrop, *Area Handbook for Pakistan* (Washington, D.C.: U.S. Government Printing Office, 1975), 194. Cf. John A. Lent, ed., *Third World Mass Media: Issues, Theory, and Research*, College of William and Mary Studies in Third World Societies 9 (Williamsburg, Va.; 1979).

44. Cf. Peter Berger, Brigitte Berger, and H. Kellner, *The Homeless Mind: Modernization and Consciousness* (New York: Random House, 1973).

45. See Stuart Auerbach, "Nightlife in Pakistan," *Washington Post*, 26 August 1981. "The Government is moving to ban the use of women as models in television and magazine advertisements, and women TV newscasters now must cover their heads with scarfs when they appear on the air."

46. The material covered here confirms the speculations of earlier studies such as that of Eric Klinger, who wrote, "There is reason to believe that television viewers develop a sense of having personal relationships with the characters of television programs much as they would with people with whom they actually interact." *Meaning and Void: Inner Experience and the Incentives of People's Lives* (Minneapolis: University of Minnesota Press, 1977), 254.

Chapter 3

1. Peter Ovennell, ed., *Byron: Selections from Poetry, Letters, and Journals* (London: Nonesuch Press, 1959), 170.

2. Robert L. Van De Castle, *The Psychology of Dreaming* (New York: General Learning Press, 1971), 34.

3. Robert W. McCarley, "Where Dreams Come From: A New Theory," *Psychology Today* 12 (1978) 54–141.

4. Cf. John G. Kennedy and L. L. Langness, "Introduction" to a special issue on dreams, *Ethos* 9 (1981), 249–50.

5. Cf. Vincent Crapanzano, *The Hamadsha: A Study in Moroccan Ethnopsychiatry* (Berkeley: University of California Press, 1973), 174.

6. Van De Castle, *Psychology of Dreaming*, 4–5.

7. Ibid., 4.

8. Ibid., 2.

9. Ibid., 10.

10. Sigmund Freud, *A General Introduction to Psychoanalysis* (New York: Washington Square Press, 1952), 120.

11. Sigmund Freud, *The Interpretation of Dreams* (New York: Basic Books, 1953), 354–59.

12. Ibid., 403–04.

13. Carl Jung, *Man and His Symbols* (New York: Dell, 1964), 34.

14. Anthony F. C. Wallace, "Dreams and the Wishes of the Soul: A Type of Psychoanalytic Theory Among the Seventeenth Century Iroquois," *American Anthropologist* 60 (1958), 235.

15. Ibid., 244–45.

16. For reviews of anthropological studies of dreams, see Benjamin Kilbourne, "Patterns, Structure, and Style in Anthropological Studies of Dreams," *Ethos* 9 (1981), 165–79; Kennedy and Langness, "Introduction"; and Erika Bourguignon, "Dreams and Altered States of Consciousness in Anthropological Research," in Francis L. K. Hsu, ed., *Psychological Anthropology* (Cambridge, Mass.: Schenkman, 1972), 403–34. Where an "ethnographic" or "emic" (actor-oriented) approach is taken, this usually involves attention to the way in which the people of a given culture *interpret* their dreams, not to the way in which the dream actor *experiences* the dream. Cf. Kennedy and Langness, "Introduction," 252–53.

17. Kilbourne, "Patterns, Structure, and Style," 166.

18. This figure, like those cited below, is drawn from a series of 222 dreams I have collected.

19. In their sample of 1,000 dreams, Calvin S. Hall and Robert Van De Castle also point out that the self is a virtual constant in American dreams. *The Content Analysis of Dreams* (New York: Appleton-Century-Crofts, 1966), 52. Sometimes the individual views the dream doings from an observer perspective, more often from the eyes of himself as actor within the dream drama.

20. Hall and Van De Castle also found that 95 percent of their dream sample involved other characters in addition to the dream self. Ibid., 163. In this sense, Berger and Luckmann are wrong in suggesting that the individual is "alone" in his dreams. *Social Construction of Reality*, 23.

21. Hall and Van De Castle, *Content Analysis of Dreams*, 59 and 166, also point out that unmet "prominent persons" (Orphan Annie, Winston Churchill, Hamlet) occur in American dreams. In their sample these figures constitute only 1.3 percent of the total sample of dream figures. In my sample media figures seem more common. They occur in 10.8 percent of the dreams collected. This apparent difference could be due to a number of factors. It might be partially due to the difference in coding, or it might reflect a bias in my sample—given that some of my informants were aware of my interest in such dreams. On the other hand, it may also be partially due to an increase in the significance of such figures since 1947–50, when the Hall and Van De Castle sample was collected.

22. Marylouise Oates, "The Woody of their Dreams," *Washington Post*, 5 January 1981.

23. David M. Schneider and Lauriston Sharp provide a useful comparative sample of Australian tribal dreams. Their study shows the strong influence of culture on dream interactions. This applies even to sexual relations. When men dream of sexual encounters, the women are usually of the appropriate social category (opposite moiety, different clan) and when they are not, obstacles to intercourse reflect the severity of the taboo violated. *The Dream Life of a Primitive People* (Ann Arbor: University Microfilms, 1969), 51.

24. These figures parallel those found in other studies of American dreams. For example, Hall and Van De Castle found that aggression occurred in 47 percent of their dream sample. *The Content Analysis of Dreams*, 171. Cf. Calvin Hall and Vernon Nordby, *The Individual and His Dreams* (New York: Signet, 1972), 19.

25. Schneider and Sharp, *The Dream Life of a Primitive People*, 55–56.

26. For example, one study found that of 556 characters presented on television shows, 45 percent were basically violent. George Comstock et al., *Television and Human Behavior* (New York: Columbia University Press, 1978), 41.

27. Sigmund Freud, *Civilization and Its Discontents* (London: Hogarth, 1930).

28. Cf. Ward Goodenough, *Culture, Language, and Society* (Reading, Mass.: Addison-Wesley, 1971), 29–30.

29. The social situation factors that make individuals more or less susceptible to nightmares may well be generalizable to cultural groups. Cf. John E. Mack, *Nightmares and Human Conflict* (Boston: Little, Brown, 1970), 214.

30. This may be true of the differences between men's and women's dreams. See Johanna King, "Characteristics of Women's Dreams," in Gayle Kimball, ed., *Women's Culture* Metuchen, N.J.: Scarecrow Press, 1981), 215–28.

31. Cf. Edward Sapir, "Culture: Genuine and Spurious," in David G. Mandelbaum, ed., *Selected Writings of Edward Sapir* (Berkeley: University of California Press, 1968), 308–31.

32. Burton Watson, trans., *Chuang Tzu: Basic Writings* (New York: Columbia University Press, 1964), 45.

33. For a discussion of this and other dream and sleep disorders, see Howard P. Roffwarg, "Diagnostic Classification of Sleep and Arousal Disorders," *Sleep* 2 (1979) 1–137.

34. Van De Castle, *Psychology of Dreaming*, 2.

35. Wallace, "Dreams and the Wishes of the Soul," 239.

36. "How to Interpret Your Dreams," pamphlet of the Reader's Digest Association (Far East, Ltd., 1979), 5, 10, 22, and 35. The title page indicates that the material was drawn from Friedrich W. Docet, *The Dream and Dream Interpretation* (Munich: Wilhelm Heyne Verlag, 1973).

37. Ann Faraday, *The Dream Game* (New York: Harper and Row, 1974), xiv-xv.

38. Ibid., 253–54.

39. Stephen P. LaBerge, "Lucid Dreaming," *Psychology Today* 15 (1981) 48–57.

40. Kilton Stewart, "Dream Theory in Malaya," in Charles Tart, ed., *Altered States of Consciousness* (New York: John Wiley, 1969), 160.

41. Ibid., 162.

42. Ibid., 162–63.

43. Ibid., 163.

44. Ibid., 166.

45. Ibid.

46. Rosalind D. Cartwright, "Happy Endings for Our Dreams," *Psychology Today* 12 (1978), 66. Cf. Patricia L. Garfield, *Creative Dreaming* (New York: Simon and Schuster, 1974).

Chapter 4

1. Wallace, "Driving to Work," in James P. Spradley, ed., *Culture and Cognition* (San Francisco: Chandler, 1972), 319.
2. Erving Goffman, *Behavior in Public Places* (New York: Free Press, 1963), 69.
3. Neglected during the reign of behaviorism, the stream of consciousness has become an important area of investigation in recent psychology. See, for example, Kenneth S. Pope and Jerome L. Singer, eds., *The Stream of Consciousness* (New York: Plenum, 1978); Jerome L. Singer, *The Inner World of Daydreaming* (New York: Harper and Row, 1975); and Mary Watkins, *Waking Dreams* (New York: Gordon and Breach, 1976). Little similar interest is yet evident in anthropology or American Studies.
4. Psychological researchers tend to be preoccupied with outside, etic, quantitative forms of analysis and pay relatively little attention to actor-oriented phenomenological, emic exploration of stream texts.
5. Robert Humphrey, *Stream of Consciousness and the Modern Novel* (Berkeley: University of California Press, 1954), 44–46. Cf. Dorrit Cohen, *Transparent Minds: Narrative Modes for Presenting Consciousness in Fiction* (Princeton: Princeton University Press, 1978).
6. On methods of study, see Eric Klinger, "Modes of Normal Consciousness Flow," in Pope and Singer, *Stream of Consciousness*, 228–32. Cf. Jerome L. Singer, "Ongoing Thought: The Normative Baseline for Alternate States of Consciousness," in Norman E. Zinberg, ed., *Alternate States of Consciousness* (New York: Free Press, 1977); Wallace, "Driving to Work," 311–12; and John L. Caughey, "Ethnography, Introspection, and Reflexive Culture Studies," *Prospects* 7 (1982).
7. Jerome L. Singer, "Experimental Studies of Daydreaming and the Stream of Thought," in Pope and Singer, *Stream of Consciousness*, 199.
8. Cf. John L. Caughey and J. Michael Mahar, "Ritual Remedies at a Sufi Shrine," paper presented to the seventy-sixth annual meeting of the American Anthropological Association (Houston, 1977). For a general discussion of the stream of consciousness in Asian cultures— based on analysis of religious texts—see Eugene Taylor, "Asian Interpretations: Transcending the Stream of Consciousness," in Pope and Singer, *Stream of Consciousness*, 31–54.
9. For historical interpretations, see George Steiner, "The Distribution of Discourse," in his *On Difficulty* (New York: Oxford, 1978); Singer,

The Inner World of Daydreaming; Watkins, *Waking Dreams*; and Singer and Pope, *The Stream of Consciousness*.

10. Fred Matthews, "In Defense of Common Sense: Mental Hygiene as Ideology and Mentality in Twentieth-Century America," *Prospects* 4 (1979) 459–516.

11. A. I. Hallowell, "The Self and Its Behavioral Environment," in his *Culture and Experience* (Philadelphia: University of Pennsylvania Press, 1955), 99.

12. Eric Berne, *Games People Play: The Psychology of Human Relationships* (New York: Grove Press, 1964).

13. Goffman, *Behavior in Public Places*, 69.

14. Robert S. DeRopp, *The Master Game* (New York: Dell, 1968), 77.

15. Donald Norman, "Post Freudian Slips," *Psychology Today* 13 (April 1980), 43–46.

16. Cf. Aaron T. Beck et al., *Cognitive Therapy of Depression* (New York: Guilford, 1979).

17. Lloyd B. Lewis, "The 'Thousand Yard Stare': A Socio-Cultural Analysis of the Viet Nam War Narratives," unpublished Ph.D. dissertation, University of Maryland, 1982.

18. George Miller, Eugene Galanter, and Karl Pribram, *Plans and the Structure of Behavior* (New York: Holt, Rinehart, 1960), 5.

19. George J. McCall and J. L. Simmons, *Identities and Interactions* (New York: Free Press, 1966), 69.

20. Peter Berger and Thomas Luckmann, *The Social Construction of Reality* (New York: Anchor, 1966), 152–53.

21. Laura Bohannan [Elenore Smith Bowen], *Return to Laughter* (New York: Anchor, 1954), 174.

22. Peter Berger, *Invitation to Sociology* (New York: Doubleday, 1963), 56.

23. Ibid., 58–61.

24. On the waitress role, see James P. Spradley and Brenda Mann, *The Cocktail Waitress* (New York: John Wiley, 1975).

25. James Morgan and Thomas Skovholt, "Using Inner Experience: Fantasy and Daydreaming in Career Counseling," *Journal of Counseling Psychology* 24 (1977), 394.

26. Ibid., 396.

27. Cf. Adaline Starr, *Rehearsal for Living: Psychodrama* (Chicago: Nelson Hall, 1977).

Chapter 5

1. *Webster's New World Dictionary* (1959).
2. Ernest R. Hilgard, *Introduction to Psychology* (New York: Harcourt, Brace, and World, 1962), 619.
3. American Psychiatric Association, *A Psychiatric Glossary* (Washington: American Psychiatric Association, 1975), 55.
4. Lawrence C. Kolb, *Noyes' Modern Clinical Psychiatry* (Philadelphia: W. B. Saunders, 1968), 78.
5. For a psychological approach, see Eric Klinger, *Structure and Functions of Fantasy* (New York: John Wiley, 1971). Much of what I am here calling fantasy has been studied in psychology as part of the stream of consciousness or daydreaming. Cf. references in Chapter Four, especially Jerome Singer, *The Inner World of Daydreaming*.
6. Freud as quoted by Kolb, *Noyes' Modern Clinical Psychiatry*, 78.
7. Caryl Rivers, "I Fell in Love With Montgomery Clift," *New York Times*, 2 August 1973.
8. Ted Morgan, "Everything but the Reason," *New York Times Book Review*, 3 January 1982.
9. Rivers, "Montgomery Clift."
10. Tom Wolfe, *The New Journalism* (New York: Harper and Row, 1973), 7–8.
11. Robert White, *The Abnormal Personality* (New York: Ronald, 1948), 180. Cf. general attitudes to daydreaming and the stream of consciousness in references cited in Chapter Four. An interesting discussion of American antagonism to fantasy is also offered by Ursula K. LeGuin, *The Language of the Night: Essays on Fantasy and Science Fiction* (New York: Berkeley, 1979), 29–36.
12. Anthropologists have studied fantasy through projective methods such as Rorschach and TAT tests. However, these approaches do not yield the kind of data with which I am concerned here. Cf. Robert B. Edgerton, "Method in Psychological Anthropology," in Raoul Naroll and Ronald Cohen, eds., *A Handbook of Method in Cultural Anthropology* (New York: Columbia University Press, 1973).
13. Cf. Jerome L. Singer and Vivian McCravern, "Some Characteristics of Adult Daydreaming," *Journal of Psychology* 51 (1961), 151–64.
14. Cf. Evon Z. Vogt and Ethel Albert, "The 'Comparative Study of Values in Five Cultures' Project," in Evon Z. Vogt and Ethel Albert, eds., *The People of Rimrock* (New York: Atheneum, 1966).
15. See, for example, the discussion of fantasy and television consump-

tion as "removal activities" for inmates of total institutions in Erving Goffman, *Asylums* (New York: Anchor, 1961), 50 and 68–70. But cf. E. Katz and D. Foulkes, "On the Use of Mass Media as 'Escape'," *Public Opinion Quarterly* 26 (1962) 377–88.

16. Anthony F. C. Wallace, "Revitalization Movements," *American Anthropologist* 58 (1956) 264–81.

17. Jerome L. Singer, *Daydreaming: An Introduction to the Experimental Study of Inner Experience* (New York: Random House, 1966), 16.

18. Nora Ephron, *Crazy Salad* (New York: Bantam, 1976), 14.

19. James Morgan and Thomas Skovholt, "Using Inner Experience: Fantasy and Daydreaming in Career Counseling," *Journal of Counseling Psychology* 24 (1977), 391.

20. Havelock Ellis, "Erotic Daydreaming," in his *Psychology of Sex* (New York: Harcourt Brace, 1938), 109.

21. E. B. Haviton and Jerome Singer, "Women's Fantasies During Sexual Intercourse: Normative and Theoretical Implications," *Journal of Consulting and Clinical Psychology* 42 (1974), 313–22.

22. Nena and George O'Neil, *Open Marriage* (New York: Avon, 1972), 133.

23. Hanja Kochansky, ed., *The Sexual Phantasies of Women* (New York: Ace, 1973), 200–01.

24. Ibid., 198.

25. Gerald and Caroline Green, *S-M: The Last Taboo* (New York: Grove, 1974), 209.

26. Garson Kanin, *Hollywood* (New York: Viking, 1974), 314.

27. Ibid., 316–17.

28. John Eric Holmes, "Confessions of a Dungeon Master," *Psychology Today* 14 (November 1980), 93–94.

29. Ibid., 88.

30. On the cowboy hero from a woman's perspective, see Joan Didion, "John Wayne: A Love Song," in her *Slouching Towards Bethlehem* (New York: Dell, 1968), 29–41.

31. Cf. Nancy Friday, *Men in Love: Men's Sexual Fantasies* (New York: Delacorte, 1980).

32. Sigmund Freud, "The Relationship of the Poet to Daydreaming," in Benjamin Nelson, ed., *On Creativity and the Unconscious* (New York: Harper and Row, 1958). On fiction as daydream, see also Charles Elkins and Darko Suvin, "Preliminary Reflections on Teaching Science Fiction Critically," *Science Fiction Studies* 6 (1979) 263–70.

Chapter 6

1. This is why, for example, there was reluctance to admit CAT (Computerized Axial Topography) scans of Hinckley's brain as evidence in his trial. Such methods are not generally accepted as reliable means for diagnosing schizophrenia.
2. John L. Caughey, "Identity Struggles in the Mental Status Examination," paper presented at the seventy-seventh annual meeting of the American Anthropological Association (Los Angeles, 1978).
3. James C. Coleman, *Abnormal Psychology and Modern Life* (Glenview, Illinois: Scott Foresman, 1976), 741 and 744.
4. Berger and Luckmann, *The Social Construction of Reality* (New York: Anchor, 1966), 175.
5. Ibid., 113.
6. Thomas J. Scheff, *Being Mentally Ill: A Sociological Theory* (Chicago: Aldine, 1966), 7.
7. Bert Kaplan, ed., *The Inner World of Mental Illness* (New York: Harper and Row, 1964), viii.
8. Ibid., x–xi.
9. Robert White, *The Abnormal Personality* (New York: Ronald, 1948), 81–82, 90.
10. Ibid., 89.
11. Ibid., 82.
12. Kaplan, *Inner World*, 133–34.
13. Ibid., 134–35.
14. Ibid., 136.
15. Ibid.
16. White, *Abnormal Personality*, 83.
17. Ibid.
18. Kaplan, *Inner World*, 136–37.
19. Ibid., 140–41.
20. White, *Abnormal Personality*, 86.
21. Ibid.
22. Ibid., 84.
23. Norman Cameron, "Paranoid Conditions and Paranoia," in S. Arieti, ed., *American Handbook of Psychiatry* (New York: Basic Books, 1959), 518–19.
24. Norman Cameron, "The Paranoid Pseudo Community Revisited," *American Journal of Sociology* 65 (1959), 56.
25. Milton Rokeach, *The Three Christs of Ypsilanti* (New York: Random House, 1964), 196.

26. Cameron, "Paranoid Conditions," 525.
27. Kaplan, *Inner World*, 171.
28. Cameron, "Paranoid Conditions," 520.
29. Ibid., 521.
30. Ibid., 525.
31. White, *Abnormal Personality*, 89.
32. Ibid., 88
33. Cf. Morton Schatzman, "Paranoia or Persecution: The Case of Schreber," in Thomas Scheff, ed., *Labeling Madness* (Englewood Cliffs, N.J.: Prentice-Hall, 1975), 112.
34. White, *Abnormal Personality*, 89–90.
35. Kaplan, *Inner World*, xi.
36. James A. Brussel, *The Layman's Guide to Psychiatry* (New York: Barnes and Noble, 1967), 66–67.
37. Maya Pines, "Invisible Playmates," *Psychology Today* 12 (September 1978), 42.
38. Ibid.
39. Ibid., 38.
40. Ibid.
41. Ibid.
42. Ibid.
43. Ibid., 42.
44. R. E. L. Masters and Jean Houston, *The Varieties of Psychedelic Experience* (New York: Holt, Rinehart, 1966), 265.
45. Andrew Greeley, *Ecstasy: A Way of Knowing* (Englewood Cliffs, N.J.: Prentice-Hall, 1974), 2–3, 11.
46. Cf. Ihsan Al-Issa, "Social and Cultural Aspects of Hallucinations," *Psychological Bulletin* 84 (1977), 573.
47. June Macklin, "A Connecticut Yankee in Summerland," in Vincent Crapanzano and Vivian Garrison, eds., *Case Studies in Spirit Possession* (New York: John Wiley, 1977), 44.
48. Ibid.
49. Ibid., 45.
50. Ibid., 48.
51. Ibid., 50.
52. Ibid., 49.
53. Ibid., 51.
54. Ibid., 43.
55 Ibid., 50–51.
56. Ibid., 45, 54.
57. Ibid., 65–66.

58. Ibid., 56.
59. Ibid., 63.
60. Ibid., 69.
61. Ibid., 69–70.
62. Cameron, "Paranoid Conditions," 520.
63. Ibid., 521.
64. Robert Lindner, *The Fifty Minute Hour* (New York: Bantam, 1958), 159.
65. Ibid., 171–73.
66. Ibid., 175–77.
67. Ibid., 178, 180.
68. Ibid., 198.
69. Ibid., 199.
70. Ibid., 205.
71. Robert Lindner, as quoted by Rokeach, *Three Christs*, 34–35.
72. Rokeach, *Three Christs*, 197.
73. Berger and Luckmann, *Social Construction of Reality*, 109.
74. Anthony F. C. Wallace, "Revitalization Movements," *American Anthropologist* 58 (1956), 265.
75. Anthony F. C. Wallace, "Mazeway Resynthesis: A BioCultural Theory of Religious Inspiration," *Transactions of the New York Academy of Sciences*, Ser. II, 18 (1956), 628.
76. Ibid.
77. Wallace, "Revitalization Movements," 270.
78. Edward F. Foulks, "Schizophrenia and Revitalization in Pre-Modern Societies," in John Brady, ed., *Psychiatry: Areas of Promise and Advancement* (New York: Spectrum, 1977), 140.
79. Ibid., 137.

Chapter 7

1. Cf. Herbert Blumer, *Symbolic Interactionism* (Englewood Cliffs, N.J.: Prentice-Hall, 1969), 185.
2. David Shribman, "A Love That Can Kill," *Washington Star*, 4 April 1981.
3. Michael R. Real, "Media Theory: Contributions to an Understanding of American Mass Communications," in *American Quarterly* 32 (1980), 241.
4. Cf. John Wicklein, *Electronic Nightmare: The New Communications and Freedom* (New York: Viking, 1981).

5. Cf. Laura Kiernan, "Clashing Portraits of Hinckley Offered," *Washington Post*, 5 May 1982.

6. Several would-be imitators appeared shortly after the assassination attempt. See Daniel Schorr, "Go Get Some Milk and Cookies and Watch the Murders on Television," *The Washingtonian*, October 1981, 190. Other recent cases of aggression against media celebrities include the "aggravated harassment" of Caroline Kennedy by a fan who wanted to marry her, described by Joyce Wadler, "Caroline Kennedy's Pursuer Found Guilty," *Washington Post*, 17 October 1981; and the stabbing of actress Theresa Saldana by an "allegedly lovesick fan," noted in "People," *Washington Post*, 19 March 1982.

7. "A Report to Felony Court," reproduced in Charles Einstein, ed., *The Fireside Book of Baseball* (New York: Simon and Schuster, 1956), 121.

8. Laura Kiernan, "Psychiatrist says Hinckley Believes in Link to Foster," *Washington Post* 26 May 1982.

9. Jerome Johnston and James S. Ettema, *Positive Images: Breaking Stereotypes With Children's Television* (Beverly Hills: Sage, 1982).

10. Cf. Ihsan Al-Issa, "Social and Cultural Aspects of Hallucinations," *Psychological Bulletin* 84 (1977), 573.

11. "Positive Denial: The Case for Not Facing Reality," Richard S. Lazarus interviewed by Daniel Goleman, *Psychology Today* 13 (November 1979), 57.

12. Aaron T. Beck et al., *Cognitive Therapy of Depression* (New York: Guilford, 1979).

13. Cf. Eugene Taylor, "Asian Interpretations: Transcending the Stream of Consciousness," in Kenneth S. Pope and Jerome L. Singer, eds., *The Stream of Consciousness* (New York: Plenum, 1978).

14. Jerome Singer, *Imagery and Daydream Methods in Psychotherapy and Behavior Modification* (New York: Academic Press, 1974) and Jerome Singer and Ellen Switzer, *Mind-Play: The Creative Uses of Fantasy* (Englewood Cliffs, N.J.: Prentice-Hall, 1980).

15. Cf. Ira Progoff, *At a Journal Workshop* (New York: Dialogue House, 1975).

Index

Krebs, Maynard G., 68–69
Krim, Seymour, 171

Landon, Michael, 74
Language: in imaginary experience, 55, 125–26, 133–35, 144, 146–47, 214, 216, 252
Lazarsfeld, Paul, 49
Lennon, John, 3–4, 46, 66
Lewis, Lloyd, 143
Lindner, Robert, 228–34, 235
Lombard, Carole, 192
Love relations: in dreams, 101, 113–14, 116; in fantasy, 159–60, 166, 182–84; in hallucinations, 19, 208, 209–10, 224; with media figures, 1–2, 4–6, 7, 37–38, 40–51, 64, 65, 72–73, 249; in the stream of consciousness, 143, 148–49, 153. *See also* Sexual relations
LSD, 217
Luckmann, Thomas, 27, 33, 146, 198
Luther, Martin, 80

M., Mrs. Rita, 219–26, 227–28
McCartney, Paul, 43, 46, 65
Macklin, June, 219, 224, 225
Manson, Charles, 62–63
Maquet, Jacques, 24
Marriage, 138–39, 183–84
Materialism, 50, 172, 175–77, 186
Mazeway resynthesis, 200, 239
Media consumption, 33–39, 52, 56–57, 247; self in, 36–38, 50–51, 54, 56–59, 65; social relations in, 35–39, 41–43, 45, 49, 52
Media effects, 39, 58–59, 67, 69, 70, 75–76, 243, 247, 249, 252; antisocial, 53, 60–63, 247–48;

prosocial, 66–69, 248–49, 252; social, 32, 44–45, 46–47, 55–56, 58–60, 63–64, 73
Media figures, 21–22, 31–33, 35, 36, 39–40, 53, 54, 65, 71–76, 247, 250, 259 n. 4; in dreams, 91–92, 93–94, 97–98; in fantasy, 45–48, 50–52, 56–58, 73, 161, 162, 167–69, 178, 184, 190–93, 195; in hallucinations, 206, 214, 230; in the stream of consciousness, 136, 137, 143
Memories, 123–25, 136, 142, 147–50, 153, 154, 155, 158
Mental illness, 2, 4, 5, 6–7, 31, 197–99. *See also* Hallucinations; Paranoid schizophrenia; Schizophrenia
Mental map, 119
Mental status examination, 31, 197–200, 204–5, 226–27
Micronesia, 20, 71, 176, 212. *See also* Fáánakkar
Miller, George, 144
Mimieux, Yvette, 48
Mitchell, Margaret, 73
Monroe, Marilyn, 58
Moore, Mary Tyler, 54, 59
Morgan, James, 151, 189

Newman, Paul, 190
Nicklaus, Jack, 167
Nightmares, 89, 265 n. 29. *See also* Dreams
Noone, H. D., 114
Norman, Donald, 141
Novak, Kim, 58
Neurosis, 226. *See also* Mental illness

Occupational achievement, 152, 164–72, 186, 187, 188, 211, 225